**Department of Economic and Social Affairs**
Division for Social Policy and Development

# MEN IN FAMILIES
## and Family Policy in a Changing World

**United Nations**
New York, 2011

## DESA

The Department of Economic and Social Affairs of the United Nations Secretariat is a vital interface between global policies in the economic, social and environmental spheres and national action. The Department works in three main interlinked areas: it compiles, generates and analyses a wide range of economic, social and environmental data and information on which Members States of the United Nations draw to review common problems and to take stock of policy options; it facilitates the negotiations of Member States in many intergovernmental bodies on joint courses of action to address ongoing or emerging global challenges; and it advises interested Governments on the ways and means of translating policy frameworks developed in United Nations conferences and summits into programmes at the country level and, through technical assistance, helps build national capacities.

## Note

The views expressed in the present publication are those of the authors and do not imply the expression of any opinion on the part of the Secretariat of the United Nations, particularly concerning the legal status of any country, territory, city or area or of its authorities, or concerning the delimitation of its frontiers or boundaries. The assignment of countries or areas to specific groupings is for analytical convenience and does not imply any assumption regarding political or other affiliation of countries or territories by the United Nations. The designations "developed" and "developing" are intended for statistical and analytical convenience and do not necessarily express a judgment about the stage reached by a particular country or area in the development process.

United Nations publication
Sales No. E.11.IV.1
ISBN 978-92-1-130306-3

Printed by the United Nations, New York

This publication is available for download at
http://www.un.org/esa/socdev/ family/docs/men-in-families.pdf
Photo credits: UNICEF

# Contents

## Tables

## Figures

# Introduction

Over the past two decades, major United Nations world conferences and summits have called attention to the issues affecting families, including family roles and responsibilities, gender equality and men's greater participation in family life. As noted by the General Assembly resolutions, the family-related provisions of the outcomes of those conferences as well as their follow-up processes continue to provide policy guidance on ways to strengthen family-centered components of policies and programmes as part of an integrated comprehensive approach to development.

The 1995 World Summit for Social Development acknowledged the importance of providing help to families so as to enable them to perform their supporting, educating and nurturing roles. Such support involves enacting social policies and programmes designed to meet the needs of families and their individual members, including those promoting equal partnership between women and men in the family and ensuring opportunities for family members to understand and meet their social obligations.

The General Assembly resolution on the Follow-up to the tenth anniversary of the International Year of the Family and beyond encouraged "the United Nations programme on the family to support and conduct action-oriented research, including through the issuance of research and publications on relevant topics, with the aim of supplementing the research activities of Government" (A/RES/60/133, para. 3).

In keeping with the objectives of the International Year of the Family, and based on existing research, the current publication aims to promote the knowledge of trends affecting families and increase awareness of family issues among Governments as well as in the private sector. It is also hoped that the study will stimulate efforts to develop family-oriented policies focusing attention upon the rights and responsibilities of all family members. Promoting knowledge of the economic, social and demographic processes affecting families and their members is indispensable to design appropriate course of action to assist families in fulfilling their numerous functions. These overall considerations have guided the preparations of the current publication, which addresses the issue of the evolving roles of men in families and the corresponding need to develop social policies supporting these new roles for the benefit of families.

The growing interest in the role of men in the family has been triggered by diverse demographic, socio-economic and cultural transformations that have occurred over the past several decades, impacting the formation, stability and overall well-being of families. Profound changes have been also occurring in the perceptions of the role of women and men in families. Women are still the main providers of care at home even as they assume greater work responsibilities outside their homes. Nevertheless, as women enter the labour market in growing numbers, men have been newly confronted with demands that they become more engaged in performing family responsibilities. Although men are still seen mostly as economic providers, disciplinarians and protectors within their families, they are increasingly taking on new responsibilities, including caregiving, and providing emotional support to children, offering guidance so as to enable children to connect with their extended family and community members and participating in a variety of household activities.

With the broadening of paternal roles, there is a greater attention being paid to the effects of men's involvement on the well-being of their families. The initial focus of research in this area was on the role of men in the achievement of gender equality and an equal sharing of domestic responsibilities. Further research centred on programme and policy initiatives designed to engage men in many areas of family life, including in reproductive health, especially family planning and maternal and newborn health. More equitable partnerships and the greater role of men in the rearing of children were also considered, with considerable research focusing on paternal contributions to positive social and education outcomes for children.

Despite an increasing worldwide focus on the role of men in families and burgeoning research documenting men's contribution to gender equality, the importance of their engagement for work-family balance, and the numerous positive paternal contributions to children's development, policy-makers have been slow to recognize the need for effective public policy that is supportive of men's involvement in their families.

Historically, social policies reflected a somewhat narrow view of men's contribution to family life, focusing on them mainly as economic providers. Moreover, many policies unintentionally presumed men to be deficient with regard to the discharging of their family responsibilities, which resulted in their exclusion from policy considerations. What is more, social policy often attempted to deal with problems in such a way as to ensure the perpetuation of the very constructions of masculinity that had produced those problems in the first place.

Notwithstanding those difficulties, new policies facilitating greater involvement of men in the lives of their families have been enacted, in particular in the area of reconciliation of work and family life. Many countries have introduced paternity leave to encourage men's participation in the care and education of their children. In granting such leave, Governments and societies at large recognize the importance of fathers in care work. A number of other policies, however, are needed to encourage greater participation of men in families, be it in the labour market, family law, health and social services as well as education and media.

This publication has been financed by the United Nations Trust Fund on Family Activities, which provides funding support for research activities with an overall aim of promoting the objectives of the International Year of the Family. The five independent chapters were commissioned to focus on a number of relevant current international issues affecting families and the role of men in addressing them. The areas of analysis include gender equality, participation in care work, fatherhood, migration and HIV/AIDS. The study also highlights problems associated with the presence of fathers and other male figures in families, such as domestic violence and substance abuse, while arguing for greater inclusion of vulnerable fathers in support services. By and large, the present publication provides an overview of existing national and regional research on the issue of men in families and related policy considerations. It aims to stimulate the debate on the best means to develop social and economic policies that recognize men in their role as valuable contributors to the well-being of their families. The study also seeks to assist Governments in integrating a family perspective into their overall policymaking. The publication reflects the views of the authors and does not imply the expression of any opinion on the part of the United Nations Secretariat.

# Chapter overviews and policy implications

## Chapter I

### Men, families, gender equality and care work

Chapter I provides a global review and analysis of trends in men's participation in care work and its importance for achieving gender equality. For a new generation of younger men, the world today is not the world of their fathers. This is true on two levels. First, pathways to adult manhood, particularly stable employment, are in flux—and, in some parts of the world, even in crisis—to a greater extent than in the past. Second, social expectations about men's involvement in the care of children, and reproduction in general, and about fatherhood itself are changing, albeit slowly, worldwide. The chapter emphasizes the importance of men's employment status for their social identity as it relates to family formation, support and stability. It also observes that beyond income provision, men's roles as fathers and caregivers are being recognized more in many parts of the world. Consequently, policies in some countries encourage greater participation by men in family life. Further, the authors discuss the changing dynamics of families and the role of men, including changing notions of manhood itself. Efforts to engage men in the area of sexual and reproductive health are highlighted. Men are becoming more involved in family planning, maternal care and childbirth. They are also more likely to be present at prenatal health check-ups and witness the birth of their children. Further, the chapter focuses briefly on family-based strategies to alleviate poverty, noting that poverty and joblessness may separate men from their families. The authors warn that strategies to alleviate poverty focusing solely on women and children may treat men as marginal to families and inadvertently reinforce gender stereotypes. Pursuant to summarizing the available data, the authors argue that, although progress in establishing a work-life balance and redressing the unequal distribution of income between men and women is slow, change can be accelerated with appropriate strategies and policies.

Reflecting on social policy implications, the chapter observes that policies related to health, poverty alleviation and gender equality have not adequately considered ways of promoting men's involvement in care work and parenting. The recommendations centre on expanding paternity leave, currently more appropriate in middle-income countries owing to the high cost of such policies and the large number of men in informal employment in low-income countries. Other policy recommendations include offering flexible working arrangements for men (and women) with small children, including the option to work part-time as well as expanding the provision of childcare. It is also important to enact changes in family laws encouraging joint custody and recognizing men as caregivers. Implementing educational programmes in the public education system so as to give boys and men the skills and knowledge needed to take on new roles in households, including school-based «life skills» courses for boys, can be another useful means of speeding up necessary modifications in social norms regarding men's roles. Other policy recommendations include developing training curricula for teacher training colleges, social work programmes nursing programmes, and other forms of care work, and undertaking campaigns to increase men's involvement in caregiving in general. Educational policies that encourage men's involvement with their children in school and day care and support men's involvement in teaching and early childhood care are needed as well. Finally, livelihood and poverty alleviation policies should recognize the roles of men and women (and the need to achieve equality between them) and acknowledge the diversity of family configurations. They should support both women and men in their efforts to achieve joint household control of assets and joint household decision-making to ensure adequate and dignified livelihoods for their families.

## Chapter II
### Fatherhood and families

Chapter II considers the subject of fathers and father figures, and their changing roles in different cultural contexts, with attention being drawn to the concept of "social fatherhood", which encompasses the care and support of males for children who are not necessarily their biological offspring. The chapter reviews different forms of father engagement and their implications for children and families, including the evidence of the beneficial educational, social and psychological effects on children. It looks at men and fathers across generations, while considering the consequences of the growing numbers of older persons for families, intergenerational relations and childcare. The chapter further explores what is known about work-family balance with respect to men, and the role of policy in advancing men's engagement with children in the context of employment policies. Men's mental and physical health is also considered and research pointing to the benefits to men arising from their engagement in family life and their relationships with their children is reviewed. The final section outlines the implications of these issues for social and family policy within the context of the labour market, law, education and health and social services.

All social and family policies should contribute to creating an environment in which men, and women, have family time and the opportunity to care for and engage with their children, and the support needed to do so. Consistent with the Convention on the Rights of the Child, laws and policies must ensure that children are protected and cared for by both parents, including under conditions of adoption, fostering, custody and maintenance. It is especially important that labour laws and housing and financial regulations facilitate men's involvement with and support for their children and families. In addition, government, the private sector and civil society must enable and encourage men to take advantage of legal, labour and other provisions that support men's participation in childcare and family life. Formal education and informal sources of influence, including the media, play a critical role in constructing and maintaining social norms and attitudes, including regarding the roles of fathers in the lives of children. Health services should recognize that men make many health-related decisions affecting their families and target them by nutrition, immunization and other health-promoting messages. Social services facilitating fathers' participation in childcare, early child development programmes, school and after school programmes should be advanced as well. Lastly, as significant changes occur in the domain of social and family policy, it is essential that they facilitate men's contribution to children's health and development and family well-being—but only in ways that do not unwittingly lead to a further entrenchment of men's tradition-based control over women and children.

## Chapter III

### Fathers in challenging family contexts: a need for engagement

Chapter III examines the wealth of research on vulnerable fathers, male carers and fathers in vulnerable family contexts. It charts a range of problematic family environments facing contemporary men and related father figures in the lives of children. A major issue for men across the world is separation from their children, through either the relatively common breakdown of relationships or the rarer occurrence of paternal imprisonment. Despite relationship fragility or discord, more fathers are attempting to sustain relationships with their non-residential children and may need support when they are met with difficulty in fulfilling their aspirations in this regard. The chapter also focuses on the problematic family environment where, through domestic or child abuse, men endanger the lives of women and children with whom they live and to whom they are related. Fathers and male kin who fail their families through engagement in physical, emotional or sexual abuse are a source of global concern, although the dimensions of the issue have still not been fully charted. Although most men do not abuse children or their partners, there is surprisingly little systematic study of the minority of fathers and male partners who do. Nevertheless, understanding of a range of factors is evolving which, in turn, is enlarging the understanding of male perspectives on family violence. The research evidence on paternal risk factors for families in terms of mental health, alcohol and substance abuse, and the presence of unrelated males is also reviewed. There is a substantive body of research highlighting the marked failure of health and social care professionals to engage with fathers and men in cases of child protection and domestic abuse. This neglect of fathers and male instigators of family violence can lead to a culture of "mother and female blaming", where overlooked fathers may be lost to the public social care system and go on to establish new relationships with women and mothers of young children within which they repeat previous patterns of abusive behaviour. The chapter also discusses fatherhood in the contexts of youth, disability and older ages and examines cases where men's family care and earning capacities are at risk of being compromised or challenged. Of particular note is the underresearched impact of increased longevity and lower mortality rates in many parts of the world for men.

Although family policies are becoming more father-inclusive, there is a long way to go in most countries, especially developing nations, which are most in need of harnessing men's caring competencies. Evidence has revealed how vulnerable fathers, male carers and fathers in vulnerable family contexts tend to be excluded from support services as if they did not have family support needs. In many countries, men's "caring" or "need for care" roles are relatively hidden, with more attention and responsibilities given to women and mothers. The support deficit is a reflection of the consistent underplaying of men's caring responsibilities and obligations to children and partners. The chapter recommends that Governments and local service providers ensure greater inclusion and enhanced visibility of men's parenting and care responsibilities throughout the life course. More research is needed on how to engage male kin and fathers in caregiving and child protection so as to prevent unnecessary institutionalization and inappropriate alternative care placement. There is also more need for research, programme development and discussion to improve the means by which social systems care for and protect fathers with disabilities, fathers in prison, substance- and alcohol-abusing fathers, young fathers and non-residential fathers, so that they can continue to care for their families and support them economically, where appropriate. Well-established international organizations working on gender, the child, employment and family welfare need to become more "father-inclusive" in their research design and strategies.

## Chapter IV

### Migration, families and men in families

Chapter IV focuses on families and men in the context of labour migration. It stresses that migration is usually a family affair and that migration patterns have become increasingly complex over the past generation. There have been notable increases in short-term and circular migration, in migration of skilled workers, and in female labour migration. The author focuses on the ways in which migration can lead to significantly increased economic and social well-being for families and communities, and the changes it can precipitate in family relations for families living in destination countries and for those remaining behind in countries of origin. The chapter examines the small body of literature on men and fatherhood in relation to migration, as well as the somewhat more substantial literature on the significant differences in remittance behaviour between male and female migrants. A major argument running throughout this chapter is that while a focus on migrant women over the past 20 years or so has counteracted a male-oriented bias in previous thinking about migration, men now tend to be left out. Many men are quite literally left behind in home communities as international labour markets privilege female labour migrants; and men also tend to be underrepresented in research, programmes and policy discussions.

Inadequate social and working conditions often experienced by migrant workers in destination communities have negative effects on families and on men. They play a role in determining the types of jobs migrant men can do, and types of neighbourhoods in which they live, and affect even the self-image of the people who experience them, which, in turn affects their ability to be good parents. One basic policy recommendation stemming from this observation is to allow migrants to work in the first place and to respect the rights of migrant workers and their families. Another is to ensure decent housing and living conditions, and to fight discrimination, xenophobia and racism. Policy and programme recommendations include improving migration data so as to better recognize families as well as men in development discourse and policy. It is necessary to simplify the channels and procedures through which people are permitted to seek work abroad and ensure their basic rights when they have migrated. Both out-migration and in-migration should be more friendly to families, for example, by strengthening support and information programmes for departing migrant workers, and by addressing the extremely complex conundrums associated with the issue of family reunification. This may mean not only facilitating migration for the families of migrant workers, but also ensuring that individuals are protected, and that policies do not end up having damaging and abusive consequences. The chapter concludes by defining some extremely troubling questions raised by recent migration patterns, and observing that those questions would be more effectively addressed if policy and programmes stressed resilience rather than deficits, and if they focused on both men and women, rather than on women alone.

## Chapter V

### Men, families and HIV and AIDS

Chapter V looks closely at the impact of HIV and AIDS on the family, as the illness, death and stigma resulting from HIV and AIDS have profound consequences not only for infected individuals but also for their families. Understanding the experiences and responses of affected families is then crucial for efforts to successfully strengthen and support families. As most affected families include men, it is important to consider the way in which family policies take into account and benefit men and their families. While the value of engaging men in family interventions is generally recognized, it is argued that family research and programmes on HIV and AIDS have been hindered by assumptions related to men and HIV, and men's involvement in families, and by messages that assign blame and emphasize innocence with respect to particular family members. The chapter examines the assumptions on which policies have been based—for example, that men have little or no involvement in the care of children or of family members who are ill. It further discusses the utilization of negative images of men in efforts to raise awareness and financial support for HIV and AIDS programmes and services targeting women and children; and considers the opportunities created by family policies that recognize and engage men as members of affected families.

Family policies on HIV and AIDS that relate to men should, essentially, seek to promote and support men's positive engagement with and involvement in families, and to initiate and improve efforts to increase men's engagement with health services targeted at addressing their own health concerns as well as those of their partners, children and other family members. Such policies should also foster positive social and service sector attitudes towards the involvement of men in providing support and care (including intimate personal care) for children and other family members, as well as recognition of the full range of parenting and childcare roles and responsibilities that men assume. Making progress on these goals requires encouraging an openness of mind and innovation in approaches to engaging men and their families. For family policies to have a positive impact, attitudes and assumptions of a whole range of actors may need to be modified. Promoting positive involvement by men in families is crucial; however, if policy benefits for HIV affected men and their families are to be realized. The adoption of similarly positive attitudes by policymakers and service providers is also required.

# Men, families, gender equality and care work

Gary Barker and Piotr "Peter" Pawlak

# The authors

**Gary Barker** is International Director and founding Director of Instituto Promundo, a Brazilian non-governmental organization, based in Rio de Janeiro, which works locally, nationally and internationally to promote gender equity and to reduce violence against children, women and youth. He has carried out research on men, violence, gender, health and conflict in Latin America, sub-Saharan Africa and Asia. He is based at Promundo's Washington, D.C., office since 2011. He has co-authored numerous training materials, including the Program H series for use in working with young men to promote gender equality and reduce violence against women. He has served as a consultant to the World Bank, the World Health Organization, the Joint United Nations Programme on HIV/AIDS (UNAIDS), the United Nations Population Fund, the United Nations Children's Fund, the United Nations Commission on the Status of Women, the Ford Foundation, the MacArthur Foundation and the Government of Brazil on issues related to gender, engaging men, health promotion and violence prevention. He holds a Master's in public policy and a Ph.D. in child development and is an Ashoka Fellow. Some of his recent publications include *Dying to Be Men: Youth, Masculinity and Social Exclusion* (Routledge, 2005) and *Engaging Men and Boys in Changing Gender-Based Inequity in Health: Evidence from Programme Interventions* (World Health Organization, 2007). He is co-chair and co-founder of MenEngage, a recently formed global alliance of nongovernmental organizations and United Nations organizations working to engage men and boys in gender equality. He is co-principal investigator for the International Men and Gender Equality Survey (IMAGES), a nine-country study on men, women and gender equality which is being carried out in Africa, Asia, Europe and Latin America. From 2008-2010, he served as Director of Gender, Violence and Rights at the International Center for Research on Women in Washington, D.C.

**Peter Pawlak** is Program Officer based at the Washington D.C. office of Instituto Promundo. He is a researcher and advocate with expertise in international public health and international human rights, and focuses on gender equality, ending violence against women and children and youth, and the role men and boys can play in the improvement of health and development outcomes. Piotr's work experience spans international and multilateral organizations, as well as both government and non-governmental institutions, and he has served as a consultant to the International Center for Research on Women, MenEngage Alliance, Sonke Justice Gender Network, Open Society Institute, Population Action International, as well as Amnesty International USA. He holds a Joint M.A. and B.A. in International Relations from University of Warsaw in Poland, and a M.A. in Political Science from University of Idaho. He recently worked with the International Center for Research on Women on the Men and Gender Equality Policy Project, and co-authored a report on public policies involving men to promote gender equality titled, "What Men Have to Do With It" (ICRW and Institute Promundo, 2010), and contributed to the development of the International Men and Gender Equality Survey (IMAGES), a nine-country study on men, women and gender equality which is being carried out in Africa, Asia, Europe and Latin America.

We would like to thank Margaret Greene, Jennifer Schulte and Manuel Contreras of the International Center for Research on Women, and Fabio Verani and Marcos Nascimento of the Instituto Promundo, Brazil, for their contribution to the formulation of various ideas presented here.

# Introduction

The attainment of gender equality requires examining men's and women's participation, roles and inequalities of power in various dimensions of political, social and family life—ranging from the household to the statehouse. It entails redressing inequalities in women's pay and their lower participation in the paid, out-of-home labour market as well as achieving change in social expectations regarding men's roles in families. That men should be co-contributors to gender equality may seem obvious. After all, gender as a concept refers to masculinities *and* femininities, and women *and* men, the power relations that exist between them, and the structural contexts that reinforce and create those power relations. In practice, however, gender frequently refers exclusively to women and girls and the disadvantages they face (International Center for Research on Women and Instituto Promundo, 2010). Similarly, public policies seeking to promote gender equality have often perceived men as obstacles, as constituting a homogeneous group, or as being static and unchanging. Only recently have policymakers in some settings begun to view and understand men as "gendered"—that is, as shaped by dynamic gender norms and structures, and as co-contributors to gender equality.

One of the core enduring symptoms of gender inequality globally is the unequal work-life divide—stemming from the fact that men are generally expected to be providers and breadwinners (who work mostly outside the home) and women and girls are generally expected to provide care or to be chiefly responsible for reproductive aspects of family life. This inequality is revealed most strikingly by two statistics. First is that globally, women earn on average 22 per cent less than men (World Bank, 2007). Second is the unequal burden of care work. Recent multi-country study including lower, middle and higher-income countries found that the mean time spent on unpaid care work by women is from 2 to 10 times greater than that spent by men (Budlender, 2008). These realities persist even as women have begun working outside the home in unprecedented numbers and as their roles have changed in households and political life, albeit with tremendous variation by region and social class. The bottom line is that men's participation in care work has not kept pace with women's increased contribution to household income and their work outside the home, and that women's income is still less than men's (even when they perform similar kinds and amounts of work).

However, as the title of the present chapter suggests, change is occurring—more slowly in some settings, more quickly in others—and is being prodded in large part by global economic trends, including the recent global economic recession. At the same time men's roles as fathers and caregivers are becoming more visible. Policies in some countries are slowly recognizing men's roles as fathers and caregivers and encouraging greater participation by men in family life. The global data and trends seem to indicate that change is slow but inevitable and that steps can be taken to speed it up. For the generation of younger men, the world is not the world of their fathers. This is true at two levels. First, conditions framing pathways to adult manhood, particularly to stable employment, are in flux and, in some parts of the world–even in crisis—to a greater extent than in the past. Second, social expectations about men's involvement in the care of children, reproduction in general and fatherhood are also changing, albeit slowly, nearly everywhere we look. We can affirm that the work-life balance and the unequal distribution of income between men and women have been slow to change, but they are changing.

This chapter seeks to provide a global review and analysis of these issues, while recognizing that it is impossible to capture all the nuances in these trends globally—and how they interact with other factors such as social class, urban/rural differences, educational attainment and age (including generational change). Discussed specifically are: (a) the changing dynamics of families and the role of men; (b) changing notions of manhood, manhood in crisis and the transition to manhood; (c) trends in engaging men in sexual and reproductive health; (d) poverty alleviation strategies and men's roles in families, and (e) the implications of these trends in terms of social policy for the United Nations, national Governments, local government, civil society and researchers.

The chapter is framed within the context of masculinities, a concept through which to understand how men are socialized, how men's roles are socially constructed (in constant interaction with women's roles) and how these roles change over the lifecycle and in different social contexts (Connell, 1994). The concept of masculinities also enjoins us to examine the diversity of men, and the pressures they may feel to adhere to specific versions of manhood—particularly the version shaped by widespread belief that being a man means being a provider or having stable employment—and to understand how such roles change historically and by social context, and within the various domains where social meanings of gender and gender-based power inequalities are constructed.

This chapter is also framed within the context of the key United Nations conventions and conferences related to gender equality. Specifically, the 1994 International Conference on Population and Development held in Cairo affirmed that achieving gender equality and empowering women are key components of eradicating poverty and stabilizing population growth. The Conference also established the importance of involving men in improving sexual and reproductive health, and emphasized the need to increase men's involvement in the care of children (World Health Organization, 2007). The Programme of Action of the International Conference on Population and Development (United Nations, 1995) calls for leaders to "promote the full involvement of men in family life and the full integration of women in community life" (para. 4.29) ensuring that "men and women are equal partners" (para. 4.24).

Pursuant to the International Conference on Population and Development, the Commission on the Status of Women at its forty-eight session reiterated and expanded on these issues, recognizing that men and boys can and do make contributions to gender equality, and urging greater involvement of men as fathers.[1] The Commission also acknowledged the need to develop policies, programmes and school curricula that encourage and maximize men's positive involvement in achieving gender equality. Furthermore, it urged Governments to adopt and implement legislation and policies designed to close the gap between women and men in terms of occupational segregation, parental leave and working arrangements and to encourage men to fully participate in the care and support of others, particularly children.[2]

1   See agreed conclusions of the forty-eighth session of the Commission on the Status of Women on the role of men and boys in achieving gender equality contained in Economic and Social Council resolution 2004/11, available at: http://www.un.org/womenwatch/daw/csw/csw48/ac-men-auv.pdf

2   An overview of these policies is presented in the final section of this chapter.

Similarly, the Millennium Development Goals encompass time-bound targets for achieving key health and development indicators, with many of those focused on achieving gender equality and improving women's lives (in terms of maternal health, education, poverty eradication, HIV/AIDS prevention and support, and reducing violence against women). Analysis using 12 indicators to measure progress on priorities of the MDGs (International Center for Research on Women, 2008) shows that clear advances have been made in empowering women, especially in education, and increasing women's political representation in national parliaments and local governments. However, improvements in women's lives in other areas—reducing violence against women, increasing women's income, and reducing inequalities related to the care burden, all of which are areas that require engaging men—have yet to be achieved.

With some notable exceptions, Governments have been slow to act on these United Nations recommendations to engage men as allies in achieving gender equality. There have been, however, in the years since Cairo, a growing number of programme experiences with men and boys in areas related to health and gender equality. A 2007 World Health Organization (WHO) review of these experiences confirmed that group education, counselling and health promotion activities carried out by community-based non-governmental organizations, in health clinics, in school settings and via mass media can influence men's attitudes and behaviours in gender-equitable ways (Barker, Ricardo and Nascimento, 2007). These changes have been documented in a wide variety of areas including sexual and reproductive health, HIV prevention and AIDS care and treatment, reducing gender-based violence, maternal and child health, men's participation as fathers and men's own health-seeking behaviour (International Center for Research on Women, 2010). While these experiences provide an important programme base on which to build and inform policy development, in and of themselves they are clearly not sufficient to drive the large-scale change necessary to achieve gender equality.

Within this introduction we can affirm: (a) that a United Nations consensus exists for engaging men in gender equality (even if this mandate has yet to be fully implemented) and (b) that there are programme interventions (and a few at the policy level) that have been evaluated and show some evidence of positive outcomes when men are engaged in the issues described above. What then do we know about the global trends related to men's participation in family life? And what implications does such evidence have for policy development directed towards engaging men in achieving gender equality?

# The changing dynamics of families and the role of men

While trends vary tremendously by region and country, the emergence of several tendencies can be affirmed: (a) slight increases in men's time allocation to care activities in some contexts; (b) decreasing fertility rates globally (with implications for men's time use and their financial investment in children); and (c) increased rates of marital dissolution and growing rates of female-headed households in some contexts, also with implications for men's participation in families. What all of these trends suggest is that there is a move towards smaller families and potentially increased participation by some men in the lives of their children. The present section will also discuss trends related to educational attainment and urbanization and their implications for men's involvement in families.

## Who does the care work?

The fact that women carry out a disproportionate share of care-related activities world-wide, including domestic work and childcare, limits their potential to earn income and perpetuates income inequalities between men and women. A recent multi-country study including lower, middle and higher-income countries found that the mean time spent on unpaid work by women is more than twice that spent by men, with unpaid care work done by women in India and other low-income settings being 10 times greater than that done by men (Budlender, 2008). Similarly, a review of studies from Latin America and the Caribbean showed that men are not dramatically increasing their role in household work and unpaid caregiving activities, even when they live in the same households with their partners, and even as women's participation in the paid labour market has increased dramatically in the region while that of men has stagnated or declined (Barker, 2006 in Bannon and Correia, eds., 2006).

In much of the world, women are increasingly earning income outside the home in both the informal and formal sectors, but they (or other women or girls in the household) continue to carry the greatest burden of care for other family members, including children, the ill or those with disabilities, and community members in need of care. Various studies confirm that women's almost universal gender-specific responsibility to provide unpaid care underpins their lower rates of labour force participation and their lower pay. This inequality is compounded by a greater burden of care for the elderly which is increasing owing to demographic shifts as populations in much of the world grow older. Indeed, numerous studies from countries as diverse as Kyrgyzstan and Brazil demonstrate that a key factor in women's labour market decisions continues to be the issue of juggling work outside the home along with care for children and other family members (Morrison and Lamana, 2006).

The increasing burden on women in combining productive and care work is reflected in these and other time-use studies showing that the increase in the number of hours they spend working outside the home has not been compensated for by men's participation in care work. This is occurring at the same time that men in many low-income countries are experiencing greater difficulty in earning a living, and yet not significantly increasing their contributions to unpaid care activities and household labour (Chant, 2007). This being said, researchers from diverse settings are finding that men do participate in caregiving, albeit sometimes in ways that are not always counted in time-use surveys (National Center on Fathers and Families, 2002; Brown and Chevannes, 1998). Specifically, the ways in which men may be involved with their children by providing guidance or financial support from abroad or from afar if they have migrated for work, accompanying children to school or on outings or activities enabling them to participate outside the home, or working extra hours to pay school fees or other costs associated with the rearing of children—are not always counted as care work.

Much of the lingering inequality in the care burden is associated with the determination of who, under traditional norms is most apt to care for children, along with decisions at the household level based, at least in part, on men's higher income as well as the lower status and value given to care work. An attitude survey conducted in 23 participating European countries found that women frequently reduce their working hours in order to work part-time when they have children. Across the countries surveyed, 50–70 percent of respondents agreed that a woman with a child of school-age should work part-time (International Social Survey Programme, 2002). At the same time, research indicates that the proportion of women aged 25–49 working part- time varies from 70 per cent in the Netherlands to 11 per cent in Portugal. Men in the same countries work, on average, longer hours than women, particularly when they have young children.

Additional data from Europe show the diversity of the care burden. Across Europe, women do more of the care work than men; but while differences are much smaller in Denmark, Finland and Sweden, they are striking in Italy and Austria. The differences between men and women in respect of time devoted to care work or domestic activities are generally smaller in families where both the man and the woman work full-time (Duyvendak and Stavenuiter, 2004). In sum, a common trend for families with young children in the context of higher-income countries is for women to reduce out-of-home working hours while men often increase theirs.

Other research affirms that women are more likely to make long-term, radical changes in their professional lives as a result of having children which, generally, involve working part-time or by changing assignments to better cope with the needs of children and the demands of family life. Men, in contrast, often maintain their full-time employment, take parental leave only for short periods of time and opt for temporary cash benefits; they concentrate instead on short-term efforts to resolve the conflicting demands that arise between work and family life (World Health Organization, 2007).

Is there evidence of changes in these trends? In some higher-income countries, there is evidence of change on the part of men. In the United States of America, for example, research has shown that women spend substantially more time than men in care work, even though women do less and men do slightly more now than they did 20 years ago (Bianchi, and others, 2000, as cited in Lee and Waite, 2005). Similarly, recent research from Norway has revealed an increase in men's participation in domestic activities compared with 20 years ago (Holter, Svare and Egeland, 2009). Studies in Sweden found that fathers with young children had reduced their working hours during the past decade (Statistics Sweden, 2003). Similarly, it was found that men in the United Kingdom of Great Britain and Northern Ireland spent 44 minutes per day on child-care in 1987 compared with 90 minutes in 1999 (Duyvendak and Stavenuiter, 2004). In addition, studies also suggest that it is no longer a "given" that women provide care work and men increase working hours when they have children; instead, these arrangements are now much more open to negotiation now than in the past, which means that "traditional" patterns of inequalities in the care burden exist alongside newer arrangements whereby these dual roles are shared (Ahrne and Roman, 1997).

The International Men and Gender Equality Survey (IMAGES), recent multi-country study carried out with household samples of men in seven countries to date, suggests that changes are expanding beyond high-income countries and that both men

3    Preliminary analysis of
IMAGES, International Center for Research on Women
and Promundo (2010)

and women value greater participation by men in the lives of children.[3] As shown in table I.1, data from five of the countries surveyed (Brazil, Chile, Croatia, India and Mexico) indicate that the vast majority of men think that it is important for them to play a role in their children's lives. The results also show that 20-65 per cent of men said that they had taken some leave when their last child was born. As is frequently seen in such studies, the amount of time devoted by men to caring for children was greater as reported by men, than as reported by their spouses. Nonetheless, 14-46 per cent of women in the five countries analysed so far reported that their husband or male partner spent the same amount or more time caring for children than they did.

Taken as a whole, the data in this section suggest that while there are persisting patterns of inequality in the care burden, there is some evidence in some settings that the time devoted by men to domestic activities and care work may be increasing.

Table I.1
**The father's early involvement in the life of the child, data from Brazil, Chile, Croatia, India and Mexico** (*percentage*)

|  | Brazil | Chile | Croatia | India | Mexico |
|---|---|---|---|---|---|
| Took leave after last child was born | 61.7 | 23.4 | 40.5 | 68.8 | 66.3 |
| Of men who took leave: This early period with the child let to better relationship later | 92.8 | 99.1 | 91.4 | 84.5 | 96.5 |
| Own report: He plays equal or greater role in daily care of child | 39.0 | 36.3 | 62.7 | 37.1 | 45.8 |
| Women's report: Male partner plays equal or greater role in daily care of child | 10.0 | 10.1 | 17.3 | 17.7 | 31.1 |

**Source:** Preliminary data from
IMAGES survey, using household
samples (men and women aged
18-59).

## Marital dissolution, women-headed households and men's participation in family life

Data from many parts of the world show slight increases in marital dissolution, increasing ages at first marriage (often associated with lower fertility), increases in the number of women who never marry and corresponding increases in the proportion of female-headed households, which are all trends with implications for men's participation in families and in care work. In the United States, for example, the crude marriage rate had risen from 8.5 in 1960 to a high of 10.6 in the early 1980s; then, however, the rate has dropped to 7.3 in 2007, a 31 per cent decline from the early 1980s (United States Census Bureau, 2010, table 78). Similarly, in Japan, in 2008, the marriage rate (per 1,000 population) was 5.8 in the same year the mean age of first marriage was 30.2 for men and 28.5 for women representing a rise of 1.7 years and 2.7 years, respectively, over the previous 20 years (Japan Ministry of Health, Labor and Welfare, 2008). Across the 27 member countries of the European Union, the number of marriages per 1,000 persons decreased: the rate in the years after 2000 was about 5 per cent lower than that during the late 1990s.

In many parts of the world, data also suggest that more marriages and unions are ending in divorce or separation. From a gender-equality perspective, this implies that women (and men) in many parts of the world have more freedom to leave negative relationships or to not marry at all; but in some settings (as described below) couples (and men in particular) may be seen as not having the social and financial means to marry. Given that mothers are more likely to obtain full custody of their children in cases of separation and divorce, these trends mean that a larger proportion of children spend time away or live apart from their biological fathers than in the past. For example, the number of divorces in the European Union has grown steadily exceeding 1 million in 2005, the equivalent of about 42 divorces per 100 marriages, or in terms of an annual rate, 2 divorces per 1,000 persons.

Similarly, most of Latin America has experienced increasing rates of marital dissolution. In Panama, divorce rates nearly doubled from 3.8 per 1,000 persons in 1986 to 6.2 per 1000 persons in 1996 (Alatorre, 2002). In Nicaragua 16 per cent of women were divorced in 1998 and the divorce rate in Costa Rica in 1999 was 29 per cent, up significantly from previous years (ibid.). In Australia, 1 in 4 marriages ends in divorce and a high proportion of divorced males, 64.2 per cent as compared to 26.1 per cent of divorced females, remarry (Australian Bureau of Statistics, 2004b).

These trends (and others) have led to an increase in the number of women-headed households and the number and proportion of men who do not live with their biological children. Currently, between 15 and 45 per cent of households in Latin America and the Caribbean are classified as female-headed, these potentially being two-parent or single- parent households although in general female-headed households are often single-parent households (Inter-American Development Bank n.d.). The country with the highest proportion of female-headed households in Latin America is Brazil where the figure is 33.81 per cent (ibid.). In Mexico, 25 per cent of households are headed by a single adult, the vast majority of those adults being women (Cunningham, 2001). Similarly, about one fourth of households in Central America were headed by women: 28.24 per cent in Nicaragua, 18.4 per cent in Guatemala, 26 per cent in Honduras and 33.56 percent in El Salvador (Inter-American Development Bank n.d.). In the English-speaking Caribbean—characterized by a high rate of migration of men and by a matrifocal family structure—the proportion of female-headed households is even higher, ranging from 37-49 per cent (Alatorre, 2002).

Similarly, about 8 per cent of United States households can be categorized as female-headed with children. These trends can be seen in other regions as well. For example, approximately 26 per cent of all households in Viet Nam (Food and Agriculture Organization of the United Nations, Regional Office for Asia and the Pacific; United Nations Development Programme, 2002) and 29.5 per cent in Japan are female-headed (Japan Population Census, 2005). It follows then that many men live apart from at least some of their children for a significant portion of those children's lives. The combination of higher rates of marital dissolution and later average ages at first marriage has also resulted in higher proportion of children who are born outside formal unions in some countries.

Globally, a sizeable minority of fathers do not live with their children. Data from a survey conducted in 43 countries on five continents show that as many as 3 in 10 men aged 25–39 and as many as 2 in 10 men aged 30–39 who fathered a child do not live with their children. This situation is more common among men living in urban areas than among those living in rural areas, with men moving from their rural homes to look for work (Alan Guttmacher Institute, 2003). Other factors accounting for the fact that men do not live with their children include marital break-ups; the custom of sending some children from rural areas to school in urban areas; and cases where parents send their biological children to live with another family—an arrangement common in parts of West Africa.

National surveys in the United States indicate that more than one fourth of children living in single-mother families did not see their fathers in the previous year. Some studies also find that post-divorce father involvement is higher among fathers who had close relationships with their children prior to divorce, fathers who live in close proximity to their children, and fathers who have joint custody (Arditti and Keith, 1993; Mott, 1990). These studies provide further evidence suggesting that characteristics of families prior to and after divorce ultimately influence the extent of father-child interaction. Recent research shows that non-residential fathers may remain involved in many ways that are not measurable by the frequency of contact, and that at least a minority of fathers are particularly likely to remain involved even after divorce or separation (Argys and others, 1998; Cabrera and others, 2008; Hofferth and others, 2007; King and others, 2004 as cited in Hofferth and others, 2007; and King, Harris and Heard, 2004, all cited in Hofferth, Forry and Peters, 2010). The motivation for non-residential fathers to be involved is less clear than for residential fathers. Non-residential fathers have somewhat more choice with respect to how much an investment they make in their children and how often they make it (McDonald and Koh, 2003); and they may not expect to benefit as much from future income or other support from their children (Hans, Ganong and Coleman, 2009; Sheng and Killian, 2009). While many studies have found decreased participation of fathers after divorce and separation, it has been shown that, in fact, many fathers in diverse settings living apart from their children continue to spend time with and money on them (Hofferth and Anderson, 2003).

Some divorced or separated fathers also start new families. With the decrease in contact with their non-residential children from previous unions and with new children and spouses vying increasingly for their attention, fathers are likely to experience a decline in their voluntary emotional involvement with and financial investments in their non-residential children (Hofferth Forry and Peters, 2010). Child support enforcement mechanisms, such as automatic pay withholding, may make some fathers' financial contributions through child support payments less dependent on the relationship with their children and former spouse than in the past (ibid.). On the other hand, relationships with children are affected by the stresses commonly associated with conflicts with former spouses over responsibilities towards and involvement with children are more costly to maintain and often lead to gradual disengagement (Amato in Gilbreth, 1999; Eldar-Avidan, Itaj-Yahia and Greenbaum, 2008). Consistent with this hypothesis, most studies have shown a gradual decline in a father's contact with children after separation (Argys and others, 2007) with notable exceptions however. For example, a study of the Agincourt subdistrict of Mpumalanga, South Africa, showed that children are as likely to receive financial support from fathers who are not members of the same household as from fathers with whom they reside. The study also found that children who receive support from their fathers during any part of their lives are likely to receive support consistently throughout their lives (Madhavan, Townsend and Garey, 2008).

Further, policies related to child support, divorce and paternity leave and those that promote men's involvement in childbirth also influence men's involvement in the lives of their children. Child support laws and laws recognizing the rights of children born outside formal unions have had an impact on men and their participation as fathers, although systematic research on the issue is scarce. Similarly, policies and practices in the public-health system influence whether fathers are allowed or encouraged to be present at the birth of their children and whether they are encouraged to participate in meeting children's health needs (Lyra, 2002).

## Other trends affecting men's participation in care work and in family life

In addition to marital dissolution, at least two other major trends are affecting men's participation in care work, notably, urbanization and increases in educational attainment. The impact of urbanization on men's participation in family life is not always clear. On the one hand, men's migration for work (as mentioned earlier) often affects their contact with children and their availability for at home care work. While urbanization can weaken the supports of traditional community life, especially when it separates poor men from their families, it can also create the desire for smaller families (Allan Guttmacher Institute, 2003). Exposure to new attitudes in urban areas—such as those that favour gender equality—may encourage men to be more active in family life. Furthermore, urban settings may also trigger changes in household arrangements with fewer extended families available to provide child care, for example), which could lead to changes in childcare arrangements.

Educational attainment also impacts men's participation as fathers, as well as in other domestic activities (Hernandez, 1996 as quoted in Barker and Verani, 2008). A recent study of men in major urban centres in Mexico found that higher educational attainment and having been born in urban areas, as well as positive attitudes toward men's participation in domestic chores, were associated with men's participation in domestic tasks; however, income level and employment status were not found to be associated with such participation (Garcia and Oliveira, 2004). Another study in Mexico found that 79 per cent of men with university education, compared with only 22 per cent of men with no or low education, believed that domestic chores should be jointly shared by men and women (Salles & Tuirán, 1996). Still another study in Mexico found that middle-class men with higher educational attainment and whose wives work, are more likely to participate in childcare tasks (Hernandez, 1996). Other authors, on the other hand, have found that men with low incomes are also taking on new tasks in the household, including childcare (Gutmann, 1996).

Studies have shown that educational levels among men in developing countries have increased considerably over the past 20–30 years, with implications for men's participation in families. In countries as disparate as Nigeria and Mexico, for example, between 60-70 per cent of men in their early twenties have completed primary school, compared with only 20-30 per cent of men aged 40–54 (Alan Guttmacher Institute, 2003). While education in urban areas has increased, over the past 20–30 years, levels of schooling in rural areas have often remained unchanged, suggesting that trends towards more positive attitudes regarding gender equality on the part of men (and possibly more participation in care work) may be greater among those with more education in urban areas.

Increased educational attainment, which often creates the desire for a more "modern lifestyle" (a term that has different meanings in different contexts), tends to result in a rise in the average age at which young people marry and first have a child, as more educated couples decide to wait until they are established economically before starting families. In sum, studies in diverse settings have found a correlation between higher levels of education and the holding of more positive attitudes towards gender equality, which again suggests that increasing educational attainment for young men may be associated with greater participation in care work (and other manifestations of acceptance of gender equality) at least in some settings.

While these data in and of themselves suggest tremendous changes in family and household structures, they do not provide a complete picture nor do they capture individual and household differences. Data consistently show that single parent female-headed households are poorer than two-parent ones. However, these data are limited in that they often do not tell us about connections and networks of social support that may exist for families beyond the household nor about individual differences within households (Bruce and others, 1995; Budowski, 2006 and Budowski and Bixby, 2003, as cited in Barker and Verani, 2008; Katapa, 2006). Indeed, some research findings show that when there is a man in the household or the household is headed by a male, a woman's burden can increase rather than decrease. A study in Nicaragua of mothers of children 12-18 months of age found that women spent more time in household production when a father was present than when he was absent (Bruce and others, 1995). Moreover in situations where men use alcohol or perpetuate violence, it may turn out that women effectively head the households even when men are present, or that the higher income men bring in is offset by the social costs of their presence. Finally, the contributions of fathers who migrate to female-headed households may be rendered invisible.

In sum, we should avoid making simplistic assumptions or generalize about men's participation in care work, whether in female-headed households or in two-parent/worker households. Some data show that when women work, men increase their relative participation in routine housework, and the influence of women's employment status operates in part by increasing women's support for egalitarianism with respect to the roles of spouses (Cunningham, 2001). These examples suggest the need for caution when making generalizations about household behaviour in cases where men or fathers are absent or in cases of divorce or separation. Furthermore, it is important to realize that the fact that men simply devote more hours per week to care work or strengthen their ties to their children does not mean that they fully embrace, support or live gender equality. While activities like washing dishes, playing with children and cooking are important in the short run, we should be careful not to assume that such actions carried out by men mean that gender equality has been achieved, either at the household level or on a societal level. Box I.1 below provides another example of the complexity of gender roles within the context of household headship trends and men's participation in the lives of their children.

## Men, masculinities and families: changing manhood, manhood in crisis, transition to manhood

It may appear obvious that the concept of adult manhood is defined perhaps universally, by societies, institutions, individuals and public policies in terms of the role of provider, breadwinner or working man. The underlying *syllogism* is as follows: *If adult*

Box I.1

**Jamaica: adaptive strategies for men's participation in the lives of children in the face of income instability**

In Jamaica, only 16 per cent of women in their childbearing years are married. The majority of first children are born into visiting unions of young unmarried partners. Women and men may have multiple unions and have children who may or may not live with them. On aggregate, men give more income to the children they live with, but diverse patterns make generalizations difficult (Brown and Chevannes, 1998). The case is common of the young man who fathers children as a symbol of his manhood before he has the means to support them, and subsequently forms a more permanent union, devoting consider-able resources to those children with whom he currently lives. Researchers argue that this is a functional and historically based pattern established to ensure family survival in the face of post-slavery poverty and lingering social exclusion, and given the nature of the Jamaican economy which provides insufficient sources of income for many low-income men and women (ibid.). Women-headed households are sometimes preferred by women because they cherish their independence and not necessarily because men use violence against them or are negligent in their roles as providers (Barrow, 1998 and 2001). Similarly, another study in Jamaica found that women preferred visiting unions because such unions gave them greater freedom from control by a spouse, while still allowing the fathers to spend time with their children (reported to be 14-15 hours per week on average) (Chevannes, 2001).

**Source:** The World Bank (2006).

*manhood equals work, not having work means not being socially recognized as an adult man.* For many men not having work results in shame, stress, depression, lack of social identity, and for some young men in some settings, increased likelihood of engagement in delinquency, armed violence or other antisocial behaviours. Men's employment status also plays a role in determining when they can form families, whether they are able to contribute financially to their families and in some cases, whether they live with their children.

If men globally derive their identities and chief social function from their role as providers, what happens when men are without work, or do not have sufficient income to meet the social expectations placed on them as providers? Specifically, what happens under such conditions in terms of men's participation in family life, involvement with their children and family formation?

These issues are particularly salient in the face of a global economic recession and ongoing restructuring in the labour market. According to the International Labour Organization (2009), in middle and upper-income economies, there are signals that the global economic crisis may be at least as detrimental for men as for women, and possibly more so initially, as witnessed by the stronger increase of the unemployment rate in developed economies for men compared with women in 2008 (1.1 percentage points for men versus 0.8 percentage points for women). This led to a narrowing of the gender gap in the unemployment rate in 2008, but only because the situation of men in the labour market had worsened, not because of women's gains.

Similarly, according to the United States Bureau of Labor Statistics, more than 80 per cent of job losses in the United States during the recent recession have been among men. More than 6 million jobs have been lost in the United States and Europe in sectors traditionally dominated by men (construction and heavy manufacturing), and they continue to decline further and faster than in those sectors in which women traditionally have predominated (public-sector employment, healthcare, and education). Furthermore, men in many middle and upper-income economies are falling behind in respect of acquiring the educational credentials necessary for success in the knowledge-based economies.

In many parts of the world, unemployment and underemployment of men, economic stress due to the global recession and income instability are associated with negative mental health. Emerging results from the International Men and Gender Equality Survey, mentioned previously, indicate that a relatively high proportion of men report that they are frequently ashamed to face their family, or are stressed or depressed as a result of having too little income or being unemployed or underemployed. In India, for example, out of 1,552 men interviewed in the household survey in two cities, 30 per cent (regardless of their current employment status) said they were ashamed to face their family because they had been out of work or did not have enough income. Those men who reported being stressed or ashamed as a result of unemployment were nearly 50 per cent more likely to have used violence against a partner and twice as likely to have used sexual violence, and had had less consistent condom use (putting them and their partners at risk of HIV), and higher rates of alcohol use than men who did not report economic stress (International Center for Research on Women and Insituto Promundo, 2010).

To be sure, women's increased participation in the labour market and increased income relative to men exemplifies success in achieving gender equality. The evidence is also clear that in addition to being a cornerstone of gender justice, women's greater economic participation contributes to overall economic development. In 2006, the Organization for Economic Cooperation and Development, OECD (which devised the Gender, Institutions and Development Database to measure the economic and political power of women in 162 countries) concluded that the greater the economic and political power of women, the greater the country's economic success. Similarly, at the level of corporations, greater participation by women is associated with greater profits. For example, researchers at Columbia University Business School and the University of Maryland analysed data on the top 1,500 United States companies in the period from 1992 to 2006 to determine the relationship between firm performance and female participation in senior management. They found that firms that had women in top positions performed better (Rosin, 2010).

As women enter the workforce in greater numbers, some men in certain parts of the world are embracing women as equal partners and participating in more equitable ways in all aspects of social and family life. Others, however, have expressed resistance to women's entry into the workplace, whether at the individual level or at the level of trade union policies that have hindered women's entry into specific work settings (Segal, 1990). In low-income countries, studies focused on women beneficiaries of microfinance programmes and other economic empowerment initiatives have found that greater income for women can often lead to more respect from male partners, in addition to a reduction of their victimization from violence. Other men, however, as we saw from the data from the International Men in Gender Equality Survey, while experiencing stress in the face of economic instability and the resulting inability to be socially recognized as providers, are, apparently not rushing back home to increase their participation in childcare nor necessarily accepting women as fully equal partners in the workplace.

For the majority of young men worldwide, stable employment is the pathway to being socially recognized as adult men, which in most parts of the world is associated with family formation. However, as the world faces its largest-ever youth cohort combined with a global economic recession, many young men are not able to acquire stable employment. In consequence their paths to family formation are often blocked or otherwise obstructed. Furthermore, an increasing proportion of young men are unemployed or have low-paying jobs. For example, among 15–24-year-olds, rates of unemployment (defined as the proportion of men who say they have no work and are searching or are available for work) are 29 per cent in Sri Lanka; 30 per cent in Greece; 33 per cent in Italy; 34–35 per cent in Jamaica, Egypt and Morocco; and 56 per cent in South Africa (see table I.2 for more examples of these trends).

Table I.2

**Unemployment rates of young men aged** (15-24), **various regions 1997, 2006 and 2007** (percentage)

| | 1997 | 2006 | 2007 |
|---|---|---|---|
| World | 10.7 | 12.0 | 11.6 |
| European Union, EU | 14.5 | 13.4 | 12.7 |
| Central and South-Eastern Europe (non-EU) and Commonwealth of Independent States | 20.4 | 17.9 | 17.2 |
| South Asia | 6.6 | 11.1 | 10.7 |
| South-East Asia and the Pacific | 9.5 | 16.2 | 15.0 |
| East Asia | 8.5 | 7.9 | 7.8 |
| Latin America and the Caribbean | 11.5 | 11.9 | 11.5 |
| Middle East | 20.7 | 17.1 | 17.1 |
| Northern Africa | 23.0 | 20.2 | 20.1 |
| Sub-Saharan Africa | 11.6 | 11.2 | 11.1 |

Source: International Labour Organization (2008)

However, many young men have occasional jobs in the informal labour sector and are thus not counted in official labour statistics. These young men may wash cars, load and unload trucks, run errands or carry messages, sell goods on the street or scavenge in garbage dumps (Alan Guttmecher Institute, 2003). In Latin America and the Caribbean, the United Kingdom of Great Britain and Northern Ireland and the United States, many young men in the low-income category are combining school and employment. However, in some countries, sizeable proportions of young men are involved in neither activity (ibid.).

As noted earlier, numerous studies confirm that young men face societal pressure to conform to gender stereotypes as "breadwinners", incurring shame if they cannot live up to such expectations (Leahy and others, 2007). If they have difficulty finding employment, young men may opt to prolong their education, if possible, or may migrate in search of work, either within their own countries or to other countries. In certain circumstances, rapid population growth and expanding youth cohorts in search of jobs and social identities may be risk factors for social and political instability.[4]

The Middle East is clearly faced with such a situation. Studies show that recent high economic growth in the Middle East did not sufficiently resolve the region's

4 The vast majority of new civil conflicts in recent decades have occurred in countries in which young people account for at least 60 per cent of the entire population.

education and employment problems. The global economic slowdown is hitting the Middle East at a time when the youth share of the total population is at a historic high (nearly 32 per cent of the population is between the ages of 15 and 29), which means that a large number of new job seekers will continue to exert pressure on the region's labour markets for years to come (Dhillon and Tarik, 2009).

Unable to secure the economic independence and social status that comes with gainful employment, young people in the Middle East make adjustments by delaying their plans to marry and form families. While early marriage continues to be the norm in a few poorer countries and in rural areas, the regional trend is towards an involuntary delay of marriage. This is particularly true for young men in the Middle East, who are delaying marriage for longer periods than their counterparts in other developing regions. Young men there and in other regions report delaying marriage because they cannot accumulate the capital or goods (for example apartments and appliances) considered necessary to be able to marry. In a region where marriage and family formation are considered fundamental rites of passage to adulthood, the involuntary delay of marriage is a form of exclusion and, by protracting the transitions of young people, is generating new social and economic difficulties (Egel and Salehi-Isfahani, 2010).

All of these trends suggest that the traditional gendered social identity for men—that of being the breadwinner—is no longer a certainty (if it ever was). Certainly, many low-income men have had trouble historically finding and holding on to stable work. However, the changing nature of job markets, the end of many forms of career employment on a near global basis, increasing income inequality, global labour and economic shifts and the size of the current global youth cohort all interact to leave millions of young men in a prolonged "waithood" or "youthhood." The diverse consequences of these trends range from exacerbation of armed conflict (as seen in some parts of Africa) to domestic violence (as noted earlier, there is evidence that violence against women by male partners is associated with economic stress).

These issues must be taken into consideration in any attempt to understand the nature of men's participation in families. Again, in citing these data, we must affirm that such trends also leave young women vulnerable, particularly those with low-income. In focusing on the effects of these trends on young men and family formation, we are not in any way implying that the lives of young women in the same settings are stress-free. Their historical exclusion from some forms of employment and their lower income and lower educational attainment compared with those of young men have, to be sure, put young women in low income countries in particular at a disadvantage.

## Trends in engaging men in sexual and reproductive health

Related to men's participation in the lives of children is the extent to which men participate in planning or exercising control with respect to when they have children and how many children they have. Indeed, if we expect men to assume the care of children, we must start by increasing men's participation in the spacing and controlling of reproduction and encouraging them to see themselves as reproductive beings.

There is evidence of changes in this regard. As a result of at least 20 years of efforts by non-governmental organizations, Governments and the United Nations to increase men's involvement in family planning (and in large part owing to economic and social change, including women's increased income and educational attainment), there has been some improvement in terms of men's increased support for their female partners' use of contraceptives and their own increased use of certain male contraceptive methods (condoms and vasectomies). This having been said, women continue to account for nearly 75 per cent of global contraceptive use.

Studies from around the world have found an increased awareness of contraceptive methods on the part of men, even in countries with high fertility (Abraham and others, 2010). Similarly, men's fertility preferences are clearly declining. One study with data from 43 countries (Alan Guttmacher Institute, 2003) representing all regions of the world found that young men aged 15-34 prefer fewer children than their older male peers (aged 50-54). Table I.3 presents these trends.

Even as men are becoming more aware of their need to participate in contraceptive use and even when public-health systems offer such services to men, men's involvement with such issues continues to be far less than women's. For example, in Brazil, national data from the public health system (SUS) show that between 1996 and 2006, the number of women who sought tubal ligations in the national public health system was about three times greater than the number of men who sough vasectomies, although these data may be incomplete inasmuch as many vasectomies are performed in private clinics (Penteado and others, 2001).

Despite these disparities, many men around the world are already active and responsible family planning partners and many share the belief that reducing unwanted pregnancies saves women's lives. Similarly, a number of studies show that many men desire access to better contraceptives and would use male hormone-based contraceptives should any of several such products currently in the early stages of development ultimately prove effective. For example, in a recent study of British men, 80 per cent identified a hypothetical male pill as one of their top three contraceptive choices (Brooks, 1998). Another study found that over 60 per cent of men in Germany, Spain, Brazil and Mexico were willing to use a new method of male contraception and as many as 49 per cent in the United States, and more than 25 per cent in Asia showed a willingness to use male hormone-based contraceptives if and when they become available (Heinemann and others, 2005).

These few examples suggest that men's participation in family planning, like their participation in care work and their reactions to economic stress, takes various forms which are changing in some settings. Policies and national health systems (and non-governmental organizations) that have worked to engage men to a greater extent in issues of sexual and reproductive health can claim at least modest success. These trends are linked in turn to a growing participation by some men (particularly younger men) in care work and a greater acceptance of more gender-equitable lifestyles.

## Men's presence and involvement in maternal care and childbirth

In many Western European countries, national health systems have made efforts to involve men to a greater extent in maternal health and in childbirth. The most common

Table I.3

## Men's fertility preferences in selected countries, 1991-2006

| Country and survey year | Mean number of children desired | Percentage of men who are fathers | | Mean number of children desired by men aged 25-39 | | | Percentage of men who are fathers | | Mean number of children | | | Mean Number of children desired |
|---|---|---|---|---|---|---|---|---|---|---|---|---|
| | Men 15-34 | Men 15-19 | Men 20-24 | Total | Rural | Urban | Men 25-29 | Men 30-39 | Men 40-44 | Men 45-49 | Men 50-54 | Men 50–54 |
| **Sub-Saharan Africa** | | | | | | | | | | | | |
| Benin Republic, 2001 | 6.0 | 2 | 1.8 | 7.6 | 8.9 | 5.9 | 61 | 89 | 7.4 | 9.5 | 10.8 | 15.4 |
| Ethiopia, 2000 | 4.9 | 0.3 | 14 | 6.5 | 6.9 | 4.3 | 59 | 87 | 5.9 | 8.0 | 8.5 | 9.1 |
| United Republic of Tanzania, 1999 | 4.6 | 1 | 24 | 5.4 | 5.9 | 4.4 | 66 | 91 | 6.0 | 7.6 | 9.1 | 7.8 |
| Uganda, 2000-2001 | 4.7 | 5 | 40 | 5.8 | 6.1 | 4.4 | 82 | 95 | 7.3 | 9.0 | 9.6 | 7.7 |
| **Asia** | | | | | | | | | | | | |
| Bangladesh, 1999-2006 | 2.3 | .. | .. | 2.3 | 2.4 | 2.2 | .. | .. | 4.2 | 4.7 | 5.9 | 2.6 |
| Kazakhstan, 1999 | 2.9 | 0.2 | 20 | 3.3 | 3.5 | 3.1 | 62 | 87 | 2.8 | 2.9 | 3.9 | 3.2 |
| Nepal, 2001 | 2.5 | .. | .. | 2.7 | 2.8 | 2.2 | .. | .. | 4.1 | 4.5 | 4.5 | 3.0 |
| **Middle East and North Africa** | | | | | | | | | | | | |
| Egypt, 1992 | 3.1 | .. | .. | 3.1 | 3.3 | 2.8 | .. | .. | 5.0 | 5.8 | 6.6 | 3.4 |
| Morocco, 1992 | 2.6 | .. | .. | 3.3 | 3.7 | 2.9 | .. | .. | 5.3 | 6.3 | 6.1 | 4.5 |
| Turkey, 1998 | 2.6 | .. | .. | 2.6 | 2.7 | 2.6 | .. | .. | 3.6 | 4.4 | 5.1 | 3.0 |
| **Latin America and Caribbean** | | | | | | | | | | | | |
| Plurinational State of Bolivia, 1998 | 2.6 | 3 | 29 | 3.0 | 3.1 | 2.9 | 62 | 86 | 4.6 | 5.2 | 5.5 | 3.2 |
| Haiti, 2000 | 3.2 | 1 | 21 | 3.1 | 3.4 | 2.8 | 47 | 83 | 5.3 | 6.7 | 6.4 | 3.7 |
| Mexico, 1996 | 2.6 | 2 | 34 | 3.7 | 4.0 | 3.5 | 63 | 93 | 4.6 | 5.4 | 6.1 | 3.8 |
| Nicaragua, 1997-1998 | 2.6 | 4 | 46 | 3.2 | 3.4 | 3.0 | 76 | 90 | 5.2 | 5.9 | 5.9 | 3.6 |
| **Industrialized Countries** | | | | | | | | | | | | |
| United Kingdom, 1990 | .. | 2 | 13 | .. | .. | u. | 36 | 70 | 1.8 | 2.1 | 2.2 | .. |
| Hungary, 1993 | 1.9 | 3 | 13 | 0.7 | 0.6 | 0.7 | 47 | 79 | 1.8 | .. | .. | .. |
| Japan, 1997 | 1.9 | .. | .. | 2.3 | 2.4 | 2.2 | 19 | 56 | 1.7 | 1.9 | .. | 2.3 |
| United States, 1991 | 2.3 | 3 | 17 | 2.5 | .. | .. | 35 | 36 | 2.0 | 2.2 | 2.4 | 2.6 |

Source: Alan Guttmacher Institute (2003) appendix tables 2-4.

Note: Two dots (..) signify that data are unavailable.

approach, among others, is to invite men to be present at regular prenatal checkups as well as parent training. A study of fathers in Denmark (Madsen, Lind and Munck, 2002) showed that 80 per cent participate in prenatal preparation courses and preventive health care consultations. In Sweden, the corresponding figure is 90 per cent. In several countries, mainly in Scandinavia, parent groups are offered, specifically targeting expectant fathers. Further, in Sweden the interest among men in participating in parent education has increased significantly during the past 20–30 years. Almost 90 per cent of the men who visit maternal and child health services take part in their parent education programmes (Ministry of Health and Social Affairs, 1997). Evaluations show that men who have taken part in these groups react positively; most of them however, are primarily first-time middle-class fathers (Blom, 1996). Similar findings are reported in England (Lewis, 1987).

Some research stresses the importance of focusing not only on parent education classes but also of encouraging men to participate in prenatal visits, particularly ultrasound examinations. A study in the United Kingdom found that presence at ultrasound examinations was important for the men, as it helped them to "visualize the baby and realize their transition to fatherhood" (Draper, 2002), and a study in Sweden concluded that that many men viewed the ultrasound experience as providing confirmation of the existence of a new life and therefore "an important milestone" in developing a paternal identity (Ekelin Crang-Svalenius and Dykes, 2004).

In some middle-income countries in Latin America, there have also been efforts to engage men in prenatal care and in childbirth. Data from Chile, for example, show that the presence of fathers in the delivery room had increased dramatically owing in part to changes in policy and an overall "humanization" of the childbirth process. In 2001, 20.5 per cent of Chilean fathers had been present at the birth of their child, while in 2008, 71 per cent of women reported having had a partner present during childbirth (nearly always the father).

Overall, these data provide evidence from European settings, and some parts of Latin America (and to a limited extent from other parts of the world), that the younger generation of boys and men have developed attitudes that are more supportive of gender-equitability than those of their older peers and relatives. Emerging data from the International Men and Gender Equality Survey cited earlier, for example, reveal that the views of younger men are slightly more supportive of equitability suggesting a shift in attitudes, driven at least in part by their having grown up seeing their mothers work outside the home and their sisters study alongside them in school. On the whole, however, such issues have not been examined systematically (Bannon and Correira, eds. 2006).

## Poverty alleviation strategies and men's roles in families

What impact do poverty alleviation strategies have on men's participation in families? Given that many poverty alleviation programmes often target women as beneficiaries or as "administrators" of their benefits, what do we know about the impact of those programmes on men's participation in family life?

In some low and middle-income countries, such as Brazil and Mexico, conditional cash transfers (CCTs) have become the basis of the largest social assistance programs, reaching millions of households. Such transfers have been hailed as a means to reduce inequality and poverty, as well as to improve child health, nutrition and school enrolment (World Bank, 2009). The fact that conditional cash transfers are, with a few exceptions, given to mothers is a reflection of the efficiency argument which maintains that women are more likely to be living with children and to use additional income to benefit the household.

There is some evidence that targeting families with conditional cash transfers positively affects family well-being. Extensive analysis of such programmes as *Bolsa Familia* (in Brazil), *Oportunidades* (in Mexico) and *Chile Solidario*, among others, by the World Bank suggests that conditional cash transfers generally help reduce poverty levels, income inequality and children's participation in the workplace (World Bank, 2009). In addition, results from various evaluations of conditional cash transfers suggest there were positive programme effects on growth-and-development monitoring visits to health centres by children. Overall, the conclusions so far are that conditional cash transfers reduce family poverty and child labour, which contributes to both mothers' and fathers' participation in the workforce.

Moreover, research findings from Mexico show a decrease in domestic violence when families benefit from conditional cash transfers (Bobonis, Castro and Gonzales-Brenes, 2009; Working Paper 362). Other research results from Mexico indicate that women beneficiaries of conditional cash transfers had a slight increase in marital turnover, in terms of both separation and the formation of new unions for women, suggesting that the additional household income held or controlled by women allows them to leave unsatisfactory relationships and makes them attractive prospects with respect to formation of new, presumably more satisfactory relationships. In the long run, as men perceive these changes in settings where women-focused conditional cash transfers are implemented, they may increase their participation in care work, as has been the case in some higher income countries where women's income increased relative to men's (Bobonis, 2009).

One of the major findings to have emerged from gender analyses of household dynamics has been the lower proportion of income dedicated to their families by men compared to women. Various studies suggest that men devote less of their income as a proportion of their earnings, to the household and therefore that investing in women's income- generation generally offers better returns for family well-being. For example, a study in Guatemala found that a relatively small increase in the mother's income was necessary to improve child nutrition, while an increase in the father's income nearly 15 times as large was required to produce the same benefit in children's health (Bruce and others, 1995). Similarly, a study in Jamaica found that households without men devote a higher percentage of their income to child-specific goods (Wyss, 1995).

While it is true (as affirmed by these studies) that men in aggregate contribute a lower percentage of their income to the household and to children than do women, conditional cash transfers and other women-focused poverty alleviation strategies based on these findings may inadvertently reinforce gender stereotypes. By virtue of their clearly positive and necessary focus on women's income, such programmes and policies may nevertheless reinforce the stereotypical view that women should and will provide for their households (and not necessarily for themselves) and that men will be derelict in supporting their households. The question remains whether it is possible to implement policies designed to increase women's income and at the same time to encourage men to reconsider their responsibility and contribution to their households. The other relevant question is how to promote income and employment generation with specific groups of low-income or socially excluded men and how to encourage them to contribute more of their earnings to the household. A case study of South Africa (see box I.2) provides insights regarding the complexity of this issues. Similarly, data from the United States and Costa Rica suggest that social policies that focus on women as heads of households may inadvertently deter men from assuming family responsibilities, thereby serving in effect to engender self-fulfilling prophecies (Chant and Gutmann, 2002; National Center on Fathers and Families, 2002).

When considering men's financial contributions to the household, existing research would appear to suggest caution when making broad conclusions or generalizations. In addition, there are questions still to be answered regarding the meaning of the fact that men's economic participation has fallen in some settings, both in terms of the global recession (in North America and Europe) and over a longer period (as seen in Latin America).

The conclusion that emerges is that work and poverty as they relate to men must be examined and understood beyond their economic implications. As seen in the previous section, work for men entails more than income: it is very much bound up with social identity and the ability to acquire those items seen as necessary for forming and maintaining families. However, such considerations are rarely taken into account in social policy. For example, child support enforcement—while fundamental to women's rights and children's well-being—is often carried out punitively based on the view that men who do not pay child support are intentionally derelict (in some countries, including Brazil, non-payment is a crime), even if in many cases they may be out of work for reasons beyond their control. In other cases, social policies, including conditional cash transfers may support not the family as a unit but rather children (or mothers and children). Thus, we can see that poverty and joblessness may separate men from their families and that the policies designed to alleviate poverty (particularly child poverty) may treat men as marginal to families. While there is significant research on this issue in terms of welfare policies in the United States and the United Kingdom, for example, there is far less research in low-income settings, including on the gender impact of conditional cash transfers.

## The micro-finance revolution and gender roles

In low-income countries, women-focused microfinance programmes are widely implemented based on the premise that women's lower income on aggregate leaves them vulnerable and perpetuates their limited agency, mobility and social status compared with those of men. In turn, evidence has confirmed that women's participation in microfinance and other economic empowerment approaches can lead to a number of positive benefits for women -including reduced risk of HIV, reductions in violence from male partners, and increased social status and mobility, in addition to the benefits of the income itself (Kabeer, 2009).

However, microfinance programmes and other women's empowerment programmes are also often based on the number of premises—partly sustained by research, and partly not—that men are already economically empowered, that they are not as reliable at paying back loans, that they are not interested in *micro* credit (seeing the income there from as too limited) and that income in the hands of a woman benefits the household more on average than income in the hands of a man. While all of these assertions are supported by research, there are many examples of men's behaviours that challenge them (Ahmed, 2008a). There are men in many settings whose behaviour gives credence to these assertions, but there are also men who act differently contributing high portions of their wages to family income, supporting their wives or partners in their employment, and reacting positively when their wives or partners benefit from microfinance initiatives. As in the case of conditional cash transfers, there is limited research on whether microfinance approaches should focus on couples or families, or on each partner as an individual. Most approaches are based on the assumption that an affirmative action approach focusing on women is necessary to empower women and to allow them to control the microfinance groups in which they participate.

## Men's participation in families in especially vulnerable situations, such as in post-conflict and post-disaster settings

In considering specific contexts of men and families, special attention should be paid to the issue of men and women in conflict settings. While trends and realities vary tremendously by context, the militarization of societies in the context of conflict too often exacerbates violent or militarized versions of manhood, leaving women and girls vulnerable and at the same time suppressing non-violent, more equitable and care-oriented versions of manhood. Furthermore, conflict destroys economies and livelihoods. Often, there are simply no jobs or fewer jobs in a conflict-affected or post-conflict economy, or the jobs that are available are not appealing to most men. Men may see the livelihood options associated with post-conflict reality as a step down from the opportunities that had fostered a sense of powerful male identity during war. For unemployed and out-of-school young men, (re)joining the fighting forces can offer the status, identity, sense of belonging and remuneration that are unavailable in a displacement camp or a devastated and economically weak post-conflict country (Barker and Ricardo, 2003). Thus, in post-conflict settings we see men feeling even more acutely that they lack a positive social identity as providers. This feeling, in turn, sometimes translates into antisocial behaviour and violence directed at women. Other studies affirm that war or conflict leave men with "either an eroded sense of manhood or the option of a militarized masculine identity with the attendant legitimization of violence and killing as a way of maintaining a sense of power and control" (Sideris, 2000, as cited and quoted in Bouta, Frerks and Bannon, 2005). The erosion of male identity as a result of post-conflict unemployment can be exacerbated when there is a sense that men have somehow failed as providers by "losing the war" or have been powerless to prevent the displacement from taking place (Holtzman and Nezam, 2004; Correia 2003 as cited in Baingana, Bannon and Thomas, 2005).

Various studies in recent years have examined how gender, and specifically masculinities, play into the militarization of young men, their recruitment into armed conflict and their perpetration of gender-based violence. For some men, participation as combatants and use of armed violence become means to obtain income and to achieve and wield power, income and power being two commodities that are often difficult to acquire (Barker and Ricardo, 2005). Hence, through the process of taking up arms or becoming soldiers or combatants some boys and young men attain status and are socially recognized as "men" even when they have acquired this status through the use of violence. In addition, young and adult men may also find a sense of connection with male peers in armed insurgency groups and in having access to sexual companionship (albeit forced) as provided, for example by "bush wives" or via transactional sex or forced sex (ibid.).

Particularly for young men, who may have achieved status in armed conflict by being part of militias or standing armies, resiliency in post-conflict settings may depend upon the community elders' behaviour and attitudes towards them in those settings. Many male youth are seen as adults during war, yet return to face social exclusion owing to the fact that they are young, unmarried and out of work. These are trends that have only begun to be studied. In respect of disarmament, demobilization and reintegration (DDR) programming, United Nations Development Programme, the World Bank and other organizations are now paying more attention to the gendered needs of ex-combatants and those affected by conflict, and are beginning to incorporate their findings into programme development. However, discussions have not, for the most part, included extensive examination of men's roles in families or as fathers. Similarly, although there is a growing inclusion of the issue of men in post-conflict settings in discussions on reducing gender-based violence, so far they have not included consideration of men's broader roles in families and the promotion of men's roles as fathers and caregivers.

---

Box I.2
**South Africa: engaging fathers to financially support their children**

South African law recognizes fathers primarily as providers, not as caregivers, and Maintenance Act 99 of 1988 establishes that the biological father of a child, married or not, must maintain or support his child in proportion to his means. Men who do not make payments are criminally liable upon conviction to imprisonment for up to one year or to a fine, although this is very rarely imposed. For low-income or unemployed fathers[a], a compliance with maintenance rulings is a challenge, and the law provides limited support to them in their roles as caregivers.

However, in addition to placing this strong emphasis on men's role in maintaining their children financially, the law now also explicitly recognizes unmarried fathers' rights, particularly in cases where mothers are unwilling or unable to raise their children. Children's Act 38 of 2005 provides that fathers who demonstrate involvement in their children's lives acquire full parental rights and responsibilities, and the default for custody in divorce is now shared custody.

On the other hand, Basic Conditions of Employment Act 75 of 1997 provides only three days' paid leave per year for family responsibility for men, to be used at the time of the birth of a child or sickness or death of a family member. Existing policy in South Africa, as in many other settings, in terms of men's roles as caregivers thus fosters entrenchment of notions of women as primary caregivers and too often fails to support efforts to increase men's involvement in care work.

a  In 2006, 21.2 per cent of men and 30.7 per cent of women aged 15-65 years were unemployed. There has been little progress in reducing unemployment since the end of apartheid, and no progress in reducing wealth disparities in the country. From 1995 to 2005, the average annual growth rate of employment was 3.5 per cent for women and 2.0 per cent for men.

**Source:** International Center for Research on Women and Instituto Promundo (2010).

# Social policy implications for the United Nations, national Governments, local government, civil society and research

This chapter has set out the many ways in which men's participation in families and care work is changing. For some men, particularly in the low income category, shifts in the labour market—short-term and long-term—mean that traditional pathways to achieving the socially recognized role of provider have been narrowed or cut off. In other settings, increased participation by women in the labour market (along with changes in social norms and legislation in some places) has led to shifts in men's behaviours and to at least modest increases in men's participation in care work. For the most part, as we have seen, policies related to health, poverty alleviation and gender equality have not adequately considered ways of promoting men's involvement in care work and parenting. What then can be done to speed up the process of achieving gender equality? How can policies engage men and women in achieving greater gender equality, measured at least in part by men's greater participation in care work?

The forty eighth session of the Commission on the Status of Women in 2004 convened an expert group that provided a clear, far-reaching blueprint for the kinds of policies necessary to achieve these changes and promote men's greater involvement in caregiving. The main recommendations of that expert group are summarized. Following these recommendations, we offer a handful of examples of specific policies that have been implemented in some countries.

Specifically, the Commission called for:

- Expanding paternity leave, building on successful examples of such policies, which have been implemented mostly in middle- and upper-income countries (see table I.3). The large number of men in informal employment in low-income countries, not to mention the cost of such policies, means that they may be more appropriate in middle-income countries but, as discussed below, this is a powerful policy option which has provided strong evidence of positive impact in many settings.
- Offering flexible work options, for example opportunities for men to be able to work part-time when they have children. Data cited earlier from several European and North American settings show that men tend to work more hours when they have children. For many low- and middle-income men, working less when they have children is simply not an option; on the other hand, flexible work hours can allow men to spend time with their families while they maintain their current working hours and income.
- Changing family laws, including laws regarding custody of children so as to enable men to be more active partners and caregivers in the context of the lives of children and dependants. Given the apparently increasing rates of divorce and marital dissolution, an increasing proportion of men are not living with at least some of their biological children. Laws that encourage joint custody and view men as caregivers play an important role in changing such norms and practices.
- Expanding the provision of childcare, including providing work-based day-care centres in all enterprises with a certain number of employees, and counting

men as well as women in calculating childcare needs. Childcare has often been hailed as central to allowing women to work outside the home and increase their income. However, if such benefits are also tied to men's work and if men are involved in childcare, including dropping children off and negotiating such benefits, they may be more likely to view care work as being their obligation as well.

- Implementing programmes in the public education system to give boys and men the skills and knowledge needed to take on new roles in households, including school-based "life skills" courses for boys. A few rigorous impact evaluation studies have provided evidence that some of those programmes were able to change boys' attitudes and practices. However, few of these initiatives have been implemented on a large scale.

- Developing training curricula for teacher training colleges, social work programmes and nursing programmes so as to encourage men's involvement in HIV/AIDS care and other forms of care work. Numerous studies have affirmed the importance of the attitudes of public health staff about men behaviours. Including such issues in tertiary and continuing education programmes can help change institutional norms and practices which too often continue to view men as having no interest in or giving little importance to their children.

- Developing campaigns to increase men's involvement in caregiving in general, and specifically in HIV/AIDS care and support activities in particular. Well-designed mass media campaigns, when combined with group education or discussion sessions about those campaigns have shown evidence of having led to changes in men's attitudes about such issues; those that have demonstrated such impact should be expanded and implemented in additional settings.

To these recommendations, we would also add the need to implement:

- Education policies designed to encourage men's involvement with their children in school and day care, and encouraging more men to become involved in teaching and early childhood care. Specifically, ensuring communication with and involvement of parents of school-going children is too often focused only on mothers. Education policymakers and school staff should promote the involvement of men as fathers in such activities. Furthermore, in many countries the care and teaching of young children are considered "women's work", thus becoming, in essence, an extension of the gendered pattern of domestic care work. Increasing salaries of teachers (whether women or men) and active recruitment of men as primary school and early childhood development teachers can constitute an important pathway towards changing the societal perception of care work as the work of women.

- Health policies that encourage men to participate in maternal and child care, including during childbirth and in all matters involving reproductive and sexual health. As noted earlier, there are programmes that have shown evidence of impact in engaging men in matters of sexual and reproductive health as well as maternal and child health. Such programmes experiences can and should inform national and local-level health policies and practices to engage men at all appropriate levels in such issues.

- Livelihood and poverty alleviation policies that recognize the roles of men and women (and the need to achieve equality between them), that recognize varying family configurations, including the needs and realities of women and men who migrate and single-parent households, and that support both women and men in achieving joint household control of assets and joint household decision-making, and adequate and dignified livelihoods. As noted in the previous section, conditional cash transfers and microfinance programmes have shown tremendous promise and impact in terms of reducing family poverty and reducing short-term economic crises or vulnerabilities at the family level. The majority of such programmes are women-focused, for the reasons described above. Policies can and should explore ways to encourage greater involvement by men in families and care work and complementary activities through which men might contribute a greater portion of their income to households and support joint household decision-making.

Among the many policy areas discussed above, paternity leave may be the one offering the most experience and the most evidence of impact. As can be seen in table I.4, paternity leave policies vary considerably among countries according to whether it is paid or unpaid, as well as in terms of length and flexibility (Duyvendak and Stavenuiter, 2004). In most European countries, parental leave is a statutory right available to either parent (and is known as family-based parental leave) (Drew, 2004). This is distinct from individual leave, which is generally added on to family leave and cannot be transferred. For example, Finland has a six-month quota for the father, Norway four weeks of paternal leave and Sweden two months reserved for each parent. In Iceland, the parental leave is divided into three parts: three months for the mother, three months for the father and three months that both can share. Some countries outside Scandinavia, also have special paternity leave. Belgium, France, the Netherlands, Portugal, Spain and the United Kingdom, for example, all offer paternity leave of 2–11 days (Duyvendak and Stavenuiter, 2004). However, as table I.4 shows, most countries continue to offer only a few days or a week at the most of paternity leave. In the process, such policies continue to reinforce the notion that men are "helpers" and continue to impose care work on women.

Clearly, paternity leave is not a one-size-fits-all mechanism for engaging men in care work but in granting such leave, societies state publicly and in the strongest possible terms that they value the care work of men, and value care work in general. It also has the added benefit of reducing gender-based work inequalities in that both male and female employees or prospective employees can request (and be entitled to) time off to care for children. In addition, in advocating for more paternity leave to encourage men's greater participation in caregiving activities, the intention should never be to reduce maternity leave. Furthermore, the diversity of childcare arrangements worldwide means that such issues must be context-specific and take into account the availability of other home-based help and what men do with the leave when they take it.

The good news is that these policies should no longer seem utopian. Some experiences with these policies provide (modest) evidence of changes related to gender equality. If in the past, too many policies had inadvertently assumed that men were deficient and derelict with regards to their family responsibilities, now, some countries understand that the needs and realities of men should to be reflected in gender-equality policies. In boxes I.3-I.6, we provide examples of the challenges associated with changing policy as well as the modest successes that have resulted.

Box I.3
## Norway: paternity leave and gender-equality policies

Since 1986, Norway has enacted and revised a series of gender-equality policies and made gender equality a central part of its social welfare policies. These policies have included subsidized childcare, family leave that benefits both, mothers and fathers, promotion of pay parity for women, and the promotion of the advancement of women in politics, business and academic life. One indicator of Norway's success is its having been ranked first in the world in gender equality using the International Gender Gap Index developed by the World Economic Forum. In 1986 and in 2006, the government carried out a Gender Equality and Quality of Life Survey, to assess the impact of 20 years of gender-equality policies. The findings were the following:

Seventy per cent of women and 80 per cent of men were satisfied with their current division of home chores, and overall, women and men who reported more equality in time use reported more satisfaction with their partner.

As of 1993 Norwegian policy offered 1 month of non-transferable paid leave for fathers out of 11 months total parental leave. In 2000, the policy was amended so that men's pay during leave was based on their own salary, not that of the mother. The result showed an increase in the number of men taking more and longer parental leave. Fathers whose youngest child was born after 2000 took an average of 6.1 weeks paid leave, compared with an average of 4.2 weeks for fathers whose younger children had been born before 2000. The vast majority of men and women viewed fathers' use of paternity leave positively, saying it helped them have closer relationships with their children. In 2009, the non-transferable father's quota was extended to 10 weeks out of 12 months total parental leave.

Pay disparities between women and men continue, and nationwide, women earn about 15 per cent less than men. Furthermore, several workplaces continue to be gender-segregated, with more men valuing higher-paying positions, and more women valuing professions involving helping others. About 30 per cent of men work in the industrial, building and construction sector compared to about 10 per cent of women, and 60 per cent of women say they work in places where the majority of employees are women. Nonetheless, when both men and women appreciated workplaces that were more gender-balanced.

Men's time and women's time devoted to domestic activities have become nearly equal. As a result, women and men report more satisfaction with the household.

In general, increased gender equality has resulted in lower rates of violence perpetuated by men against women and by men (and women) against children, and to the conclusion that the father's role as the agent of physical punishment or violence is disappearing from the average Norwegian home. Women and men in Norway perceive the increased gender equality as having brought more happiness and greater quality of life. Both support greater gender equality (including increased leave for fathers), and see it as a public good for all. This experience was associated with wide-ranging social welfare policies and a political commitment to social equality. Thus, whether such levels of gender equality can be achieved without also attaining other kinds of social equality, particularly income equality, along with additional wide-reaching reforms in democratic participation, is a major and lingering question as other countries seek to learn from the Norwegian experience.

Source: International Center for Research on Women and Instituto Promundo (2010).

Box I.4
## Brazil: engaging men in childbirth onward

In Brazil, a national policy in place since 2005 has given women the right to have a person of their choice present during childbirth (with the idea that, in many cases, this would be the father of the child). In practice, however, health practitioners (rang-

Box I.4
**Brazil: engaging men in childbirth onward** (*continued*)

ing from hospital administrators to doctors and nurses) are opposed to the practice or do not facilitate its implementation. They argue that they cannot guarantee women's privacy in crowded delivery wards; others think men get in the way.

To raise awareness about men's involvement in childbirth and childcare, in 2008 the Network of Men for Gender Equality (RHEG), a national network of non-governmental organizations, some affiliated with MenEngage, started a national campaign whose title, *Dá licença, eu sou pai,* involved a play on words: "give me leave, I'm a father." The campaign included a national public service announcement featuring prominent Brazilian actors and awareness-raising material distributed via non-governmental organizations and in public spaces such as hospitals, schools and transportation hubs.

In addition, there have been increasing public discussions in Brazil about expanding paternity leave. Currently, men who become fathers (including via adoption) have 5 days of paternity leave under the 1988 federal constitution (compared with mothers who have 120 days of leave guaranteed by law, which has been extended to 180 days in some workplaces and regions of the country since). These five days of paternity leave include the weekend. For example, if a child is born on a Thursday, the father is required to be back at work on the following Tuesday. Some women's rights advocates in Brazil have questioned whether increasing paternity leave will improve women's lives, citing national household data that show that women spend on average 21.8 hours a week on domestic chores (including childcare activities) compared with 9.1 hours for men, and that women with children under age 14 who live with a man spend 2 hours more per week on average than women in households where a man is not present. However, some States and cities in Brazil have increased paternity leave to between 15 and 30 days for Government employees; and in 2007, discussions started regarding the introduction of a law seeking to extend paternity leave to up to 30 days.

**Source:** International Center for Research on Women and Instituto Promundo (2010).

Box I.5
**Sweden: paternity and maternity leave**

For nearly four decades, the Government of Sweden has legislated to give women equal rights at work, and men equal rights at home. As Swedish mothers take almost four times as much time off with children than men, laws also reserve at least 2 months of the generously paid, 13-month parental leave exclusively for fathers. The government also guarantees the parent on leave a full salary for a year before he or she returns to a guaranteed job. Both mothers and father can work six-hour days until children entered school. The country has adopted an approach based on the notion that the only way to achieve equality in society is to achieve equality in the home. Increasing fathers' share of parental leave is an essential part of this approach. A study by Goteborg University showed that 41 per cent of companies reported in 2006 that they had made a formal decision to encourage fathers to take parental leave, up from only 2 per cent in 1993. In 2009, the proportion of male and female employees who took leave was as high as 24 per cent. Since 1995, more than 8 men in 10 have taken parental leave. The addition of a second non-transferable father month in 2002 only marginally increased the number of men taking leave, but the amount of time they took more than doubled, with benefits for men and women. A study by the Swedish Institute of Labour Market Policy Evaluation showed that a mother's future earnings increase on average 7 per cent for every month of leave taken by the father. It noted that a growing number of couples with university degrees split the leave evenly; some switch back and forth every few months to ensure that neither parent assumed a dominant role or was away from his or her job for too long.

Other countries tried to adopt similar parental-leave policy models. The United States, with lower taxes and traditional wariness of State meddling in family affairs, is not among them. Portugal is the only country where paternity leave is mandatory but only for a week. As noted earlier, Iceland has arguably gone furthest, reserving three months for father and three months for mother and allowing parents to share another three months. In 2007 Germany adapted Sweden's model and reserved 2 out of 14 months of paid leave for fathers. Within two years, the proportion of fathers taking parental leave surged from 3 to more than 20 per cent. Eight fathers in 10 in Germany now take one third of the total 13 months of leave; and 9 per cent of fathers take 40 per cent of the total or more, up from 4 per cent a decade ago.

**Source:** Bennhold (2010).

Box I.6
## Chile: increasing men's participation during childbirth

Owing to demand by women and men, and public-health reform efforts such as those advocating breastfeeding and changes designed to humanize childbirth, a growing number of pregnant women giving birth in the public health care system of Chile are now accompanied by their male partners. For example, in 2001, 20.5 per cent of women had been accompanied by a person of their choice during birth. In 2008, 71 per cent of women reported the presence of a partner during childbirth (nearly always the father). Until 2009, this increase was due not necessarily to a specific policy to encourage men's involvement but to the fact that the public-health system permitted men to be present during childbirth. In September 2009, a law institutionalized the Childhood Social Protection System ("Chile Grows with You" *Chile Crece Contigo*) created during the tenure of President Bachelet. The health component of this system is a programme that aims to support the holistic development of children, which promotes increased in the participation of fathers in childcare, pregnancy and birth.

**Source:** International Center for Research on Women and Instituto Promundo (2010).

# Final comments

The examples and policy recommendations presented above suggest concrete steps that may be taken by national and local governments to change the notion that caregiving is exclusively the work and role of women. The examples demonstrate that promoting large-scale change requires changing the way in which public and private institutions– including the workplace, schools, and the public health system–treat families, men and women. Perhaps key to achieving these changes is acknowledging at the highest levels of policy men's roles in families, and changing our deepest held assumptions about men's (and women's) contributions to families. As the ILO Committee of Experts has noted, «measures designed to promote harmonization of work and family responsibilities, such as childcare services, should not be specific to women». Indeed, excluding men's participation in such issues too often perpetuates the idea that women alone are responsible for childcare, and continues to devalue care work in general, and thus often increases or maintains discrimination against women in the workplace broadly (International Labour Organization, 2004).

Finally, we must also acknowledge that these changes will not occur quickly. As Lynne Segal cogently asserts in her insightful and influential book entitled *Slow Motion: Changing Masculinities, Changing Men:*

State policy, and expansions and contraction of welfare, as well as patterns of paid employment for men and for women, affect the possibilities for change in men. The competitive, individualistic nature of modern life in the West exacerbates the gulf between what is seen as the feminine world of love and caring and the masculine world of the market-place—wherever individual men and women may find themselves. As some socialist feminists have always known, the difficulty of changing men is, in part, the difficulty of changing political and economic structures (Segal, 1990, p. 309).

Indeed, policymakers who take seriously the need to engage men to a greater extent in family life and care work and should be prepared to test, evaluate and modify their approaches over the long term. They should also be prepared to invest in long term structural change which combines social justice with gender justice. Finally, we must acknowledge that engaging men in more equitable ways in care work is not simply changing the behaviour of small groups or small numbers of men—however powerful men's and women's individual experiences in this regard may be. It is fundamentally about changing the conditions that shape and structure the lives of women, men and families.

Table I.4
**Paid paternity and maternity leave, selected countries, various regions**

| Country | Paid paternity leave | Paid maternity leave | Restrictions/comments |
|---|---|---|---|
| **Africa** | | | |
| Cameron | 10 days paid leave for family events related to worker's home | 14 weeks (paid 100 per cent) | |
| Djibouti | 10 days family-related leave | 14 weeks (paid 50 per cent for private sector and 100 per cent for public employees) | |
| Rwanda | 2 days paternity leave | 12 weeks (paid 67 per cent) | Employer provides 67 per cent maternity coverage |
| South Africa | 3 days' paid family responsibility leave | 4 months (up to 60 per cent depending on the level of income) | Unemployment insurance fund covers required percentage of maternity leave |
| **Asia and the Pacific** | | | |
| Philippines | 7 days paid paternity leave for married workers | 60 days | Social security provides 100 per cent maternity coverage |
| Cambodia | 10 days special leave for family events | 90 days | Employer provides 50 per cent of maternity coverage |
| Australia | 18 weeks federal minimum wage (from 1 January 2011, pending parliamentary approval) | | The 18 weeks paid and the 52 weeks are shared 50-50 between the parents. Parental leave: 1 year, unpaid. Can be shared or taken by one parent but is available only to employees on the payroll for 12 months prior to birth |
| **Latin America** | | | |
| Paraguay | 2 days paid paternity leave | 12 weeks (50 per cent for 9 weeks) | Social security provides maternity coverage |
| Bahamas | 1 week family-related leave | 13 weeks | Social security or employer provides maternity coverage |
| Argentina | 2 days' paid paternity leave | 90 days | Social security provides 100 per cent maternity coverage |
| Guatemala | 2 days at birth of child | 84 days | Social security or employer provides 100 per cent maternity coverage |
| **Europe** | | | |
| Norway | Each parent can take an extra full year of unpaid leave after the paid period ends. Paid paternity leave–45 weeks at | 42 or 52 weeks parental leave (9 weeks reserved for the mother) | Social security provides 80 per cent or 100 per cent maternity coverage. Parental leave: 2 weeks after birth but most are paid by employer. Father must take a |

| Country | Paid paternity leave | Paid maternity leave | Restrictions/comments |
|---------|---------------------|---------------------|----------------------|
| **Europe** (*continued*) | | | |
| | 80 per cent of pay or 35 weeks at 100 per cent shared with mother | | minimum of 6 weeks or lose the paid leave. Each parent has to have worked for his or her employer for at least 6 of the 10 months prior to birth or any leave is unpaid |
| Portugal | 5 days paternity leave | 120 days (100 per cent paid) | Social security provides 100 per cent maternity coverage |
| United Kingdom of Great Britain and Northern Ireland | 2 weeks paid paternity leave | 26 weeks (90 per cent for the first 6 weeks and flat rate after) Increased statutory maternity pay from £55 per week in 1997 to £102.80 and rising to £106 per week from April 2005 | Employer refunds for 92 per cent from public funds. The person requesting paternity leave must have worked for his or her current employer for at least 26 weeks before the fifteenth week before the due date (and received a salary that is higher than a fixed minimum). He or she must give the employer notice before the fifteenth week before the child is due |
| Turkey | 3 days paternity leave in public sector | 16 weeks (67 per cent for 12 weeks) | Social security provides maternity coverage |
| **North America** | | | |
| Canada | 55 per cent up to $447/week for 35 weeks parental leave (shared with mother) | 17-18 weeks depending on the Province (paid 55 per cent up to a ceiling) | Employment insurance provides maternity coverage. Part time work as percentage of total employment: parents can work part-time without losing benefits if they are earning 25 per cent or less of their usual income or Canadian dollars 50 per week, whichever is greater |
| United States of America | | There is no statutory maternity leave, paid or unpaid (the United States of America has a right to leave for family and medical reasons, which could include care of a new-born baby, but this is unpaid) | The federal Family and Medical Leave Act of 1993 (FMLA) protects workers' job security during leave taken for the employee's own disability or illness (including pregnancy and childbirth); the care of the employee's newly born, adopted, or foster child; or the care of an immediate family member (spouse, child or parent) with a serious health condition. The FMLA applies to employees who work 20 or more weeks in a year and have worked at least 12 months for their current employer and who work for a firm employing at least 50 workers. This federal policy ensures that eligible employees receive:<br>• Up to 12 weeks of unpaid leave annually (leave may be taken all at once or intermittently, and for part or all of a day)<br>• Continued health insurance benefits (if ordinarily provided by the employer)<br>• a guarantee of return to the same, or an equivalent, job |
| **Middle East** | | | |
| Saudi Arabia | 1 day of paid leave | 10 weeks (paid 50 per cent or 100 per cent depending on the duration of employment) | Employer provides maternity coverage |
| **Central Europe and Russian Federation** | | | |
| Russia | Following the after birth portion of maternity leave, up to 18 months after birth: 1,500-6,000 roubles per month for the first child, 3,000-6,000 roubles a month for any subsequent child, but not exceeding 100 per cent (could be shared with father, grandparents, guardians or actual caregivers of the child) | | Social security provides 100 per cent maternity coverage |
| Estonia | 14 calendar days | 140 calendar days (paid 100 per cent) | Social Security provides 100 per cent maternity coverage |
| Romania | 5 days' paid paternity leave | 126 calendar days (paid 85 per cent) | Social Security provides maternity coverage |
| Latvia | 10 calendar days | 112 days (paid 85 per cent) | Social Security provides 100 per cent maternity coverage |

# References

Abraham, W., A. Adamu, and D. Deresse (2010). The involvement of men in family planning an application of the transtheoretical model in Wolaita Soddo Town South Ethiopia. *Asian Journal of Medical Sciences,* vol. 2, No. 2, pp. 44-50, 2010.

Ahmed, F. (2008). Microcredit, men and masculinity. NWSA Journal, vol. 20. No. 2 (summer), pp. 122-155.

Ahrne, G. and C. Roman (1997). Hemmet, Barnen och Mmakten: Förhandlingar om Arbete och Pengar i Familjen. Statens offentliga utredningar, No. 39 (arbetsmarknads-departementet). Stockholm: Fritzes.

Alan Guttmacher Institute (2003). In Their Own Right. Addressing the Sexual and Reproductive Needs of Men Worldwide. New York: Alan Guttmacher Institute. Avaialble from http://www.guttmacher.org/pubs/itor_intl.pdf

Alatorre, J. (2002). Paternidad responsable en el istmo centroamericano. Document No. LC/MEX/L.475/ Rev. 1. Mexico City: United Nations, Economic Commission for Latin America and the Caribbean (CEPAL).

Amato P. and J. Gilbreth (1999). Nonresident fathers and children's well-being: a meta-analysis. *Journal of Marriage and the Family*, vol. 61 (August), pp. 557–573.

Arditti, J. A. and T. Z. Keith (1993) «Visitation Frequency, Child Support Payment, and the Father-Child Relationship Postdivorce.» *Journal of Marriage and the Family* vol. 55, No. 3, pp. 699-712.

Argys, L., and others (1998). The impact of child support on cognitive outcomes of young children. *Demography*, vol. 35, No. 2 (May), pp. 159-173.

_____ (2007). *Measuring contact between children and nonresident fathers*. In *Handbook of Measurement Issues in Family Research,* S.L. Hofferth and L. M. Casper, eds., pp. 375–398. Mahwah, New Jersey: Erlbaum.

Australian Bureau of Statistics (2006). *2006 Census QuickStats: Australia*. Available from http://www.abs.gov.au/AUSSTATS/abs@.nsf/web+pages/statistics?opendocument#from-banner=GT.

Baingana, F., I. Bannon and R. Thomas (2005). Mental health and conflicts: conceptual framework and approaches. Health, Nutrition and Population (HNP) Discussion Paper. Washington, D.C.: World Bank.

Bannon and Correira (2006). *The Other Half of Gender. Men's Issues in Development.* Available from http://www-wds.worldbank.org/external/default/WDSContentServer/WDSP/IB/2006/06/20/000090341_20060620141950/Rendered/PDF/365000Other0ha101OFFICIAL0USE0ONLY1.pdf

Barker, G. (2006), Men's participation as fathers in the Latin American and Caribbean region: critical literature review and policy options. In *The Other Half of Gender: Men's Issues in Development,* I. Bannon and M.C. Correia, eds., pp. 43-72. Washington, D.C.: World Bank.

Barker, G. and K. Ricardo (2003). Young men and the construction of masculinity in sub-Saharan Africa: implications for HIV/AIDS, conflict and violence. Social Development Papers, Conflict Prevention and Reconstruction, No. 26. Washington, DC.: World Bank, June, 2005.

_____ (2005). Engaging boys and men to empower girls: reflections from practice and evidence of impact. Document EGM/DUGC/2006/EP.3. United Nations, Division for the Advancement of Women in collaboration with UNICEF. Available from http://un.org/womenwatch/daw/egm/elim-disc-viol-girlchild/ExpertPapers/EP.3%20%20%20Barker.pdf .

_____ and M. Nascimento (2007). Engaging Men and Boys in Changing Gender- based Inequity in Health: Evidence from Programme Interventions. Geneva: World Health Organization. Available from http://www.who.int/gender/documents/Engaging_men_boys.pdf.

Barker, G. and F. Verani (2008). *Men's Participation as Fathers in the Latin American and Caribbean Region: A Critical Literature Review with Policy Considerations.* Brazil: Instituto Promundo and Save the Children. Available from http://www.promundo.org.br/wp-content/uploads/2010/03/Mens%20Participation%20as%20Fathers%20in%20the%20Latin%20American(2008)-ING.pdf

Barrow, C. (1998). Caribbean masculinity and family: revisiting marginality and «reputation». In *Gender Portraits: Essays on Gender Ideologies and Identities*, C. Barrow, ed., pp. 339-358. Kingston: Ian Randle Publishers, in association with the Centre for Gender and Development Studies, University of the West Indies.

_____ (2001). Children's rights and Caribbean family life: contesting the rhetoric of male marginality, female-headed and extended family breakdown. In *Children's Rights: Caribbean Realities*, C. Barrow, ed., pp. 189-213. Kingston: Ian Randle publishers.

Bennhold, K. (2010). The female Factor: in Sweden, men can have it all. *New York Times*, Available from http://www.nytimes.com/2010/06/10/world/europe/10iht- sweden.html.

Binzel, C., and R. Assaad (2008). Pathways to marriage in Egypt: how the timing of marriage for young men is affected by their labor market trajectory. Economic Research Forum, November 2008.

Blom, U-L. (1996). Pappautbildning. Utvärdering av ett forsook med pappautbildning I fyra landsting och en kommun. Stockholm: SPRI, Socialdepartementet och Landstingsförbundet.

Bobonis G. (2009). The impact of conditional cash transfers on marriage and divorce. Working Paper No. 359. Toronto: University of Toronto, Department of Economics.

_____., R. Castro and M. González-Brenes (2009). Public transfers and domestic violence. the roles of private information and spousal control. Working Paper, No. 362. Toronto: University of Toronto, Department of Economics.

Bouta, T., G. Frerks and I Bannon (2005). *Gender, Conflict and Development.* Washington, D.C.: World Bank.

Brooks, M. (1998). Men's views on male hormonal contraception: A survey of the views of attendees at a fitness centre in Bristol. *British Journal of Family Planning*, vol. 24, No. 1, pp. 7-17.

Brown, J. and B. Chevannes (1998). Why man stay so: an examination of gender socialization in the Caribbean. Kingston: University of the West Indies.

Bruce, J., and others (1995). *Families in Focus: New Perspectives on Mothers, Fathers and Children.* New York: Population Council.

Budlender, D. (2008). The Statistical Evidence on Care and Non-Care Work across Six Countries. *Gender and Development Programme Paper*, No.4. Geneva: United Nations Research Institute for Social Development.

Budowski, M. (2006). *Dignity and Daily Practice: The Case of Lone Mothers in Costa Rica.* Berlin: LIT verlag.

_____, and L.R. Bixby (2003). Fatherless Costa Rica: child acknowledgment and support among lone mothers. *Journal of Comparative Family Studies*, vol. 34, No. 2 (spring), pp. 229-254

Cabrero, N.J., and others (2008). Low-income nonresident father involvement with their toddlers: variations by fathers' race and ethnicity. *Journal of Family Psychology*, vol. 22, No. 4 (August), pp. 643-647.

Chant, S. (2007). Dangerous equations? how female-headed households became the poorest of the poor: causes, consequences and cautions. In *Feminisms in development: Contradictions, Contestations and Challenges*, Andrea Cornwall, Elizabeth Harrison and Ann Whitehead, eds., pp. 35-47. London: Zed Books.

_____ and M. Gutmann (2002). "Men-streaming" gender? questions for gender and development policy in the twenty-first century. *Progress in Development Studies*, vol. 2, No. 4, pp. 269-282.

Chavannes, B., (2001), Fatherhood in the African-Caribbean landscape: an exploration of meaning in context. In *Children's Rights: Caribbean Realities, C. Barrow, ed.,* pp. 214-226. Kingston: Ian Randle publishers.

Connell. R.W. (1994). *Masculinities.* Berkeley, California: University of California Press.

Cunningham, W. (2001). Breadwinner or caregiver? how household role affects labor choices in Mexico. World Bank Policy Research Working Paper 2743. Washington, D.C.: World Bank, Latin America and the Caribbean Region, Gender Sector Unit, December.

De Watteville, N. (2002). Addressing gender issues in demobilization and reintegration programs. Africa Region Working Paper Series. Washington, DC: World Bank.

Dhillon, N., and T. Yousef, eds. (2009). *A Generation in Waiting: The Unfulfilled Promise of Young People in the Middle East.* Washington, D.C.: Brookings Institution Press.

Draper, J. (2002). It was a real good show: the ultrasound scan, fathers and the power of visual knowledge. *Sociology of Health and Illness*, vol. 24, No. 6, pp. 771-795.

Drew, E. (2004). Parental leave in Council of Europe member states. Available from www. coe.int/equality.

Duyvendak, J. W., and M. Stavenuiter, eds. (2004). Working fathers, caring men: reconciliation of working life and family life. The Hague: Verwey-Jonker Instituut, Rotterdam.

Egel, D., and D. Salehi-Isfahani (2010). Youth education, employment and marriage transitions: evidence from the school to work transition survey. Middle East Youth Initiative Working Paper. Washington, D.C.: Wolfensohn Center for Development at the Brookings Institution and the Dubai School of Government. Washington, D.C.: March.

Eisenberg M.L, and others (2009). Racial differences in vasectomy utilization in the United States: data from the national survey of family growth. *Urology*, vol. 74, No. 5 (November), pp. 1020-1024.

Ekelin, M., E. Crang-Svalenius and A.K. Dykes, A-K (2004). A qualitative study of mothers' and fathers' experiences of routine ultrasound examination in Sweden. *Journal of Midwifery*, vol. 20, No. 4, pp. 335-344.

Eldar-Avidan D., M.M. Haj-Yahia and C.W. Greenbaum (2008). Money matters: young adults' perception of the economic consequences of their parents' divorce. *Journal of Family and Economic Issues*, vol. 29, No. 1, pp. 74–85. Eurostat (2009). Available from http://epp. eurostat.ec.europa.eu/cache/ITY_OFFPUB/KS-CD-09-001/EN/KS-CD-09-001-EN. PDF).

Fiszbein, A., and others (2009). *Conditional Cash Transfers: Reducing Present and Future Poverty.* A World Bank Policy Research Report. Washington, D.C: World Bank Available from http://siteresources.worldbank.org/INTCCT/Resources/5757608-1234228266004/PRR-CCT_web_noembargo.pdf

Food and Agriculture Organization of the United Nations, Regional Office for Asia and the Pacific and United Nations Development Programme (2002). *Gender differences in the transitional economy of Viet Nam.* Bangkok: FAO and UNDP.

Garcia, B. and O. Oliveira (2004). El ejercicio de la paternidad en México urbano. In *Imágenes de la familia en el cambia de siglo.* Mexico City: Instituto de investigaciones sociales, Universidad Nacional Autónomia de Mexico (UNAM), pp. 283-317.

Garfield C.F., and A. Isacco (2006). Fathers and the well-child visit. *Pediatrics*, vol. 117, No. 4 (April), pp. 637-45.

Grown, C., G. Rao Gupta and A. Kes (2008). Seven priorities, seven years to go: progress on achieving gender equality. Washington, D.C.: International Center for Research on Women.

Gutmann, M. (1996). *The Meanings of Macho: Being a Man in Mexico City*. Berkeley, California: University of California Press.

Hans J.D., L.H. Ganong and M. Coleman (2009). Financial responsibilities toward older parents and stepparents following divorce and remarriage. *Journal of Family and Economic Issues*, vol. 30, No. 1, pp. 55–66.

Heinemann, K., and others (2005). Attitudes toward male fertility control: results of a multinational survey on four continents. *Human Reproduction*, vol. 20, No. 2, pp. 549-56.

Hernandez, D. (1996). *Genéro y roles familiares: la voz de los hombres*. Master's thesis in social anthropology. Centro de Investigaciones y Etudios Superiores en Antropología Social, Mexico City.

Hofferth S.L, and K.G. Anderson (2003). Are all dads equal? biology versus marriage as a basis for paternal investment. *Journal of Marriage and the Family,* vol. 65, No. pp. 213–232.

Hofferth S., N.D. Forry and H. Elizabeth Peters (2010). Child support, father–child contact, and preteens' involvement with nonresidential fathers: racial/ethnic differences. *Journal of Family and Economic Issues*, vol. 31, No. 1. pp. 14–32.

Hofferth S., and others (2007). *Residential father involvement and social fathering*. In S. Hofferth and L. Casper, eds., pp. 335-374. *Handbook of Measurement Issues in Family Research*. Mahwah, New Jersey: Erlbaum; 2007. pp. 335–374.

Holter, Ø.G., H. Svare and C. Egeland (2009). *Gender Equality and Quality of Life: A Norwegian Perspective*. Oslo: Nordic Gender Institute (NIKK).

Holtzman, S., and T. Nezam (2004). *Living in Limbo: Conflict-Induced Displacement in Europe and Central Asia*. Washington, D.C.: World Bank.

Inhorn, M.C., and others, eds. (2009). *Reconceiving the Second Sex: Men, Masculinity and Reproduction*. New York: Berghahn Books.

Inter-American Development Bank (n.d.) Sociometro database. Country comparison of households headed by females. Available from http://www.iadb.org/sociometro/

International Center for Research on Women and Instituto Promundo (2010). What men have to do with it: public policies to promote gender equality. Available from http://www.icrw.org/files/publications/What-Men-Have-to-Do-With-It.pdf.

International Fund for Agricultural Development (2000). Grenada: Rural EnterpriseProject: Formulation Mission Report. Working Paper I, "Socio-economic and gender equity aspects of the target group". Rome.

International Labour Organization (2004). Addressing gender equality through work-family measures. Information sheet No. WF-2. May. Available from http://www.ilo.org/public/english/protection/condtrav/pdf/infosheets/wf-2.pdf

_____ (2009a). Conditions of Work and Employment Programme (TRAVAIL). Available from http://www.ilo.org/public/english/protection/condtrav/family/reconcilwf/natpolicies.htm

_____ (2009b). *Global Employment Trends for Women: March 2009*, p. 2. Geneva: International Labour Office.

_____ (2008). *Global Employment Trends for Youth: October 2008*. Geneva: International Labour Office.

International Social Survey Programme (GEIS) (2004). Family and changing gender roles III (34 countries). Z A Study 3880, ISSP 2002. Cologne, Germany: Zentralarchiv fuer Empirische Social forschung. UK Data Archive 5018.

Japan Ministry of Health, Labor and Welfare (2009). *Statistical Handbook of Japan 2009,* chapt. 2, "Population". Tokyo: Statistics Bureau.

Katapa, R. S. (2006). A comparison of female- and male-headed households in Tanzania and poverty implications. *Journal of Biosocial Science*, vol. 38, No. 3, pp. 327-340.

Kreider, R.M. and J.M. Fields. (2002). Number, timing, and duration of marriages and divorces: 1996, p.18. U.S. Census Bureau Current Population Reports, Washington D.C.: United States Government Printing Office.

King, V., K.M. Harris and H.E. Heard (2004). Racial and ethnic diversity in non-resident father involvement. *Journal of Marriage and the Family*, vol. 66, No. 1 (February), pp. 1-21.

Lee Y., and L. Waite (2005). Husbands' and wives' time spent on housework: A comparison of measures. *Journal of Marriage and Family*, vol. 67, No. 2 (May), pp. 328–336.

Leahy, E. and others (2007). The shape of things to come: Why age structure matters to a safer, more equitable world, p. 24, Washington D.C.: Population Action.

Lewis, C. (1987) *Becoming a Father*. Philadelphia, Pennsylvania: Open University Press.

Lyra, J. (2002). *Paternidades adolescentes. Conferencia Regional: "Varones adolescentes Construcción de Identidades de Género en América Latina. Subjetividades, prácticas, derechos y contextos socioculturales.* Santiago de Chile, 6-8 de noviembre 2002.

_____ and B. Medrado, B. (2002). *Paternidade na adolescência: construindo uma agenda política.* Regional Latin-American conference and international workshop on Young Men as Allies in the Promotion of Gender Health and Equality. Rio de Janeiro, Brazil, 27-30 August 2002.

MacDonald M, and S.K. Koh (2003). *Consistent motives for inter-family transfers: simple altruism. Journal of Family and Economic Issues,* vol. 24, No. 1, pp. 73–97.

Madsen S.A., D. Lind and H. Munck (2002). *Fædres tilknytning til spædbørn*. Copenhagen: Hans Reitzel Förlag.

Madhavan, S., N. Townsend and A. Garey (2008). Absent breadwinners: fathers' connections and paternal support in rural South Africa. *Journal of Southern African Studies,* vol. 34, No. 3, pp. 647-663.

Morrison, A., and F. Lamana (2006). Gender issues in the Kyrgyz labor market. Background paper for Kyrgyz Poverty Assessment. Washington, D.C.: World Bank.

Mott, Frank L. (1990). *When is a father really gone? paternal-child contact in father-absent homes. Demography*, vol. 27, No. 4, pp. 499-517.

National Center on Fathers and Families (2002). The Fathering Indicators Framework: A tool for quantitative and qualitative analysis. Philadelphia, Pennsylvania: NCOFF.

Olavarria, J. (2000). *La reproducción: Los padres populares en la crianza y las actividades domesticas.* Santiago de Chile: Facultad Latinoamericana de ciencias sociales (FLACSO).

_____ (2002). *Hombres: identidades, relaciones de genero y conflictos entre trabajo y familia. en Trabajo y familia: ¿conciliación? Perspectivas de género.* Santiago de Chile Flacso-Chile, Servicio Nacional de la Mujer (SERNAM), Centro de Estudios de la Mujer (CEM), Santiago de Chile.

Organization for Economic Cooperation and Development. (2009). Time use for work, care and other day-to-day activities. Family database available at www.oecd.org/els/social/family/database. Social Policy Division–Directorate of Employment, Labour and Social Affairs. Available from http://www.oecd.org/dataoecd/1/50/43199641.pdf

Penteado, L., and others (2001). Organizing a public-sector vasectomy program in Brazil. *Studies in Family Planning,* vol. 32, No. 4, pp. 315–328.

Population References Bureau. (2010). Female-headed households with children, by race/ethnicity, 1970-2002 Available from http://www.prb.org/pdf/DiversityPovertyCharacterize FemaleHeadedHouseholds.pdf

Rosin, H. (2010) The end of men. Atlantic Monthly (July/August). Available from http://www. theatlantic.com/magazine/archive/2010/07/the-end-of-men/8135).

Salam, R., The death of macho. *Foreign Policy*, 22 June 2009.

Salles, V and R. Tuiran (1996). Vida familiar y democratiación de los espacios privados. In M.L. Fuentes and L. Otero, eds. *La Família: Investigacion y Política Publica*. Mexico City: Sistema Nacional para el Desarrollo Integral de la Familia.

Segal, L. (1990). *Slow Motion: Changing Masculinities, Changing Men*. Rutgers University Press: New Brunswick, New Jersey.

Sheng X., and T.S. Killian (2009). *Over time dynamics of monetary intergenerational exchanges. Journal of Family and Economic Issues*. vol. 30, No. 3, pp. 268–281.

Sideris, T. (2000). Rape in war and peace: some thoughts on social context and gender roles. *Agenda*, No. 43, pp. 41-45.

United Nations (1995). *Report of the International Conference on Population and Development, Cairo, 5-13 September 1994*, sales No. E.95.XIII.18.

_____ (2009) Department of Economic and Social Affairs. Division for the Advancement of Women, Kabeer, N. (2009). *2009 World Survey on the Role of Women in Development: Women's Control over Economic Resources and Access to Financial Resources, including Microfinance*. Sales No. E.09.IV.7.

United States Census Bureau (2010). *The 2010 Statistical Abstract* (129th ed.) Washington, D.C. Available at http://www.census.gov/statab/.

Wambui T., A.C. Ek and S. Alehagen S. (2009 ). Perceptions of family planning among low income men in Western Kenya. *International Nursing Review*, vol. 56, No. 3 (September), pp. 340-345.

World Bank. (2006a). Gender Equality as Smart Economics: a World Bank Group Gender Action Plan. September.

World Health Organization (2007). Fatherhood and health outcomes in Europe: a summary report. Copenhagen: WHO Regional Office for Europe. Available from http://www. euro.who.int/__data/assets/pdf_file/0019/69013/E91129sum.pdf

Wyss, B. (1995). Gender and economic support of Jamaican households: implications for children's living standards. Doctoral dissertation, University of Massachusetts, Amherst.

II

# Fatherhood and families

Linda Richter, Jeremiah Chikovore, Tawanda Makusha, Arvin Bhana,
Zitha Mokomane, Sharlene Swartz and Monde Makiwane

## The authors

Professor **Linda Richter** (Ph.D.) is a Distinguished Research Fellow at the Human Sciences Research Council in South Africa, and is currently on half-time contract at the Global Fund to Fight AIDS, Tuberculosis and Malaria in Geneva. Professor Richter has conducted both basic and policy research in the field of child, youth and family development as applied to health, education, welfare and social development, and has published more than 250 papers and book chapters in the fields of child, adolescent and family development. She is the author of several books and monographs, including *Mandela's Children: Growing Up in Post-Apartheid South Africa* (Routledge, 2001) and *Baba: Men and Fatherhood in South Africa* (HSRC Press, 2006). She has devised a number of innovative intervention programmes and has advised local and international agencies on the design, implementation and evaluation of interventions for children, youth and families. Her focus in this regards has included malnourished children and their caregivers, street children, children in situations of conflict and war, support for vulnerable children provided by youth, promoting men's care and protection of children, social protection and human rights, and both mitigation and palliative care for children in the context of the HIV/AIDS pandemic.

Drs. **Jeremiah Chikovore** (sociologist), **Zitha Mokomane** (demographer), **Arvin Bhana** (psychologist), **Sharlene Swartz** (sociologist) and **Monde Makiwane** (demographer) are all senior researchers in the Human Sciences Research Council, South Africa. **Tawanda Makusha** is a PhD intern with Linda Richter. The group works together on issues of men and fatherhood.

# Introduction

The issue of men, fathers and fathering has become an increasingly important focus of family research, practice and policy. Engaged and caring men are important in the lives of women and children and supportive family life including children in turn benefits men's health and well-being. Conversely, evidence from around the world points to the adverse consequences on children of absent, dysfunctional or violent fathers.

Family formation is not random or arbitrary. The fact that, among the majority of primates, female kin coalitions rear infants, makes paternal investment in children and family life somewhat unique to human beings (Geary and Flinn, 2001). Humans have evolved a specific life strategy which involves intensive parenting of children over a long period of time, and includes the transfer of social values and competencies intergenerationally (Belsky, 1997; Geary and Flinn, 2001). Families, in all their diverse forms and including men, constitute the social context for the survival, maturation and development of children and are, in turn, embedded in wider networks of kin and thereby contribute in important ways to broader society. To a greater or lesser extent, it is within this broader context that biological parents can share parenting with others and receive assistance in protecting and nurturing of children (Taylor and others, 2000).

Viewed in this way, family formation is an expression of social "deep structure" (Bugental, 2000) encompassing motivational and behavioural dispositions within men and women to create (and recreate) social relationships that provide not only for the nurture of individual children in the immediate generation, but also for accumulated knowledge, security through lineage and the continuation of family in the future (Foley and Lee, 1989). The existence of this deeply embedded pattern of affiliation in order to support and protect children implies that both children and adult men and women will attempt to replicate parental and family arrangements of one kind or another even when misfortune occurs and families are disrupted or children abandoned. For example, adults (men and women) have a biological proclivity to respond to the cries of infants, and to console young children and attempt to relieve their distress (Boukydis and Burgess, 1982); infertility in couples is a strong predictor of their desire to adopt a child (Bausch, 2006); and generally, people show a willingness to foster and/or adopt orphaned children, including those orphaned by AIDS, especially when they are related to those children (Townsend and Dawes, 2004; Howard and others, 2006). In the same vein, in their effort to maintain family ties, older children will take on adult responsibilities in caring for disabled, sick or mentally unstable parents (Burton, 2007) as well as their younger siblings (Donald and Clacherty, 2005); and children who live on the street frequently replicate family relationships through provision of care and establishment of authority among themselves (Scanlon and others, 1998). Many men who have sex with other men have children (Baral and others, 2007) and contemporary couples, including same-sex partners, form families that comprise biological kin as well as friends (Levine, 1990). Although all of these circumstances present challenges as do changes in the family constellation throughout the life-cycle, including deaths and dissolutions (McGlodrick and Carter, 2003), all human beings have a fundamental motivation to be part of a family and will undertake whatever actions are needed to achieve this goal.

Unlike the rather typical nuclear families of the West, most families throughout the majority world are generally extended; and socialization of children is seldom left solely to one or both biological parents. In Africa, for example, a parent's siblings are often referred to as "little mother" or "big father", depending on whether they are younger or older than the parent (Chirwa, 2002; Verhoef, 2005). What remains true, however, is that men's involvement in families, whether as biological or social fathers, is of critical importance on a number of levels. Some dimensions of this subject are explored in the present chapter, together with the social policies needed to support men's engagement with children.

Throughout the world, dramatic changes are occurring within families, in the perceptions of the roles of women and men in families, at work and in the wider society; (Goode, 1963). Giddens (2000) sees these changes as being driven by globalization and the underlying spread of Western culture, including its ideal of romantic love. Birth control, the feminist movement, the expansion of democracy and increasing appreciation of human rights have led to a change in the perception of women in all but the most traditional and fundamentalist societies. These factors are changing the roles and responsibilities of men and women, socially and economically, thereby affecting family relationships and parenting. Work is globalized and both men and women participate in the workforce, often in places far from home. Men are being drawn into co-parenting and co-responsibility for household maintenance just as women move into out-of-home livelihood activities and the labour market; and some men have taken the lead in the growing advocacy movement for fathers' rights and custody, and the need for change in norms and services in support of men as caregivers. Family and employment policies, childcare, and social and other services have not kept pace with these changes. Women still feel responsible for childcare, even if they are without additional help while they work; and although some men might want to be more involved in family, workplace policies and normative views of male workers undermine their efforts.

In this chapter, we examine fathers and father figures, and their changing roles in different cultural contexts; we draw attention to the notion of "social fatherhood", which describes the care and support of men for children who are not necessarily their biological offspring; we review the evidence for the beneficial educational, social and psychological effects on children of father engagement, as well as different forms of father engagement and their implications for children, partners and families. We then look at men and fathers intergenerationally, and the implications of the growing numbers of older persons for families, intergenerational relations and childcare and explore what is known about men's work-family balance and the role of policy in advancing men's engagement with children in the context of employment policies and expectations. Men's mental and physical health is considered and research that points to the benefits to men arising from their engagement in family life and their relationships with their children is reviewed. In the final section, we outline the implications of these topics for social and family policy.

## Fathers and fathering, and other male family figures in different cultural contexts

The forms fatherhood take are not universal and unchanging but rather dynamic and interactive (Lamb, 2004; Mkhize, 2004), and need to be understood in context and over time. Fathers provide for and are involved with their children and families in different ways, and there are cultural, social and individual differences in respect of how fatherhood is defined and expressed. While notions of fathers and fathering in Western contexts place emphasis on individual factors linked to biology and psychology (Day and Lamb, 2004), in many other cultures, the concept of fathering is not focused on the character of one individual. In these cultures, fathering is viewed instead as a collective responsibility in keeping with traditional patterns of extended family formation (Mkhize, 2004).

Most of the available literature on fatherhood acknowledges that the roles of fathers are influenced by the structure of families (including marriage, paternity and co-residence); the quality of primary relationships (including the quality of the marital relationship; the relationship with the child's mother, relationship with the father's own father, the type of fathering relationship with the child, individual skill levels and motivation, the range and types of involvement, and the supports for and obstacles to involvement including those arising from the workplace); financial status (employment and income); and personal qualities (personality, health, educational level, parenting style, beliefs about the father's role, and cultural background) (Palkovitz, 2002; Day and Lamb, 2004; Rabe, 2007; Hauari and Hollingworth, 2009) The influence of these factors on the perceptions of fathers is examined below.

Extensive changes in family structures and dynamics occurred during the twentieth century, with households shrinking globally as a result of urbanization and labour migration, including shifts, to a greater or lesser degree, from co-resident extended families to nuclear ones (United Nations, 2003; Hunter, 2006; Morrell, 2006). However, in Africa, Asia and Latin America, co-resident nuclear families continue to maintain close ties with relatives in the extended family system. Though kin might live in separate houses, or even in separate towns, interdependence is fostered through marriage, collaboration in economic activities, and mutual dependencies between working adults who send home remittances and those members of the family who continue to maintain traditional land and homesteads. Children in such families are exposed to multiple adult figures all of whom participate in child-rearing to a greater or lesser extent (Townsend, 1997; Parke and others, 2004; Nsamenang, 1989). In these contexts, the conception emerges of a "social father" (Bzostek, 2008),—with an ascribed, as opposed to an attained, status.

Fatherhood occurs in the context of intimate social relationships (Roy, 2008; Lloyd and Blanc, 1996; Engle and Breaux, 1998; Foster and Williamson, 2000) in which men may play a significant role in parenting, including of children who are not biologically their own. Different men, including grandfathers, uncles, stepfathers, foster fathers, older brothers, cousins and other men may perform various fatherhood functions in relation to a child (Montgomery and others, 2006; Desmond and Desmond, 2006; Rabe, 2007) and these men, singly or collectively, may be the child's primary source of male support (Mkhize, 2006). Both biological and social fathers, as icons of culture and mythology throughout the world, embody "the father in the mind", that is to say; the attributes and expectations attached to the notion of a father, whether he is present in a child's life or not (Lindegger, 2006).

Sociological and historical analyses clearly establish that, beyond insemination, fathering is "fundamentally a social construction", with each cohort shaping its own conception of fatherhood (Doherty, Kouneski and Erickson, 1998, p. 278). Motherhood is socially constructed in the same way, although it is biologically more certain

(Phoenixl, Woollett and Lloyd, 1991). While having a child might represent evidence of masculinity for men, in most parts of the world a man becomes a father, and is treated with the respect attached to the role, when he takes responsibility for his family and becomes a model of appropriate behaviour for young children (Lesejane, 2006). Even when fathers do not play a direct role in the care of children as a result of labour migration or for other reasons, the father's authority, deriving from his acknowledged paternity, is frequently strong (even when he is absent), as reported among the Sotho and Zulu in Southern Africa and among the Nso in Cameroon (Engle and Breaux, 1998; Lesejane, 2006; Nsamenang, 1987).

### Changing conceptions of fatherhood

Although this is changing, a father's role has traditionally been defined as that of provider or breadwinner, having responsibility as well for moral oversight of children and gender role-modelling (Lamb, 2000). In traditional Arab, African and other families, the father still constitutes the authority figure, and in consequence he shoulders the major responsibilities for the members his family (Nsamenang, 1987; Nosseir, 2003). In many low- and middle-income countries, the provider role was also framed by colonialism (Hunter, 2006; Rabe, 2007). By levying monetary taxes that required people to earn money, colonial powers forced men to migrate to urban farming and mining areas to seek work in order to meet these levies with their earnings and provide for their families (van Onselen, 1976).

However, important social trends have fundamentally changed the sociocultural contexts in which this conception of fatherhood prevailed (Tamis-LeMonda and Cabrera, 1999; Cabrera and others, 2000). Increased female labour-force participation in many countries (see table II.1), has been accompanied by a shift in the conception of fatherhood. Men are beginning to share household chores with their employed female partners and are providing care for children. Conceptions of fatherhood have also changed owing to the absence of biological fathers from the lives of their children as a result of death, migration for employment or divorce or separation (Posel and Devey, 2006; Richter and Panday, 2006) and the presence of non-biological fathers in children's lives (Mkhize, 2004). The increases in female-headed households, delays and declines in marriage, attitudinal shifts about gender, and increased cultural diversity all over the world have affected family life and influenced the nature of father involvement. For example, as a result of delayed marriages, the proportion of women who were not married in age group 20-24 in Bangladesh increased from 4.6 per cent to 18.5 per cent between 1970 and 2000 (De Silva, 2003).

In the United States of America in the mid-1900s, the image of the father represented in the media had been that of as an emotionally distant breadwinner. In the 1980s this started to shift to a figure who was more emotionally engaged, more nurturing and more committed to spending time with his children, both during infancy and as they grew older (Wall and Arnold, 2007). While increases in the amount of time fathers spend with children may reflect changing conceptions of fatherhood, fatherhood is also sensitive to macro- and microeconomic circumstances. Increased rates of maternal employment, periods of economic decline, joint work schedules, flexible and irregular work-hours, part-time employment, job sharing and home-based work are all associated with increases in paternal responsibility for childcare (Casper and O'Connell, 1998).

Table II.1
**Female labour market participation in selected countries, 1980-2008**

| Country | 1980 | 1985 | 1990 | 1995 | 2000 | 2005 | 2008 |
|---|---|---|---|---|---|---|---|
| South Africa | 31.3 | 33.1 | 35.6 | 40.5 | 44.3 | 45.9 | 47.2 |
| Libyan Arab Jamahiriya | 11.5 | 12.5 | 15.3 | 18.8 | 22.7 | 24.3 | 23.8 |
| Ghana | 68.6 | 69.5 | 70 | 71.2 | 72.6 | 73.4 | 73.7 |
| Germany | 40.7 | 41.5 | 45.2 | 47.8 | 49.1 | 51.4 | 52.9 |
| France | 44.1 | 45.8 | 46 | 47.3 | 48.3 | 50.2 | 50.9 |
| United Kingdom | 44.7 | 48.3 | 52 | 51.8 | 53.5 | 54.7 | 55.2 |
| Argentina | 39.4 | 41.5 | 42.8 | 41 | 45.6 | 50.3 | 51.1 |
| Mexico | 32 | 33.6 | 34.3 | 37.6 | 38.8 | 41 | 43.4 |
| Colombia | 22.8 | 26.3 | 29.2 | 32.2 | 36.2 | 39.3 | 40.5 |
| United States | 51.1 | 54.1 | 56.9 | 58.4 | 59.5 | 58.6 | 58.9 |
| China | 71 | 71.6 | 73 | 72.3 | 70.9 | 68.5 | 67.5 |
| Japan | 47.6 | 48.6 | 50.1 | 50 | 49.2 | 48.4 | 48.6 |
| India | 32.6 | 33.2 | 34 | 34.5 | 33 | 32.4 | 33.1 |

**Source:** World Bank (2010)
**Note:** With the exception of a few countries which have had stable female labour-market participation, although at different levels (some higher than others), most countries have seen a substantial increase in female labour-market participation during the last 30 years. In general, family policies have not adapted to this change.

But attitudes are slow to change, despite increased consciousness of the need for more equal gender expectations with respect to family and childcare. In studies in Eastern Europe on family and changing gender roles 40–60 per cent of respondents in Bulgaria, Croatia, the Czech Republic, Hungary, Latvia, Poland, the Russian Federation, Slovakia and Slovenia said that they agreed or strongly agreed with the following statement: "A man's job is to earn money; a woman's job is to look after the home and family" (World Health Organization, 2007). The corresponding figures for Scandinavia were 8–9 per cent. Similarly, 20–50 per cent of the participants in Eastern Europe endorsed the following statement: "A preschool child is likely to suffer if his or her mother works full-time" (ibid.).

In the United Kingdom, the women's movement has consistently pressed for a more equal division of domestic labour, and men have increased their contribution over time, albeit slowly (Gershuny, Godwin and Jones, 1994). Nonetheless, assistance from fathers with housework and childcare is, and continues to be, more common in the United Kingdom than in many countries (Dex and Shaw, 1988). There is also research evidence that in multicultural United Kingdom men generally wish to be more involved as fathers, and desire more balance between work and home life, than in the past (Harrington, van Deusen and Ladge, 2010).

In Latin America, women's increasing education as well as their participation in the economy and politics, combined with new models of empowered women, is prompting changes in norms of femininity and masculinity (Olavarría, 2006). Growing numbers of men are sharing greater intimacy and affection with their partners and children. Traditional conceptions of fatherhood in Mexican-American cultural contexts have also undergone change. The stereotype of the Latino family comprising an authoritarian man and a dependent, submissive woman (Bozett and Hanson, 1991) has been challenged in the face of urbanization and acculturation. Traditionally, Latino fathers were depicted as fighting roosters through terms like macho, borracho (drunk) and bien gallo (fighter) (Coltrane and others 2004). An emergent model depicts an increasingly egalitarian family where men assume more progressive roles such as that of loving husband (Cabrera and others, 2000), while spending time on basic caregiving activities including bedtime routines, physical care and feeding of children (Parke and others, 2004). Fathers who live with and raise their children alone are also increasing. These men, however, tend to live in middle- and upper-income households, often with female household help (Jelin and Diaz-Munoz, 2003).

In Northern Africa, strict patriarchal traditions are also beginning to shift. Previously, the father was the authority figure with the assigned leadership role in providing for and supporting family members, while mothers looked after and educated children, trained them in religious and cultural traditions, and took care of the household (Nosseir, 2003). More recently, as a result, inter alia, of the employment of women and labour migration, more fathers now share family authority and responsibility with others.

The family in the Arab world, has tended, however, to remain patriarchal (ibid.). Traditionally, fathers exercised authority and power based on the fact that they retained possession of and controlled family property. This enabled men to impose obedience and dependency on women and children, a dynamic that characterizes other institutions of authority, such as schools, which frequently protect and sustain patriarchy (United Nations, 2003).

The characteristics of the family system prevalent in the Mashrek countries—Egypt, Jordan, Iraq, Lebanon, Syrian Arab Republic and Palestine have also changed. The situation in which the father is the provider, the mother is the "housekeeper" and there are, on average, seven or eight children, is no longer typical (Badran, 2003). Changes have occurred largely because of the massive incorporation of women into paid work. This has increased women's power vis-à-vis men and lessened men's domination. In addition, increased availability of contraception has given women more control over the timing and frequency of childbearing (see table II.2) thereby increasing their options with regard to paid work, as has the increasing influence of the women's movement (ibid.).

In Asia, families have experienced rapid transitions within a range of cultural, demographic, socio-economic and policy contexts. In China, the one-child policy has had a significant impact on gender roles, and on parent-child relationships (Asia Research Institute and Department of Sociology, 2010). The declining ability of men to earn a family wage that supports growing needs has resulted in a situation where an increasing number of women engage in economic activities (Lloyd and Duffy, 1995).

In the Philippines and Sri Lanka, as examples, large numbers of women migrate to work in other countries for long stretches of time, leaving children with their father and other female family members (De Silva, 2003). In Singapore, Japan, the Republic of Korea, Taiwan, Province of China and Hong Kong, Special Administrative Region of China, low fertility rates have altered family dynamics and changed expectations of men's roles (Asia Research Institute and Department of Sociology, 2010). However, patriarchy remains a dominant family ideology in the region despite impressive increases in women's education and labour force participation. Many men maintain a disciplinary stance and generally refrain from offering emotional support to children (De Silva, 2003).

Table II.2
**Changes in the fertility rate in selected countries, various regions, 1970-2007**

| Country | 1970-1975 | 1980-1985 | 1990-1995 | 1995-2000 | 2007 |
|---|---|---|---|---|---|
| **South Asia** | | | | | |
| India | 5.4 | 4.5 | 3.7 | 3.3 | |
| **Central Asia** | | | | | |
| Uzbekistan | 6.3 | 4.7 | 3.6 | 2.8 | |
| **Central America** | | | | | |
| Honduras | 7.1 | | 5.3 | 4.4 | |
| **Caribbean** | | | | | |
| Jamaica | 5.0 | | 2.6 | 2.4 | |
| **Latin America** | | | | | |
| Colombia | 5.0 | | 3.0 | 2.6 | |
| **Southern Africa** | | | | | |
| Botswana | 5.0 | | 2.8 | | 2.3 |

**Source:** United Nations Children's Fund (2009). The State of the World's Children. Available from http://data.un.org/Data.aspx?d=SOWC&f=inID%3A127 (accessed 9 July 2010).

## Fathering roles

With the increasing commitment of men to their families and the well-being of their children, the turn of the twenty-first century is seeing the emergence of the "new father" (Roy, 2008; LaRossa, 1997), a man who is both provider and caregiver for his children (Lamb, 2004). For example, Hauari and Hollingworth (2009), in their study on fatherhood in the modern multicultural United Kingdom, found that White British, Black Caribbean and younger parents tended towards egalitarian parenting and considered that economic necessity increasingly dictated that both parents have a role in earning and caring for their family. While all ethnic groups emphasized that mothers were "naturally" better equipped to fulfil the responsibilities for providing physical care and nurturing children, they also felt that fathers had a strong responsibility to remain accessible and available to their children as much as possible and also to ensure that they spent "quality" time with their children

In a comparison between Latino and European-American fathers, Toth and Xu (1999) found that, like African-American fathers, Latino fathers were more likely to report that they monitored and supervised their children's activities, and spent time with them in shared activities (Toth and Xu, 1999). Coltrane, Parke and Adams (2001) found that Mexican-American fathers were similar to European-American fathers in respect of the proportion of housework and child monitoring they reported, but that the former devoted more hours to those tasks and were more involved in activities with their children.

Canadian studies that had examined the amount of time fathers in dual-income families spend with their children revealed that fathers spend about two thirds as much time with preschool children as mothers even when both parents work full-time (Silver, 2000). Furthermore, fathers' time with children is dominated by play and leisure, while mothers' time is devoted to caretaking. Fathers' time with children is also more likely than mothers' to be in the presence of the spouse (Craig, 2006). That is, fathers compared with mothers spend less time and less time alone with their children. However, in the United States in 1993, more than 1.6 million preschoolers were cared for by their fathers while their mothers were at work (Marsiglio and Day, 1997). Informal observations in South Africa indicate that, because their female partners are employed, often with non-standard hours of work, men are increasingly attending health centres with children who require immunization, walking and driving children to and from school, and providing care at home (Richter, 2006).

In the present section we have considered the social construction of fatherhood and the existence of the social father, as well as the ways in which men's roles as fathers differ in varying cultural and socio-economic contexts and over time, principally along the primary axes of provider and nurturer. To be sure, men's economic situation affects the capacity of men to support children and the time men have available for interaction with children, a topic we will return to in a later section. We will now deal with the ways in which men and fathers' involvement in families impact upon children's development.

## Fathering and children's development

As indicated above, fathering is as much a sociocultural as a biological construct, and most children experience more than one type of a very wide range of fathering relationships. The continuum encompasses co-residential biological fathers who are present for the entire period of childhood at one end, as well as concerned teachers and other mentors who may take a keen interest in children and encourage them over long periods of their lives, on the other. For this reason, the term social fatherhood has emerged to describe the many ways in which children can be connected to men who take responsibility for a child's wellbeing (Mkhize, 2004). As Bachrach and Sonestein (1998, p.1) point out: "Men are now more likely than ever to live separately from their children and to father children outside marriage. Many men experience fatherhood as a series of relationships with children, some biologically theirs and some the children of spouses and partners." This state of affairs requires a fairly dramatic readjustment of our perception of fatherhood and how fathers may be involved in the lives of children.

The increasing diversity of fatherhood, and the fact that fatherhood is frequently evaluated against a "maternal template" (that is what mothers usually do for children) (Marsiglio, Amato, and Day, 2000), complicate research on the effects of fatherhood on children's development. What is clear, however, is that fathers can have both direct and indirect or mediated effects on children.

Fathers around the world have the most direct effect by virtue of the fact that they tend to contribute the major proportion of family's financial resources, and it is true almost universally that two-parent households, where fathers are present, are economically better off than single-mother households (Jarrett, 1994). Children in father-absent families have been estimated to be many times more likely to be poor than children in married-couple households (United States Census Bureau, 2003). In addition to money, men usually have access to other community resources which may not be available to women, including mutual support and influence. To illustrate this, Townsend (2002, p. 270) concluded from a study in Botswana that "Children are not necessarily disadvantaged by the absence of their father, but they are disadvantaged when they belong to a household without access to the social position, labour and financial support that is provided by men". In many parts of the world, a father who acknowledges and supports his children confers social value on them, enabling them thereby to become members of a wider circle of family and kin. Men also provide a household with protection which includes, shielding women and children from potential exploitation and abuse by other men (Dubowitz and others, 2004).

Men also have indirect effects on children through their relationships with mothers. Women who live with supportive partners report being less stressed, including about childcare issues, and fathers may lessen women's workload by assisting with household and care giving responsibilities (McLoyd and others, 1994). Importantly, on the other hand, men not only contribute to women's well-being and happiness, but in several studies have also been found to buffer children against neglectful or harsh parenting by a distant, demoralized or overburdened mother (Martin, Ryan and Brooks-Gunn, 2010).

Notwithstanding the benefits men offer to women and children, presence of a male in households sometimes has its costs. There is a 20-60 per cent incidence of domestic violence—which affects children in significant ways, including over the long term—in households around the world (Heise, Pitanguy and Germain, 1994). This issue is addressed in Chapter III.

## Men's involvement with children

Children are very conscious of the presence of their father, value his interest and guidance, and will experience emotional pain and may even bear a stigma as a result of not knowing, losing or feeling neglected or abused by him (Richter and Morrell, 2006).

Within the first three months of life babies differentiate their fathers from their mothers, in terms of smell, voice, and handling; and by the end of the first year children show a strong attachment to fathers, one that is separate from their attachment to their mothers (Cox, Owen and Henderson, 1992). In this regards, babies express a discernible recognition of their father, respond to their father's emotional cues regarding the safety of their surroundings or the threat posed by those surrounding or other people, and as they do with their mothers, turn to their fathers for comfort. Throughout their development, children convey the importance of their fathers in their lives and seek their company and approval.

The dimensions of fathering behaviour that have been studied include the amount of time men spend with children and in childcare, the kinds of household and childcare tasks they take on, the differences between paternal and maternal parenting and the differential effects of engagement in fathering on children's health, well-being and education. As little, apart from time use, is known about these aspects of fathering outside of the United States and Europe, they are clearly important areas for future study.

From all data available, it is clear that men spend less time than women with children, especially young children, and are less engaged in childcare (Barry and Paxson, 1971; Population Council, 2001). For this reason, men are sometimes depicted as "deficient women" in the context of childcare (Brown and Barker, 2004). However, time as a proxy of men's engagement with or influence on children is being challenged. Men are often the primary decision makers regarding a number of issues that significantly affect children, such as when they get taken to a health facility, how long they may be allowed to attend school and what work they may do to help to support the family. As an alternate to the simplistic assessment of time as a measure of paternal involvement with children, Lamb and others (1985) propose three categories of fathering behaviour: engagement (that is, interaction between father and child); accessibility, including emotional availability; and responsibility for childcare or actions and initiatives undertaken to care for children that are not prompted by mothers (see also Palkovitz, 2002). While it is assumed that complete involvement—engagement, availability and responsibility—is important for children and female partners, no studies could be found that had specifically test this assumption against specific child outcomes.

In many studies, almost all from the United States and Europe, the largest discrepancy between the parenting behaviours of men and women was found to lie within the dimension of responsibility—for planning, acting and following up on children's needs—which has been taken to demonstrate that even men who have shown their engagement tend to assume very little responsibility for childcare. Although men's proportional share of childcare rises when mothers work outside the home, the available data indicate that this is due to the fact that women do less, not that men do more (Pleck, 1997).

On a global scale, contemporary changes in both the work patterns of men and women and the structure of families are associated with men's increasing involvement in household work and childcare. Unemployed men with working wives often take on increased responsibility for childcare, especially in lower income families (Casper and others, 1998). According to the "availability hypothesis", the more a father is available to care for his children, the greater the likelihood of his providing that care (Levine and Pittinsky, 1997).

## The impact of father involvement on children's health, development and education

In general, the evidence is weighted in the direction of men's having an impact on young children indirectly through their effect on women and the extent of parenting and family identity rather than directly (Amato and Gilbreth, 1999). However, there is a shift to increased direct impacts on educational achievement, adjustment and health as children move into late childhood and their teens. Although there is little empirical data on the issue, certainly outside of the West, Lamb (2004) is of the view that a father influences child and adolescent outcomes in the same way as does a mother, by their degree of emotional support, security and encouragement that he provides. Conversely, father absence or disengagement is associated with a wide range of adverse effects on children.

Regardless of the mechanisms of the effects a father produces, his presence or involvement is associated with a number of benefits for children, both in the short term and over time (Sarkadi and others, 2008). For example, holding other factors constant, preschool children who experience "sensitive and responsive fathering" have been found to perform better on cognitive and language tests than those with less responsive fathers (Bronte-Tinkew and others, 2008). Early cognitive achievement is, of course, related to school outcomes but, it is precisely those children whose fathers are involved in their schooling and encourage academic achievement—regardless of the father's own level of schooling—who remain in school longer and have better educational outcomes than peers with less involved fathers (McBride, Schoppe-Sullivan and Ho, 2003). Such findings have also been reported for low- and middle-income countries. For example, Mboya and Nesengani (1999) found that boys in South Africa, who lived with their fathers, had higher academic achievements than those who did not. Fathers influence not only their children's schooling but also (especially their sons') employment, mainly through their access to intergenerational and occupational networks (Magruder, 2010).

Similar benefits of father engagement are manifest in children's socio-emotional development and adjustment. Involved fathering has been found to be associated with a number of positive child characteristics, such as increased empathy, self-esteem and social competence (Bernadett-Shapiro, Ehrensaft and Shapiro, 1996). Importantly, fathers' involvement in the lives of their children appears to enhance children's sense of happiness and gratification as well as increase their community involvement (Marsiglio and Day, 1997). Similarly, lower rates of problem behaviours in childhood, including hyperactivity, anxiety and depression, as well as lower rates of delinquent behaviour, especially among boys, are reported among samples of children with involved fathers (Carslon, 2006; Flouri and Buchanan, 2002; Schacht, Cummings and Davies, 2009; Harris, Furstenberg and Marmer, 1998). Many of the benefits conferred by engaged fathers are reported even when fathers are not resident in the same household with their children, but are nevertheless engaged with them, through the provision of, inter alia, support, and contact (King, 1994).

Effects of the father vary to some extent by gender of the child. For example, Barnett, Marshall and Pleck (1992) reported that the father-child relationship proved to be of greater significance than the mother-child relationship in predicting psychological distress among sons. Similarly, father absence or lack of contact with father appears to have its most dramatic effect on male children (Mott, 1994), particularly as regards boys' behavioural control, social competence and school success. It has been suggested that father availability and engagement have a modulating effect on boys' aggression, by providing a model of culturally appropriate male behaviour, and that boys in father-absent families tend to engage in what may be perceived as exaggerated demonstrations of masculinity in the areas of control and belligerence. Among girls, father presence shows a strong relationship with higher self-esteem (Wenk and others, 1994), lower levels of sexual risk behaviours (Ellis and others, 2003) and fewer difficulties in forming and maintaining romantic relationships. Girls reared in single-mother homes are more likely to engage in sexual activity at a young age, have an early pregnancy, a birth outside of marriage, an early marriage or divorce (Ellis and others, 2003; McLanahan & Bumpass, 1988).

Debate continues on: whether the benefits that fathers confer on children and the disadvantages arising from their absence, are due to economic factors; on whether those benefits differ from the contributions made by mothers; and on the way in which they are amplified by co-residence. Frey (2003), a strong advocate of men's involvement with their children, argues, as does Lamb, a pre-eminent scholar on father involvement, that "the contribution males can and should make to their children's development is precisely the same contribution that females make to their children's development, which is the ongoing care and nurturing of a human life" (p. 56). This means that the mechanisms through which parenting affects children are the same for men and women, but that the gender and power-related differences between men and women may account for the fact that male involvement is the source of unique inputs and benefits for children.

While this section has focused primarily on the effect fathers have on children's development, the next section considers fathering in the context of both older and younger generations.

## Fathering across generations

Fathering occurs across generations. Grandparents, for example, apart from fathering their adult children, are increasingly involved in the support and care of their grandchildren as a result of labour migration, women's participation in work outside the home, and mortality resulting from violence and HIV/AIDS. In addition, a body of research indicates that patterns of fatherhood recur across generations. For example, in the United States, early fatherhood, both during the teen years and in early twenties, was much more likely to occur if young men had not grown up with their own fathers. Young fathers were also less likely to be living with their children if their own fathers had not lived in residence with them throughout childhood (Furstenberg and Weiss, 2000). These findings have also been reported in South Africa (Swartz and Bhana, 2009).

We review below some of the reasons for increased involvement in children's lives among grandfathers, the roles grandfathers play and some of the potential benefits of grandfather engagement with children.

### The changing demographic structure of the world population

The number of older persons throughout the world is increasing at a very rapid rate, and it is estimated that it will have reached 2 billion by 2050 (Mirkin and Weinberger, 2001). The majority of older persons are resident in Asia (53 per cent), with Europe hosting the second largest portion of older persons (24 per cent); in contrast, only 5 per cent of the population in sub-Saharan Africa is aged 60 years or over (Mirkin and Weinberger., 2001). While older persons in Africa constitute a small proportion of the population, their number is significant: it is estimated to be over 38 million and it is projected that it will have reached between 203 million and 212 million by 2050 (HelpAge International, 2002). The proportion of the *oldest old*, defined as persons who are aged 80 years or over, is expected to grow much faster, from the current 1 per cent to an estimated 4 per cent of the population in 2050. The fact that ageing is of major interest today stems not only from the increase in the number of older persons but also from the changing relationship between older and younger generations, including in respect of the roles and responsibilities of older persons in family life and childcare (Nathanson, 1984). Table II.3 presents estimated life expectancy of men and women over the period 2000-2005.

Population ageing has entailed a shift in resources in many societies, including by Governments, towards pensions, health and long-term care. Rarely noted, though, are the state savings on family support and education resulting from reductions in fertility. In addition, many roles that older people, including men, play in society and family do not usually receive the recognition they deserve. Most of the work done by old men, for example, is erroneously assumed to be economically unproductive. However, sharing skills, experience, wisdom and labour contributes to productivity,

Table II.3
**Differences in life expectancy of men and women, selected countries by region, over the period 2000-2005**

| Country | Life expectancy at birth | | Expected years of life after 60 | |
|---|---|---|---|---|
| | Women | Men | Women | Men |
| **Africa** | | | | |
| Algeria | 72 | 70 | 20 | 17 |
| Burundi | 44 | 42 | 16 | 15 |
| South Africa | 51 | 47 | 18 | 14 |
| **North America** | | | | |
| Canada | 82 | 77 | 25 | 21 |
| Jamaica | 73 | 69 | 22 | 20 |
| Trinidad and Tobago | 73 | 67 | 21 | 18 |
| **South America South** | | | | |
| Argentina | 78 | 71 | 23 | 18 |
| Guyana | 66 | 60 | 19 | 16 |
| Venezuela, (Bolivarian Republic of) | 76 | 70 | 22 | 20 |
| **Asia** | | | | |
| Bangladesh | 63 | 62 | 17 | 15 |
| India | 65 | 62 | 18 | 16 |
| Jordan | 73 | 70 | 19 | 17 |
| **Europe** | | | | |
| Austria | 82 | 76 | 24 | 20 |
| Czech Republic | 79 | 72 | 21 | 17 |
| Spain | 83 | 76 | 25 | 20 |

**Source:** United Nations Statistics Division (2005).

especially in the informal economy. In fact, society stands to gain from increases in life expectancy, if most of the additional time gained comprises "healthy years" (Goldscheider, 2006).

## The changing roles of ageing fathers in supporting younger generations

Old age is seen in most societies as a time of life when people, because of physical decline, can no longer carry out their customary duties. In the Western world, however, older people, with better health, extensive social security and prolonged participation in the labour market, are able to maintain an independent life for a longer period of time, and may choose to live apart from their children and other family (Lloyd-Sherlock, 2001). When older persons undergo institutionalization in old-age establishments, a common practice in the West, there are two consequences. On the one hand, they are afforded specialized care but, on the other hand, there is a sense that they have been discarded and are no longer needed by society. Of course, this is not the case in all Western countries with Italy, for example, having a strong tradition of co-residence of older persons with their families. Many industrialized nations in Asia have also tended to retain traditional living arrangements, with older persons integrated into family life and childcare (Edlund and Rahman, 2005).

New evidence shows that intergenerational co-residence in the West has exhibited a U-shaped trend. A decline, which began in the mid-twentieth century, was triggered by a sharp reduction in dependency on farming economies. Recently, even in Western countries with a history of low prevalence of co-residence, there has been a growing trend towards children residing longer with their parents delaying the move to establish residential independence from them. Co-residence is one means through which families, including fathers, can play a role in giving financial, material and emotional support to the succeeding generation. Increased life expectancy means that many fathers spend a greater number of years exercising a much needed parental role, while the members of the younger generation are completing their education, entering the labour market, and establishing themselves as independent adults (Cobb-Clark, 2008). A sizeable proportion of young people now co-reside with parents until they are well into their early thirties. This has been reported to be the case in Australia (Cobb-Clark, 2008), Europe and the United States (Da Vanzo and Goldsheider, 1990; Whittington and Peters, 1996; Gerard, Landry-Meyer and Roe, 2006). Economic downturns and other challenges, coupled with added healthy productive years, have resulted in a situation where mothers and fathers are being required to give support to their children over a much longer time.

In addition to their providing for their own children over a longer period of time, there is a growing trend for grandparents to support grandchildren. In the United States in 2000, for instance, 4.5 million grandparents were in charge of grandchildren in the absence of parents. This was up from 2.2 million documented in 1970 (Bullock, 2005). The presence of grandparents in the lives of grandchildren has been an added advantage in underprivileged families in the United States and Europe (Gerard, Landry-Meyer and Roe, 2006). Bullock (2005) noted that children from single-mother families who lived with at least one grandparent did as well or better than children from married-parent families and that, in particular, the presence of a grandfather is associated with the availability of better economic resources to grandchildren, compared with families where there are only grandmothers.

In many African societies, there have been marked changes in the roles of older persons in multigenerational households, propelled mainly by rising morbidity and mortality of young people in the region as a result of the AIDS pandemic (Makiwane, Schneider and Gopane, 2004). Thus, in contrast with their traditional role as recipients of care and remittances from children, older persons are emerging as breadwinners and caregivers for the third generation. A stereotypic view is that the role of caregiver is to be played solely by older women. While available evidence confirms that older women are more likely to be caregivers than men, a significantly large group of men are also caregivers to the third generation. A study of a rural area of South Africa, for example, found that 32 per cent of grandfathers were caregivers to grandchildren, compared with 51 per cent of grandmothers (Makiwane, Schneider and Gopane, 2004). A similar trend has been observed in the United States (Bullock, 2005). In domains other than caregiving, the general observation is that grandfathers play a greater role than grandmothers. For instance, data from South Asia show that without being paid, more older men than older women help their children to generate income (United Nations, 2001).

*The second demographic dividend*

The changing demographics of the world population that have been impacting on men's involvement in families have been noted: globally, declining fertility and increased female labour participation; in the Western world, an ageing population, some of whose members are becoming alienated from extended families; and in the majority world, changing patterns of labour migration (see table II.4) as well as morbidity and mortality due to HIV and AIDS among the members of the middle generation. There is another emerging demographic pattern that impacts on men's involvement in families: a youth bulge occurs in the population some two to three decades following discernible declines in child mortality and fertility (Ashford, 2007). Society benefits from having a higher number of working-age adults able to support a proportionately smaller number of dependent younger and older people. This might be called a first demographic dividend, although according to Lee and Mason (2006) it is only a transitory bonus. The second demographic transition, which is linked to the process of ageing, is more likely to lead to sustainable development provided other economic and social conditions are favourable.

The second dividend occurs when a population is concentrated at older ages. It is especially likely to enhance the role of men in their traditional role as breadwinners and providers to subsequent generations. As the lifespans of the members of the older generation increase, they are able to accumulate more assets as a result of investments over a longer lifetime, including their contribution to the economy through extended participation in the labour force. Thus, the older generation is able to benefit the younger by sharing their current and lifetime resources.

Clearly much of the impetus for men's involvement in the lives of families and children, including when it is extended by healthy old age, is derived from work and the provision of resources. The next section examines the issue of balancing work and efforts to engage with family.

# Fathering and the work-family balance

The work-home balance refers to the equilibrium between the amount of time and effort devoted by a person to work and that devoted to other personal and social aspects of his or her life. The subject of work-family balance has been a source of much international and interdisciplinary interest and debate over the past three decades (Pavalko & Henderson, 2006). This interest can be attributed to a range of economic and demographic changes in contemporary societies which have implications for employees' ability to negotiate work and family responsibilities. Key among these changes are the increased labour force participation of women; increasing mobility of the labour-force; a growing reluctance to accept longer working hours; technological advances making it possible to work from home; and changes in family composition and structure, particularly decreasing fertility and an increasing proportion of older persons in the population (Janèaitytë, 2006; International Labour Organisation, 2007). For Bailyn, Drago and Kochan (2001), the most obvious implication of these changes is the increasing time squeeze, which means that many working adults, particularly single parents and those in dual-earner families have difficulty providing the daily attention needed for the well-being of children and family, including themselves.

Table II.4

**Labour migration: estimated number of international migrants at mid year, 1960-2005**

| Year | Estimated number of international migrants at midyear (both sexes) | International migrants as a percentage of the population | Estimated number of international male migrants at midyear | Estimated number of female migrants at mid year | Female migrants as percentage of all international migrants |
|------|------|------|------|------|------|
| 1960 | 75 463 352 | 2.5 | 40 135 120 | 35 328 232 | 46.8 |
| 1965 | 78 443 933 | 2.4 | 41 525 601 | 36 918 332 | 47.1 |
| 1970 | 81 335 779 | 2.2 | 42 908 824 | 38 426 955 | 47.2 |
| 1975 | 86 789 304 | 2.1 | 45 684 990 | 41 104 314 | 47.4 |
| 1980 | 99 275 898 | 2.2 | 52 391 759 | 46 884 139 | 47.2 |
| 1985 | 11 013 230 | 2.3 | 58 648 512 | 52 364 718 | 47.2 |
| 1990 | 154 945 333 | 2.9 | 78 977 842 | 75 967 491 | 49.0 |
| 1995 | 165 080 235 | 2.9 | 83 683 620 | 81 396 614 | 49.3 |
| 2000 | 176 735 772 | 2.9 | 88 978 168 | 87 757 603 | 49.7 |
| 2005 | 190 633 564 | 3.0 | 96 114 953 | 94 518 611 | 49.6 |

**Source:** United Nations, Department of Economic and Social Affairs, Population Division (2006).

A significant portion of the literature shows that interacting trends in the labour market of countries and the structure of families are catching many households in a "time-money squeeze" between family responsibilities and demands of work (International Labour Organization, 2004b). This challenge often leads to stress and work-family conflict (Greenhaus and Beutell, 1985), which is particularly important given its negative impact on family well-being; child development, care and health; gender equality; and workplace productivity. It has been shown, for example, that work pressure may force workers to resort to unsatisfactory childcare arrangements such as leaving children alone at home, taking an older child out of school to care for younger siblings, or bringing a child to the work place where the environment may be unhealthy or dangerous (International Labour Organization, 2004b). Additionally, not only can family responsibilities constrain workers' ability to maximize income-generating opportunities or career prospects or both but they can give rise to depressive irritation, anxiety, and physical illness, especially among working women, but also among men (Oomens, Geurts and Scheepers, 2007). The problems that work-family conflicts pose for workers inevitably also impact on productivity, expressed in high turnover, increased absenteeism, tardiness and decreased job satisfaction (International Labour Organization, 2004b). Achieving a work-home balance is therefore vital to enhancing the well-being of workers and their families, as well as to better labour-market outcomes (Pavalko and Henderson, 2006).

## Fathering and the work-home balance

Although both men and women experience work-home conflict, much more has been written about the conflict as experienced by working mothers. Industrialization and urbanization had seen men pursuing waged work while women stayed at home (International Labour Organization, 2004a; Hook, 2006). This altered men's role in the daily life of the family and created a "male breadwinner-female caregiver" division of labour (Hook, 2006). This separation of function endures today as men continue to be expected to be good providers for and protectors of their families (Hosking, 2006). As Haas and Hwang (2008) point out:

A "good father" has been defined as a successful breadwinner; he is supportive of his partner's participation in childcare and "helps out" occasionally, but is not expected to take any direct responsibility for children's care, spend as much time with children or develop the same type of close ties with children that mothers do.

In consequence, both research and policy on balancing work and family life still tend to focus on mothers' lives. Men's fathering roles are frequently neglected, as many employers continue to view the "ideal worker" as an unencumbered male free of domestic responsibilities (Dancaster, 2008), and hence see flexible working conditions or family-friendly working policies as benefiting women specifically rather than both men and women.

A growing literature has been showing the positive effect of the presence and active involvement of a father on a child's life chances, academic performance, and social, emotional and cognitive functioning (Engle, Beardshaw and Loftin, 2006; Richter, 2006; Kang and Weber, 2009); and in consequence, the nature of fatherhood is changing, with the emergence of a so-called new or modern father. Modern fathers are no longer mere breadwinners: they are increasingly aware of, and concerned about what they do as fathers and how they do it (Duyvendak and Stavenuiter, 2004; Kang and Weber., 2009; Grubb, 2010). While this change in their role has led to greater demands place on men in respect of sharing domestic responsibilities, breadwinning still remains central to their definition of themselves as good fathers (Winslow, 2005; Nomaguchi, 2009).

This has resulted in an increase in men's perception of work-family conflict. For example, using a global corporate sample of working fathers from 48 countries, Hill and others (2003) found that men and women reported equal amounts of work-to-family conflict. In the United States, the National Study of the Changing Workforce (Kang and Weber, 2009), which traces trends in men's and women's attitudes and actions over the past three decades, revealed that changing gender roles have significantly and specifically increased the overall level of work-life conflict experienced by men, the proportion of these men experiencing such conflict having risen from 34 per cent in 1977 to 45 per cent in 2008. Along the same lines, a 2003 survey of fathers carried out by the Equal Employment Opportunities Trust (2003) had found that 80 per cent of fathers in New Zealand reported that they wished they could spend more time with their children; 82 per cent stated that their paid work negatively affected the amount of time they spent with their children; and 52 per cent asserted that their work affected the quality of the time they spent with their children.

The literature on contemporary fatherhood therefore suggests that a growing number of men would like to have a better-balanced work-life situation, one that would enable them be more involved in the care of their children (Hobson and Fahlen, 2009). There is also evidence of a growing trend among employers throughout the world, towards finding the means to create workplaces, policies and laws that are "father-friendly". In many countries, the most common first step in this direction has been the granting of paternity, parental, or family leave. Definitions of these types of leave vary from country to country. At a very basic level, paternity leave is a statutory entitlement designed to enable a father to be absent from work for a certain period of the time commending with the birth of his child (O'Brien, 2009). Parental leave, on the other hand, is long-term leave which is made available to parents to allow them to take care of an infant or young child over time and is usually granted in addition to maternity/paternity leave (Organization for Economic Cooperation and Development, 2001). Family leave can be described as leave taken to attend to certain family responsibilities such as caring for a seriously ill family member. Other initiatives aimed at allowing men to be more involved with their children include a wide range of arrangements such as flexible work-start and finish times, working from home, annualized hours and taking time off for emergencies and making up the time at a later date (Fursman and Callister, 2009)

These provisions are based on the assumption that granting leave will help men become more actively involved in sharing childcare and family responsibilities with women (Haas and Hwang, 2008). Indeed, previous research has suggested a positive relationship between fathers' taking parental leave and their participation in childcare. For example, studies conducted in Sweden in the 1970s and 1980s showed consistently that fathers who took leave soon after the birth of a child were more likely to continue participating and sharing equally in childcare after their leave had terminated (ibid.). The same pattern has been observed in other countries such as Norway (Brandth and Kvande, 2003) and the United States (Pleck, 1993; Seward, and others, 2006).

However, even with such policies in place, there is evidence that fathers tend to take up little of the paternity or parental leave available to them (see, for example, Organization for Economic Cooperation and Development, 2001; Fursman and Callister, 2009). As a result, men still spend significantly less time in child care, and significantly more time than women in paid work. Barriers to greater participation in care by men range from the visible and clearly significant to the hidden and seemingly minor (Fursman and Collister, 2009). These include working hours; workplace cultures; occupational characteristics; the gender pay gap; culture and ideology; and a lack of "official" advocates for men as care givers in the policy arena. Institutional policies and practices—such as the creation of workplaces structured around the "ideal worker" or "unencumbered worker" who functions as if he has no family responsibilities—can also preclude men's getting involved in nurturing activities early in their children's lives (Haas and Hwang, 2008). In the same vein, gendered policies and laws can act as a barrier to men's participation in care and thus increase their work-family conflict. For example, parental leave policies that are contingent on mothers' meeting eligibility criteria, or that rely on mothers' willingness to transfer leave to their partners may hinder men's access to leave that enables them to care for their children (Fursman and Collister, 2009).

A major limitation of the available literature on the work-family interface and fatherhood is its decidedly Western focus, with the majority of studies having been conducted among white, middle-class Northern American, European and Australasian families (Poelmans and others, 2003; Spector and others, 2004; Beardshaw, 2006). The few studies conducted elsewhere have come mainly from Asia (for example, Abe, Hamamoto and Tanaka, 2003; Kim and Kim, 2004; Kusakabe, 2006) and Latin America (for example, Sorj, 2004; Reddock and Bobb-Smith, 2008). There is therefore an urgent need for research in Africa and the Middle East, from which data on fathers and their work-home situation are almost non-existent. As Korenman and Kaester (2005) caution, considerable care is needed before assuming that the more "family friendly" institutional arrangements in Western countries would, without significant other reforms, be effective in low- and middle-income countries. It is also noteworthy that research on work–family conflict tends to focus narrowly on well-educated professionals, while very little attention has been given to the experiences of low-wage, non-professional workers (Lambert, 1999).

While the concept of work-family balance is especially overlooked in the majority world context, the physical and mental health of fathers which forms the focus of the next section has also received little attention. The chapter concludes with a consideration of implications for policy.

## Mental and physical health of fathers

Epidemiological research has determined that social relationships protect people from various causes of morbidity and mortality (Berkman, 1995). For example, married individuals compared with the unmarried, have greater life satisfaction, happiness and lower risk for depression, and lower morbidity and mortality (Holt-Lunstad, Birmingham and Jones, 2008). While one might expect that there would be an extensive literature on how involvement of fathers in parenting could contribute to better health outcomes for men and their children, actually little is known about the relationship between fatherhood and health. The paucity of the literature is particularly noteworthy in majority-world contexts where the role of the father has typically been evaluated in relation to breadwinning, with little data on the value of family life and children in promoting fathers' mental and physical health. While we know that culture shapes the relationship between fathers and children, this have not been studied extensively, especially within developing-country contexts (United Nations, 2003).

The present section looks specifically at how the experience of fathering affects the mental and physical health of men. Fatherhood is a social role which exhibits significant variation, for example in terms of whether one is a first-time or an experienced father, and across class and cultural settings. While most research supports the idea that fatherhood can be beneficial to a man's health (Bartlett, 2004; Spector, 2006), the health effects of fatherhood are mediated by a number of factors, including the number and the age of children; the father's lifestyle and role competence and whether he is gainfully employed; and social class and social environment (Bartlett, 2004), as well as the quality of spousal relationships. Further, men tend to suffer from more severe health conditions than women and have consistently earlier death rates, dying at an age that is on average nearly seven years younger than that of women, reflecting the fact that socialized health-related beliefs play a critical role in the way men and women respond to their social environment. For example, men tend to show a lack of concern about their own health relative to women (Courtenay, 2000). In addition, men tend not to seek nurturance nor do they usually have an extensive social network; they seldom ask others for help, and view themselves as physically and emotionally stronger than women. These socially prescribed health attitudes and behaviours affect how men experience fatherhood and the benefits they derive from their relationships with their children.

## Fathers, parenthood and health

Giving support to others promotes longevity (Brown and others 2003), and the provision of support to children by fathers may confer similar physical and mental health benefits. The most consistent negative reports about caring for children relate to the effects of daily hassles (repeated and chronic strains of everyday life) (DeLongis, 1982), and studies that controlled for confounding factors have shown that a lower mortality rate can be predicted for fathers on the basis of the presence of children. A meta-analytic review revealed an overall beneficial effect of fatherhood on men's self-reported health (Bartlett, 2004). Holt-Lunstad and others (2009) found that having children significantly lowered blood pressure among parents compared to non-parents; and it is noteworthy that the effect was even stronger for mothers.

Mortality studies among fathers point to a similar trend. For example, Smith and Zick (1994) found that fathers aged 35-64 experienced a lower mortality risk with an increase in the number of children ever born. Hemström (1996) found that divorced Swedish men with no children had higher relative rates of mortality than men with one or two children. Similarly, in a study of British men aged 60-69, those with two children had a significantly lower risk of developing heart disease than men with one or no children. However, with each additional child after two, the risk of heart disease increased by 12 per cent. Thus, while fatherhood can be beneficial to a man's health, it is influenced by other factors as well, such as the stress associated with supporting a large family.

## Effect of transition to parenthood on well-being

Most studies report that men increase their level of involvement in family life when they become fathers. For example, Swartz and Bhana (2009) found that after the birth of their child, young unmarried fathers living in poverty in South Africa altered their pattern of socializing and the time they spent out of the home. They also spent less money on themselves, and shifted the weight of their social relationships towards family and reconnecting with their own fathers. Knoester and Eggebeen (2006) noted that the transition to fatherhood transforms men's well-being and social participation: fathers become more involved in the lives of family members and increase their participation in service-oriented activities, particularly if they live with their child. It has been suggested that the dynamics associated with being a father extend a man's social networks. Further, the extent of a man's social integration reduces individual vulnerability, and stress is believed to be mitigated by the protective role of social support (Berkman and others, 2000; World Health Organization, 2007).

## Health risks associated with single fatherhood

In a comprehensive review of risks and subsequent effects of paternal depression upon a family, single fathers living with children were noted to have better health than single fathers without children (Spector, 2006). Further, men with custody of their children or who lived in stable relationships had fewer medical and social problems than those living alone, even though men involved in custody disputes were more prone to depression from varying causes. The presence of children in a marriage offers the prospects of a positive experience for fathers, while divorce presents the prospect of reduced contact with children, besides introducing feelings of being unsupported, demeaned and demoralized when the separation is conflictual. Kendler (2001) also found that non-custodial fathers report guilt, severe anhedonia and substance abuse, sometimes sufficiently severe to require treatment. Such fathers also report lower satisfaction with their lives and a reduction in health-promoting activities, and are exposed to more health risks (Tepp, 1983). Unmarried adolescent fathers have been found to be more vulnerable to mood and anxiety disorders, psychosomatic symptoms and poor work or school performance (Girard, Coll and Becco, 1991).

## Effects of stress and loss on a father

Fathers who lose a spouse in general experience greater vulnerability to depression than women, with about 15 per cent reporting suicidal thoughts or actions. A lower level of social support among male-led single-parent households is accompanied by a reduced inclination by men to seek help (Spector, 2006).

The most critical psychological aftermath is experienced four to six years after the event of the death of a child, at which time both parents run the risk of chronic anxiety and depression (Spector, 2006). Mandell, McAnulty and Reece (1980) found that fathers experience low self-worth and tend to blame themselves and they frequently deal with this by focusing on work so as to keep themselves busy. If the child has died as a result of a chronic illness, then the father's sense of powerlessness is likely to precipitate anxiety and depression. The response of fathers to the loss of a child due to miscarriage or spontaneous abortion is often underestimated. It has been noted that anxiety and depressive symptoms could manifest anywhere between 2 and 30 months after the loss, with substance abuse being particularly noticeable (Goldbach and Lasker, 1991; Gray, 2001). Other effects of paternal depression include to lower problem-solving skills and adverse impact on the financial well-being of the family (Jacob and Johnson, 2001).

Taken as a whole, the evidence shows that children have significant positive effects on men's physical and mental health, and also seem to mitigate the negative effects of family dissolution and conflict. However, the research studies are limited to Europe and North America and provide few grounds for generalization.

## Implications for social and family policy

In this chapter, we have considered the far-reaching effects of men in the lives of children and families and, to a lesser extent, the impact of children on the well-being of men; and we have described fathering practices and roles in varying cultural contexts and drawn attention to the role of the social father and the influence of social class and other contextual factors on fathering practice. We have also examined the impact of fathering on children's development, including their health, well-being and education, and growth into sexual maturity and parenthood, and considered the role that men play in the intergenerational transfer of wealth and in intergenerational caregiving practices. In considering fatherhood and the work-family balance, we have sought to show the importance of the work environment in creating conditions that enable men adapt to changing roles in parenting and caregiving. Finally, we have provided an overview of the impact of fathering, single fatherhood, divorce and the death of a child on the mental and physical health of men.

We have sought throughout to illustrate the diversity of contexts and the contrasting experiences of men from both the Western world and those from the majority world, although the literature on the experiences of the latter is extremely limited; in many cases, men's involvement in the lives of children and families are constrained by their context, including the availability of resources, political and cultural will, and social policies. Truth be told, we simply do not know enough about men's experiences in the majority world to offer substantial conclusions or recommendations. Beardshaw (2006) argues that if men's involvement in families is to be strengthened, then particular attention needs to be paid to research, policy and programmes. Each area will be considered in turn.

## Research

It is clear that research in each of the five areas that we have considered, would enhance our understanding of men's needs and contribute towards effective policies and programmes. In particular, studies need to focus on the following topics:

1.  *Highlighting social fatherhood*: With regard to fluid and changing social and cultural roles played by men in the lives of children and families, the concept of the "social father" needs to be highlighted, and men's care work valued and recognized, whether or not they are a child's biological father, or whether or not they are co-resident with their child over long periods of time. It is important to unravel what father involvement means and which components of men's interactions with children are most critically important and how to support men in enacting them.

2.  *Men's involvement and emotional engagement with children*: With regard to the role that men play in children's development, research efforts need to be extended across cultures and class so as to reflect such factors as the manner in which migrant labourers, for example, perceive the sacrifices they make in leaving home to find work, as the strongest manifestation of their commitment to and engagement with their children. Workplace policies need to acknowledge this and support men's engagement in family life. Studies in Europe and the United States have demonstrated the stresses arising from fatherhood under conditions of immigration or work migration, but little is known about how these adverse effects can best be mitigated (Roer Strier, 1996).

3.  *Shifting demographics and migration*: Given the shifts in demographics currently at play, we need to know more about the needs of adolescent fathers, migrant male labourers, older men who are involved in providing and caring for the third generation, fathers with disabilities and other men with special needs. We also need to know how to prevent or mitigate men's loss of contact with their children when fatherhood is reached at a young age or when men are absent as a result of engagement as labour migrants. We also need to ascertain the conditions under which the intergenerational transfer of support, skills and wealth is encouraged and facilitated.

4.  *Research is required that challenges representations in the consciousness of employers of the ideal worker as an "unencumbered male"*, replaces those representations with images of the caregiving and providing father. Understanding how work norms

are generated and maintained would better enable us to challenge and change them. We need to research models that reconcile work and family life, especially in the context of men in low-wage, non-professional jobs.

5. *Studies need to consider the mediating influence of multiple social, cultural and community variables* in determining men's health and experiences of fatherhood. It is important to understand the role of the media and the potential of the internet and social networking technologies. This is especially necessary among low-income populations in majority-world countries.

## Polices

As we turn to a consideration of the implications for promoting men's involvement in families and engagement with their children, we need to ask what current policies create an environment conducive to encouraging men to engage with children and families, and which additional policy innovations and amendments might further these aims. Beardshaw (2006) describes five major areas of policy engagement, namely, the labour market, education, health, family law and social services. In each, we select one or two key examples that might have the greatest leverage and, where appropriate, address programmatic implications.

### Labour market

According to Beardshaw (2006), taxation, benefits, employment, childcare and parental leave systems should be based on the principle that both fathers and mothers are jointly responsible for children's overall health and wellbeing. A key area of labour policy where initiatives could contribute materially to men's involvement in child and family is that of parental leave. While parental leave is frequently included in current labour legislation, the extent of such leave varies widely across national contexts. According to the Human Sciences Research Council Fatherhood Project, the average number of days allowed for family responsibility leave in Africa lags behind the number granted in most European countries (Human Sciences Research Council, 2006). In South Africa fathers are entitled to three days paid family responsibility leave; and the same number of days is granted in Algeria. By comparison, in Cameroon, Chad, Côte d'Ivoire, Gabon and Togo fathers are entitled to 10 days paid family responsibility leave (see table I.3).

However, even when parental leave systems are in place, men frequently do not access these benefits. Cultural influences, family policies and workplace cultures may discourage men from taking on parenting responsibilities, especially in the context of the persisting social expectation that fathers will assume greater responsibility for breadwinning and mothers for caregiving (Barclay and Lupton, 1999), and may therefore hinder involved and responsive fatherhood. It is also important to focus on the meanings that fathers and other family members assign to activities associated with fatherhood because these can have profound consequences with regard to the nature and level of men's participation in family life (Palkovitz, 1997). On the other hand, paternity benefits, flexi-time, home work and telecommuting, and other arrangements that help to reconcile work and family life can be helpful to men who want to be involved in the care of their children.

## Education (and media)

Education—both formal education as it is provided in schools, training institutions and places of higher education, and informal education through media channels—is a key area in which societies communicate and entrench representations of men, masculinity and fatherhood. Beardshaw (2006) argues for the development of national education programmes for children that promote the sharing of domestic and care responsibilities between men and women among future generations. This is important, but without media messages to reinforce supportive underlying norms, success may be limited. Content and discourse analyses of media portrayals and advice literature often demonstrate that the identities of men may be undermined by images that position fathers as part-time, secondary and less competent parents with fewer parenting and greater breadwinning responsibilities as compared with mothers (Sunderland, 2006). In an analysis of commercials in the United States, Kaufman (1999), for instance, found that men were less likely than women to be shown with children, and that when men were pictured with children there was usually a woman present, which suggested that men were not expected to take responsibility for parenting duties.

Men are also far more likely than women to appear in commercials for electronic devices and life insurance, among other items, and are almost never shown in commercials for, say, children's medication (ibid.). In commercials for food and cleaning products, men are often portrayed as similar to children, with both frequently being served by a mother figure or passively watching her cook and clean. Kaufman concludes that "while they appear to be involved family men ... those that are involved need not know how to cook or clean or care for a sick child" (p. 456). This portrayal of men should be replaced by images that depict men as being actively involved in childcare and domestic chores. Furthermore, there is a need to utilize the role of the media and technology to enhance intergenerational cooperation. The media can also support a positive perception, including across spatial and social divides, of older people in families and society more generally including of the involvement of older men in supporting their children and grandchildren.

## Family law

1   United Nations Treaty Series, Vol. 1577, No. 27531

Consistent with the Convention on the Rights of the Child,[1] family laws should, among other things, ensure that children are protected and cared for by both parents, which requires an enabling legal environment. Family laws governing adoption, fostering, custody and provision (maintenance) ought to have as their primary aim the formation and maintenance of families, however constituted. In this regard, child and family support, access rights, inheritance laws, and other provisions need to enable and encourage men's involvement with children, whether or not they are the biological parent. Currently, custody laws tend to favour women to the disadvantage of men. Thus, while biological parents, for example, receive tax relief for having and supporting children, there is no such benefit available to social fathers—the many men who support children who are not their own. Similarly, there are seldom mechanisms to ensure that health insurance and other forms of social protection that may cover working men include nonbiological children who are dependent on them.

Easing financial transfers and relaxing exchange-control laws or providing taxation relief for men who send remittances home could contribute to a more facilitating milieu for fathers who migrate for work. In addition, offering programmes and incentives that help men regain contact with children and families after separation due to work, imprisonment or the like, may also contribute to keeping men in families. Tax incentives for economically active younger people to facilitate the provision of greater levels of support to older generations could also be considered to mutual benefit.

## Health

While research is beginning to demonstrate the mental and physical health benefits of fatherhood for men, the benefits of fatherhood are routinely underestimated in social policies affecting men. The psychological transition to fatherhood can be as dramatic as that to motherhood. However, medical and social services often fail to address men's experiences. Health services need to become more "father-friendly", and to consider that many health-related decisions affecting women and children are made by men and that, for this reason, men also need to be targeted by nutrition, immunization and other health-promoting messages. The need for specific health and support services for fathers, including in dealing with anxiety during pregnancy and depression upon loss of a child, should be recognized in work with families. Loss of child custody places fathers at significant risk of physical and psychological ill health, yet little is known about these issues and there are few services available to this high risk population. Furthermore, the beneficial effect of a healthy father on family welfare needs greater emphasis in promotional material, and a better understanding of fathers' mental health could greatly enhance policy and programmatic interventions for families.

## Social services

In a similar vein, instituting quality standards for "father-friendliness" (Beardshaw, 2006) in family, children and community services could contribute to greater involvement by men in the lives of children and families. Early child development programmes, school enrolment, after care school programmes and school and out-of-school recreation programmes are seldom designed or tailored to ensure the inclusion of men. As a result, neither children nor the services benefit from men's participation, Social services and programmes that have been shown to increase fathers' participation in childcare ought to be disseminated widely as models of good practice, along with the development of training capacities to spread development of the skills and knowledge base among programme planners and workers (ibid.).

# Last word

There are many areas in which policy affects men's involvement with children and families (a recent publication, Redpath and others, 2008) concluded that social policy "all too frequently engages with problems in a way that perpetuates the very constructions of masculinity that have given rise to the social problems in the first place" (p. 57). In this chapter, we have therefore tried to steer away from making proposals on a microlevel, for example, with regard to laws and policies concerning divorce, child custody, child maintenance, family violence, inheritance laws, and laws regarding gun possession or child maltreatment.

We recognize the potential conflicts that occur as legal and social policies are examined and changed with a view to encouraging men's involvement in families, while simultaneously serving and protecting children and women. We also recognize that social and legal polices are frequently slow in providing relief, and often encounter opposition from special interest groups. Instead we have focused in our recommendations on a few select actions that may serve, to quote Archimedes, as a lever that moves the world, if just a little, in the direction of encouraging men's involvement in the lives of children and families.

Young and old men, like women, are important in the lives of children and are an asset to family life throughout the life-cycle. Their absence and disengagement are keenly felt and are to the detriment of children's development and their transition to adulthood. Their contributions, however, are seldom encouraged or acknowledged; therefore, much more needs to be done to ensure the recognition of the value men bring to the lives of children, women and future generations of fathers. Men throughout the world have reported their experience of fatherhood as a significant formative influence in their own lives, and have spoken of their aspirations towards being fathers—and good fathers, however, the term *good father* may be defined. First and foremost a social policy environment is needed that stimulates and enables specific actions to promote fatherhood and the engagement of men by the media, services, civil society organizations and the private sector. At the same time caution must be exercised when father-friendly policies are being developed so as to prevent the opportunistic reassertion of men's authoritarian control over women and children, which is frequently associated with abuse in many parts of the world. The new vision is one of caring men who practice egalitarianism and strive within the unique context of their gender, networks, experiences and dreams to realize the potential of the family to provide support to children, women and men themselves, and to establish a strong foundation for parenting, and especially fathering, well into the future.

# References

Abe, M., C. Hamamoto, and Tanaka, S. (2003). *Reconciling work and family: Issues and policies in Japan*. Geneva: International Labour Office.

Amato, P.R. and J. Gilbreth (1999). Nonresidential fathers and children's wellbeing: a meta-analysis. *Journal of Marriage and the Family*, vol. 61 (August), pp. 557-573.

Ashford, L. (2007). Africa's youthful population: risk or opportunity? Washington, D.C.: Population Reference Bureau.

Asia Research Institute and Department of Sociology (2010). International Conference on Fatherhood in 21st Century Asia: Research, Interventions, and Policies, National University of Singapore, Singapore, 17 and 18 June 2010.

Bachrach, C. and F. Sonestein (1998). Male fertility and family formation: research and data needs on the pathways to fatherhood. In "Nurturing fatherhood: improving data and Research on Male fertility, family formation and fatherhood. Report on the Conference on Fathering and Male Fertility, 13 and 14 March 1997. Federal Interagency Forum on Child and Family Statistics, ed., Washington D.C.

Badran, H. (2003). Major trends affecting families in El Mashrek El Araby. Background document in "Major trends affecting families", United Nations, ed., New York: United

Nations Programme on the Family, Division for Social Policy and Development, Department of Economic and Social Affairs.

Bailyn, L., R. Drago and T. A. Kochan (2001). Integrating work and family life: a holistic approach. Boston, Massachusetts: MIT, Sloan School of Management.

Baral, S. and others (2007). Elevated risk for HIV infection among men who have sex with men in low- and middle-income countries 2000-2006: a systematic review. *PLoS Medicine, vol. 4*, No. 12 (December), p. 339.

Barclay, L. and D. Lupton, (1999). The experiences of new fatherhood: a socio-cultural analysis. *Journal of Advanced Nursing*, vol. 29, No. 4 (April), pp. 1013-1020.

Barnett, R., N.L. Marshall and J.H. Pleck (1992). Adult son-parent relationships and their associations with sons' psychological distress. *Journal of Family Issues,* vol. 13, No. 4, pp. 505-525.

Barry, H. and L. Paxson (1971). Infancy and early childhood: cross-cultural codes 2. *Ethnology,* vol. 10, No. 4, pp. 466-508.

Bartlett, E. (2004). The effects of fatherhood on the health of men: a review of the literature. *Journal of Men's health and Gender*, vol. 1, Nos. 2-3, pp. 159-169.

Bausch, R. S. (2006). Predicting willingness to adopt a child: a consideration of demographic and attitudinal factors. *Sociological Perspectives,* vol. 49, No. 1, pp. 47-65.

Beardshaw, T. (2006). Taking forward work with men in families. In *Baba: Men and fatherhood in South Africa*, L. Richter and R. Morrell, eds., pp. 306-316. Cape Town: HSRC Press. Belsky, J. (1997). Attachment, mating, and parenting. *Human Nature*, vol. 8, No. 4, pp. 361-381.

Berkman, L.F. (1995). The role of social relations in health promotion. *Psychosomatic Medicine,* vol. 57, No. 3, pp. *57,* 245-254.

_____ and others (2000). From social integration to health: Durkheim in the new millennium. *Social Science and Medicine,* vol. 51, No. 6, pp. 843-857.

Bernadett-Shapiro, S., D. Ehrensaft and S. Shapiro (1996). Father participation in childcare and the development of empathy in sons: an empirical study. *Family Therapy,* vol. 23, No. 2, pp. 17-23.

Boukydis, C.F. and R.L. Burgess (1982). Adult physiological response to infant cries: effects of temperament of infant, parental status, and gender. *Child Development,* vol. 53, No. 5, pp. 1291-1298.

Bozett, F.W. and S.M. Hanson (1991). *Fatherhood and Families in Cultural Context.* New York: Springer.

Brandth, B. and E. Kvande (2003). Father presence in childcare. In *Children and the Changing Family*, A.M. Jensen and L. McKee (eds.), pp. 61-75. London: Routledge Falmer.

Bronte-Tinkew, and others (2008). Involvement among resident fathers and links to infant cognitive outcomes. *Journal of Family Issues*, vol. 29, No. 9, pp. 1211-1244.

Brown, J. and G. Barker. (2004). Global diversity and trends in patterns of fatherhood. In "Supporting Fathers: Contributions from the International Fatherhood Summit 2003". The Hague: Bernard van Leer Foundation.

Brown, S.L., and others (2003). Providing social support may be more beneficial than receiving it: results from a prospective study of mortality. *Psychological Science,* vol. 14, No. 4, pp. 320-327.

Bugental, D. B. (2000). Acquisition of the algorithms of social life: a domain-based approach. *Psychological Bulletin,* vol. 126, No. 2, pp. 187-219.

Bullock, K. (2005). Grandfathers and the impact of raising grandchildren. *Journal of Sociology and Social Welfare,* vol. 32, No. 1, pp. 43-59.

Burton, L. (2007). Childhood adultification in economically disadvantaged families: a conceptual model. *Family Relations,* vol. 56, No. 4, pp. 329-345.

Bzostek, S.H. (2008). Social fathers and child well-being. *Journal of Marriage and Family,* vol. 70, No. 4 (November), pp. 950-961.

Cabrera, N.J., and others (2000). Fatherhood in the twenty-first century. *Child Development,* vol. 71, No. 1 (January/February) pp. 127-136.

Carlson, M. (2006). Family structure, father involvement, and adolescent behavioural outcomes. *Journal of Marriage and the Family,* vol. 68, No. 1 (February), pp. 137-154

Casper, L. and M. O'Connell (1998). Work, income, the economy, and married fathers as childcare providers. *Demography,* vol. 35, No. 2 (May), pp. 243-250.

Chirwa, W. C. (2002). Social exclusion and inclusion: challenges to orphan care in Malawi. *Nordic Journal of African Studies,* vol. 11, No. 1, pp. 93-113.

Cobb-Clark, D. (2008). *Leaving Home: What Economics Has to Say about the Living Arrangements of Young Australians.* Centre for Economic Policy Research *Discussion Paper* No. 568. Canberra: The Australian National University, Centre for Economic Policy Research.

Coltrane, S., R.D. Parke and M. Adams (2004). Complexity of father involvement in low-income Mexican American families. *Family Relations,* vol. 53, No. 2, pp. 179-189.

_____ (2001). Shared parenting in Mexican-American and European-American families. Paper presented at the Biennial Meeting of the Society for Research in Child Development, Ann Arbor, Michigan.

Courtenay, W. H. (2000). Engendering health: a social constructionist examination of men's health beliefs and behaviors. *Psychology of Men and Masculinity,* vol. 1, No. 1, pp. 4-15.

Cox, M., M. Owen, and V. Henderson (1992). Prediction of infant-father and infant-mother attachment. *Developmental Psychology,* vol. 28, No. 3 (May) pp. 474-483.

Craig, L. (2006). Does father care mean fathers share?: a comparison of how mothers and fathers in intact families spend time with children. *Gender and Society,* vol. 20, No. 2 (April), pp. 259-281.

Dancaster, L. (2008). Mom at work. *Mail & Guardian*, 18 September.

Day, R. and M.E. Lamb (2004). Conceptualizing and measuring father involvement: pathways, problems and progress. In *Conceptualizing and Measuring Father Involvement,* R. Day and M. E. Lamb, eds., pp. 1-14. Mahwah, New Jersey: Lawrence Erlbaum Associates.

Da Vanzo, J. and F.K. Goldscheider (1990). Coming home again: returns to the parental home of young adults. *Population Studies,* vol. 44, No.2 (July), pp. 241-255.

De Silva, I. (2003). Demographic and social trends affecting families in the South and Central Asian region. In *Major Trends Affecting Families*, Background document. United Nations (ed.), New York: United Nations Programme on the Family, Division for Social Policy and Development, Department of Economic and Social Affairs.

DeLongis, A. (1982). Relationship of daily hassles, uplifts, and major life events to health status. *Health Psychology,* vol. 1, pp. 119-136.

Desmond, C. and C. Desmond (2006). HIV/AIDS and the crisis of care for children. In *Baba: Men and Fatherhood in South Africa,* L. Richter & R. Morrell (eds.), pp. 226-236. Cape Town: HSRC Press.

Dex, S. and L. Shaw (1988). Women's working lives: a comparison of women in the United States and Great Britain. In *Women and Paid Work: Issues of Equality,* A. Hunt, ed., London: Macmillan.

Doherty, W., E. F. Kouneski and M.F. Erickson (1998). Responsible fathering: an overview and conceptual framework. *Journal of Marriage and the Family,* vol. 60, No. 2 (May), pp. 277-292. University of Minnesota.

Donald, D. and G. Clacherty (2005). Developmental vulnerabilities and strengths of children living in child-headed households: a comparison with children in adult-headed households in equivalent impoverished communities. *African Journal of AIDS Research,* vol. 4, No. 1 (May), pp. 21-28.

Dubowitz, H.M., and others (2000). Fathers and child neglect. *Archives of Pediatrics and Adolescent Medicine,* vol. 154, No. 2, pp. 56-70.

Duyvendak, J.W. and M.M. Stavenuiter (2004). Working fathers, caring men. Reconciliation of working life and family life. The Hague: Ministry of Social Affairs and Employment and Verwey-Lonker Institut, Rotterdam.

Edlund, L. and A. Rahman (2005). *Household structure and child outcomes: nuclear vs. extended families. Evidence from Bangladesh.* Mimeo. Columbia University.

Ellis, B.J., and others (2003). Does father absence place daughters at special risk for early sexual activity and teenage pregnancy? *Child Development,* vol. 74, No. 3 (May-June), pp. 801-821.

Engle, P., T. Beardshaw and C. Loftin (2006). The child's right to shared parenting. In Baba: Men and fatherhood in South Africa. L. Richter and R. Morrell, eds., pp. 293-305. Cape Town: HSRC Press.

Engle, P., and C. Breaux, C (1998). *Fathers' involvement with children: perspectives from developing countries.* Social Policy Report, vol. XII, No. 1. Ann Arbor, Michigan: Society for Research in Child Development.

Equal Employment Opportunities Trust (2003). Fathers and paid work. Auckland, New Zealand.

Flouri, E., and A. Buchanan (2002). Life satisfaction in teenage boys: the moderating role of father involvement and bullying. *Aggressive Behavior,* vol. 28, No. 2, pp. 126-133.

Foley, R.A., and P.C. Lee (1989). Finite social space, evolutionary pathways, and reconstructing hominid behavior. *Science,* vol. 246, No. 4927 (13 October), pp. 901-906.

Foster, G., and J. Williamson (2000). A review of current literature on the impact of HIV/AIDS on children in sub-Saharan Africa. *AIDS,* vol. 14, Supplement 3, pp. s275-s284.

Frey, R. (2003). Important, unique or uniquely important? In *Focus on Fathering,* R. Sullivan, ed. Melbourne, Australia: ACER Press.

Fursman, L., and P. Callister (2009). *Men's Participation in Unpaid Care: a Review of the Literature.* Wellington, New Zealand: Department of Labour.

Furstenberg, F., and C. Weiss (2000). Intergenerational transmission of fathering, roles in at risk families. *Marriage and Family Review,* vol. 29, Nos. 2 and 3 (May), pp. 181-201.

Geary, D.C. and M. V. Flinn (2001). Evolution of human parental behavior and the human family. *Parenting: Science and Practice,* vol. 1, Nos. 1 and 2 (January-June), pp. 5-61.

Gerard, J., L. Landry-Meyer and J. Roe (2006). Grandparents raising grandchildren: the role of social support in coping with caregiving challenges. *The International Journal of Aging and Human Development,* vol. 62, No. 4, pp. 359-383.

Gershuny, J., M. Godwin and S. Jones (1994). The domestic labour revolution: a process of lagged adaptation. In *The Social and Political Economy of the Household,* M. Anderson, F. Bechofer, and J. Gershuny, eds., Oxford: Oxford University Press.

Giddens, A. (2000). *Runaway World: How Globalization is Reshaping Our Lives:* New York: Routledge.

Girard, G.A., A. Coll and L. Becco (1991). The adolescent father: somebody who needs assistance: implications for health care. *International Journal of Adolescent Medicine and Health,* vol. 5, No. 2, pp. 127-133.

Goldbach, K. R., and others (1991). The effects of gestational age and gender on grief after pregnancy loss. *American Journal of Orthopsychiatry,* vol. 61, No. 3 (July), pp. 461-467.

Goldscheider, F. (2006). Family, fathers and demographic change. Washington, D.C.: Population Reference Bureau.

Goode, W. (1963). *World Revolution in Family Patterns*. Glencoe, Illinois: Free Press.

Gray, K. (2001). Grieving reproductive loss: the bereaved male. In *Men Coping with Grief*, A. Lund, ed., pp. 327-337. Death, Value and Meaning Series, J. D. Morgan, ed. Amityville, New York: Baywood.

Greenhaus, J. H. and N. J. Beutell (1985). Sources of conflict between work and family roles. *The Academy of Management Review*, vol. 10, No. 1, pp. 76-88.

Grubb, L. (2010). Fathers ruling the roost. *"Mamas and Papas"*, vol. 2, pp. 137-140. Johannesburg, South Africa.

Guma, M., and N. Henda (2004). The socio-cultural context of child abuse: a betrayal of trust. In L. Richter, A. Dawes, and C. Higson-Smith (Eds.), *Sexual abuse of young children in southern Africa*. Cape Town: HSRC Press.

Haas, L. and C.P. Hwang (2008). The impact of taking parental leave on fathers' participation in childcare and relationships with children: lessons from Sweden. *Community, Work and Family*, vol. 11, No. 1, pp. 85-104.

Harris K., F. Furstenberg and J. Marmer (1998). Paternal involvement with adolescents in intact families: the influence of fathers over the life course. *Demography*, vol. 35, No. 2, pp. 201-216.

Harrington, B., F. van Deusen and J. Ladge (2010). The new dad: exploring fatherhood within a career context. Boston, Massachusetts: Boston College, Center for Work and Family.

Hauari, H. and K. Hollingworth (2009). Understanding fathering: masculinity, diversity and change. York, United Kingdom: Josephine Rowntree Foundation.

Heise, L., J. Pitanguy and A. Germain (1994). *Violence against women: The Hidden Health Burden*. World Bank Discussion Paper, No. 255. Washington, D.C.: World Bank.

HelpAge International (2002). Gender and ageing briefs. United Kingdom: HelpAge.

Hemström, O. (1996). Is marriage dissolution linked to differences in mortality risks for men and women? *Journal of Marriage and Family*, vol. 58, No. 3 (May), pp. 366-378.

Hill, E., and others (2003). Studying «working fathers»: comparing fathers' and mothers' work-family conflict, fit, and adaptive strategies in a global high-tech company. *Fathering: A Journal of Theory, Research, and Practice about Men as Fathers*, vol. 1, No. 3, pp. 239-261.

Hobson, B., and S. Fahlen (2009). Competing scenarios for European fathers: applying Sen's capabilities and agency framework to work-family balance. *The ANNALS of the American Academy of Political and Social Science*, vol. 624, No. 1 (July), pp. 214-233.

Holt-Lunstad, J., W. Birmingham and B. Q. Jones (2008). Is there something unique about marriage? The relative impact of marital status, relationship quality, and network social support on ambulatory blood pressure and mental health. *Annals of Behavioral Medicine*, vol. 35, No. 2 (April), pp. 239-244.

Holt-Lunstad, J., and others (2009). Married with children: the influence of parental status and gender on ambulatory blood pressure. *Annals of Behavioral Medicine*, vol. 38, No. 3 (December), pp. 170-179.

Hook, J. L. (2006). Care in context: men's unpaid work in 20 countries, 1965-2003. *American Sociological Review*, vol. 71, No. 4 (August), pp. 639-660.

Hosking, A. (2006). Men, work and parenting. In *Baba: Men and fatherhood in South Africa*. L. Richter and R. Morrell, eds., pp. 216-225. Cape Town: HSRC Press.

Howard, B., and others (2006). Barriers and incentives to orphan care in a time of AIDS and economic crisis: a cross-sectional survey of caregivers in rural Zimbabwe. *BMC Public Health*, vol. 6, No. 27.

HSRC (Human Sciences Research Council) (2006). The Fatherhood Project newsletter, No. 24 (August). Pretoria.

Hunter, M. (2006). Father without amandla. Zulu-speaking men and fatherhood. In *Baba: Men and Fatherhood in South Africa*, L. Richter and R. Morrell, eds., pp. 99-107. Cape Town: HSRC Press.

International Labour Organization (2004a). Addressing gender equality through work-family measures. Information sheet No. WF-2. Geneva: International Labour Office, Conditions of Work and Employment Programmes.

_____ (2004b). Work and family responsibilities: what are the problems? Information sheet No. WF-1. Geneva: International Labour Office, Conditions of Work and Employment Programme.

_____ (2007). Global employment trends for women. Brief. Geneva: International Labour Office.

Jacob, T. and S.L. Johnson (2001). Sequential interactions in the parent-child communications of depressed fathers and depressed mothers. *Journal of Family Psychology,* vol. 15, No. 1 (March), pp. 38-52.

Janèaitytë, R. (2006). Family-friendly policies and welfare states: a comparative analysis. In *Between Paid and Unpaid Work: Family Friendly Policies and Gender Equality in Europe,* J. Reingardiene, ed. Vilnius: Social Research Center of Vytautas Magnus Universit.

Jarrett, R. (1994). Living poor: family life among single-parent, African-American women. *Social Problems,* vol. 41, No. 1 (February), pp. 30-49.

Jelin, E. and A.R. Diaz-Munoz (2003). Major trends affecting families: South America in perspective. In Major trends affecting families, United Nations, ed., New York: United Nations Programme on the Family, Division for Social Policy and Development, Department of Economic and Social Affairs.

Kang, A. and J. Weber (2009). Opportunities for policy leadership on fathers and work-family. Policy Briefing Series, No. 20. Chestnut Hill, Massachusetts: Boston College; Sloan work and Family Research Network.

Kaufman, G. (1999). The portrayal of men's family roles in television commercials. *Sex Roles,* vol. 41, Nos. 5-6, pp. 439-458.

Kendler, K.S., L.M. Thornton and C.A. Prescott (2001). Gender differences in the rates of exposure to stressful life events and sensitivity to their depressogenic effects. *American Journal of Psychiatry,* vol. 158, No. 4, pp. 587-593.

Kim, T.H. and K.K. Kim (2004). *Reconciling Work and Family: Issues and Policies in the Republic of Korea.* Conditions of Work and Employment Series, No. 6. Geneva: International Labour Office.

King, V. (1994). Nonresident father involvement and child well-being: can dads make a difference? *Journal of Family Issues,* vol. 15, No. 1, pp. 78-96.

Knoester, C. and D.J. Eggebeen (2006). The effects of the transition to parenthood and subsequent children on men's well-being and social participation. *Journal of Family Issues,* vol. 27, No. 11 (November), pp. 1532-1560.

Korenman, S. and R. Kaester (2005). Work-family mismatch and child well-being: A review of the economic research. In *Work, Family, Health and Wellbeing,* S.M. Bianchi, L.M. Casper and R.B. King, eds., pp. 293-308. Mahwah, New Jersey: Lawrence Erlbaum Associates.

Kusakabe, K. (2006). *Reconciling Work and Family: Issues and Policies in Thailand.* Geneva: International Labour Office.

Lamb, M.E. (2000). A history of research on father involvement: an overview. *Marriage and Family Review,* vol. 29, No. 2, pp. 23-42.

_____ (2004). *The Role of the Father in Child Development*, 4th ed. New York: John Wiley & Sons.

_____ and others (1985). Paternal behavior in humans. *American Zoologist,* vol. 562, No. 3, pp. 883-894.

Lambert, S.J. (1999). Lower-wage workers and the new realities of work and family. *The ANNALS of the American Academy of Political and Social Science,* vol. 562, No. 1 (March), pp. 174-190.

LaRossa, R. (1997). *The Modernization of Fatherhood.* Chicago, Illinois: University of Chicago Press.

Lee, R. and A. Mason, A. (2006). Back to basics: what is the demographic dividend? *Finance and Development*, vol. 42, No. 3 (September). Washington, D.C: International Monetary Fund.

Lesejane, D. (2006). Fatherhood from an African cultural perspective. In *Baba: Men and Fatherhood in South Africa,* L. Richter and R. Morrell, eds., pp. 173-182. Cape Town: HSRC Press.

Levine, C. (1990). AIDS and changing concepts of family. *The Milbank Quarterly,* vol. 68, pp. 33-58. Supplement I (Part 1): A Disease of Society: Cultural Responses to AIDS.

Levine, J. and T. Pittinsky, T. (1997). *Working Fathers: New Strategies of Balancing Work and Family.* Reading, Massachusetts: Addison-Wesley.

Lindegger, G. (2006). The father in the mind. In *Baba: Men and Fatherhood in South Africa,* L. Richter and R. Morrell, eds., pp. 121 131. Cape Town: HSRC Press.

Lloyd-Sherlock, P. (2001). Living arrangements of older persons and poverty, Population Bulletin of the United Nations: Critical Issues and Policy Responses, Ageing and Living Arrangement of Older Persons: Special Issue, Nos. 42/43. United Nations publication, Sales No. E.01.XII.16.

Lloyd, C B. and A.K. Blanc (1996). Children's schooling in sub-Saharan Africa: the role of fathers, mothers, and others. *Population and Development Review,* vol. 22, No. 2 (June), pp. 265-298.

Lloyd, C.B. and N. Duffy (1995). Families in transition. In *Families in Focus: New Perspectives on Mothers, Fathers, and Children,* J. Bruce, C.B. Lloyd, and A. Leonard, eds., (pp. 5-23. New York: Population Council.

Magruder, J. (2010). Intergenerational networks, unemployment and persistent inequality in South Africa. *American Economic Journal: Applied Economics,* vol. 2, No. 1, pp. 62-85.

Makiwane, M., M. Schneider and M. Gopane, M. (2004). Experience and needs of older persons in Mpumalanga. Pretoria: Human Sciences Research Council.

Mandell, F., E. McAnulty and R.M. Reece (1980). Observations of paternal response to sudden unanticipated infant death. *Pediatrics,* vol. 65, No. 2 (February), pp. 221-225.

Marsiglio, W. and R. Day (1997). Social fatherhood and paternal involvement: conceptual, data and policymaking issues. Report of the Working Group on Conceptualizing Male Parenting, prepared for and presented at the NICHD Conference on Fathering and Male Fertility: Improving Data and Research, Bethesda, Maryland.

Marsiglio, W., P.R. Amato and R. Day (2000). Scholarship on fatherhood in the 1990s and beyond. *Journal of Marriage and Family,* vol. 62, No. 4 (November), pp. 1173-1191.

Martin, A., R. M. Ryan and J. Brooks-Gunn (2010). When fathers' supportiveness matters most: maternal and paternal parenting and children's school readiness. *Journal of Family Psychology,* vol. 24, No. 2 (April), pp. 145-155.

Mboya, M. and R. Nesengani (1999). Migrant labour in South Africa: a comparative analysis of the academic achievement of father-present and father-absent adolescents. *Adolescence,* vol. 34, No. 136, pp. 763-767.

McBride, B. A., S.J. Schoppe-Sullivan and M.H. Ho (2005). The mediating role of fathers' school involvement on student achievement. *Journal of Applied Developmental Psychology,* vol. 26, No. 2 (March), pp. 201-216.

McGlodrick, M., and B. Carter (2003). The family life cycle. In *Normal Family Processes: Growing Diversity and Complexity,* F. Walsh, ed., pp. 375-398. New York: Guilford Press.

McLanahan, S. and L. Bumpass (1988). Intergenerational consequences of family disruption. *The American Journal of Sociology,* vol. 94, No. 1 (July), pp. 130-152.

McLoyd, V., and others (1994). Unemployment and work interruption among African-American single mothers: effects on parenting and adolescent socioemotional functioning. *Child Development,* vol. 65, No. 2 (April), pp. 562-589.

Mirkin, B. and B. Weinberger (2001). The demography of population ageing. *Population Bulletin of the United Nations,* Ageing and Living Arrangements of Older Persons: Critical Issues and Policy Responses, Special Issue, No. 42/43. United Nations publication, Sales No. E.01.XIII.16.

Mkhize, N. (2004). Socio-cultural approaches to psychology: dialogism and African conceptions of the self. In *Critical Psychology,* D. Hook and others, eds., pp. 53-83. Cape Town: UCT Press.

_____ N. (2006). African traditions and the social, economic and moral dimensions. In *Baba: Men and Fatherhood in South Africa,* L. Richter and R. Morrell, eds., pp. 183-198. Cape Town: HSRC Press.

Montgomery, C. M., and others (2006). Men's involvement in the South African family: engendering change in the AIDS era. *Social Science and Medicine,* vol. 62, No. 10 (May), pp. 2411-2419.

Morrell, R. (2006). Fathers, fatherhood and masculinity in South Africa. In *Baba: Men and Fatherhood in South Africa,* L. Richter and R. Morrell, eds., pp. 13-25. Cape Town: HSRC Press.

Mott, F.L. (1994). Sons, daughters and fathers' absence: differentials in father-leaving probabilities and in home environments. *Journal of Family Issues,* vol. 15, No. 1 (March), pp. 97-128.

Nathanson, C. A. (1984). Sex differences in mortality. *Annual Review of Sociology,* vol. 10 (August), pp. 191-213.

Nomaguchi, K. (2009). Change in work-family conflict among employed parents between 1977 and 1997. *Journal of Marriage and Family,* vol. 71, No. 1 (February), pp. 15-32.

Nosseir, N. (2003). Family in the new millennium: major family trends affecting families in North Africa. In Major trends affecting families. United Nations, ed. New York: United Nations Programme on the Family, Division for Social Policy and Development, Department of Economic and Social Affairs.

Nsamenang, A. B. (1987). A West African perspective. In *The Father's Role: Cross-cultural Perspectives,* M.E. Lamb, ed., pp. 273-293. Hillsdale, New Jersey: Erlbaum.

_____ (1989). Another style of socialization: the caregiving child: poster presented at the Iowa/International Conference on Personal Relationships.

O'Brien, M. (2009). Fathers, parental leave policies, and infant quality of life: international perspectives and policy impact. *The ANNALS of the American Academy of Political and Social Science,* vol. 624, No.1 (July), pp. 190-213.

Organization for Economic Cooperation and Development (2001). Balancing work and family life: helping parents into paid employment. OECD Employment Outlook 2001: June. Paris: OECD.

Olavarría, J. (2006). Men's gender relations, identity, and work-family balance in Latin America. In *The Other Half of Gender: Men's Issues in Development,* pp. 29-42, I. Bannon and M. C. Correia, eds. Washington D.C.: World Bank.

Oomens, S., S. Geurts and P. Scheepers, P. (2007). Combining work and family in the Netherlands: blessing or burden for one's mental health? *International Journal of Law and Psychiatry,* vol. 30, Nos. 4-5 (July-October), pp. 369-384.

Palkovitz, R. (1997). Reconstructing involvement: expanding conceptualizations of men's caring in contemporary families. In *Generative Fathering: Beyond Deficit Perspectives,* A. Hawkins and D. Dollahite, eds. Thousand Oaks, California: Sage.

_____ (2002). *Involved Fathering and Men's Adult Development: Provisional Balances.* Mahwah, New Jersey: Lawrence Erlbaum Associates.

Parke, R., and others (2004). Assessing father involvement in Mexican-American families. In *Conceptualizing and Measuring Father Involvement,* R. Day and M.E. Lamb, eds., pp. 15-33. Mahwah, New Jersey: Lawrence Erlbaum Associates.

Pavalko, E. K. and K.A. Henderson (2006). Combining care work and paid work: do workplace policies make a difference? *Research on Aging,* vol. 28, No. 3 (May), pp. 359-374.

Phoenix, A., A. Woollett and E. Lloyd, E. (1991). *Motherhood: Meanings, Practices and Ideologies.* London: Sage.

Pleck, J. (1993). Are "family-supportive" employer policies relevant to men? In *Men, Work and Family,* J. Hood, ed., pp. 217-237. Newbury Park, California: Sage.

_____ (1997). Paternal involvement: levels, sources and consequences. In *The Role of the Father in Child Development,* M.E. Lamb, ed., pp. 66-103. New York: Wiley.

Poelmans, S., and others (2003). A cross-national comparative study of work/family demands and resources. *International Journal of Cross Cultural Management,* vol. 3, No. 3 (December), pp. 275-288.

Population Council (2001). *The unfinished transition: gender equity–sharing the responsibilities of parenthood.* Population Council issues paper. New York.

Posel, D., and R. Devey (2006). The demographics of fatherhood in South Africa: an analysis of survey data, 1993-2002. In *Baba: Men and Fatherhood in South Africa,* L. Richter and R. Morrell, eds., pp. 38-52. Cape Town: HSRC Press.

Rabe, M. (2007). My children, your children, our children. *South African Review of Sociology,* vol. 38, No. 2, pp. 161-175.

Reddock, C. and Y. Bobb-Smith (2008). *Reconciling work and family: Issues and policies in Trinidad and Tobago.* Conditions of Work and Employment Series, No. 18. Geneva: International Labour Office.

Redpath, and others (2008). Masculinities and public policy in South Africa: changing masculinities and working toward gender equality. Johannesburg, South Africa: Sonke Gender Justice Network.

Richter, L. (2006). The Importance of fathering for children. In *Baba: Men and Fatherhood in South Africa,* L. Richter and R. Morrell, eds., pp. 53-69. Cape Town: HSRC Press.

_____ and R. Morrell (2006). Introduction. In *Baba: Men and Fatherhood in South Africa.* L. Richter and R. Morrell, eds. pp. 1-12. Cape Town: HSRC Press.

_____ and S. Panday (2006). Youth conceptions of the transition to adulthood in South Africa: barriers and opportunities. Sexuality in Africa, vol. 3, No. 1, pp. 1-4.

Roer Strier, D. (1996). Coping strategies of immigrant parents: directions for family therapy. *Family Process,* vol. 35, No. 3 (September), pp. 363-376.

Roy, K. (2008). A life course perspective on fatherhood and family policies in the United States and South Africa. *Fathering: A Journal of Theory, Research, and Practice about Men as Fathers,* vol. 6, No. 2, pp. 92-112.

Sarkadi, A., and others (2008). Fathers' involvement and children's developmental outcomes: a systematic review of longitudinal studies. *Acta Paediatrica,* vol. 97, No. 2, pp. 153-158.

Scanlon, T.J., and others (1998). Street children in Latin America. *BMJ,* vol. 316 (23 May), pp. 1596-1600.

Schacht, P.M., E.M. Cummings and P.T. Davies (2009). Fathering in family context and child adjustment: a longitudinal analysis. *Journal of Family Psychology,* vol. 23, No. 6, pp. 790-797.

Seward, R.R., and others (2006). Fathers taking parental leave and their involvement with children: an exploratory study. *Community, Work and Family,* vol. 9, No.1 (February), pp. 1-9.

Silver, C. (2000). Being there: the time dual-earner couples spend with their children. *Canadian Social Trends,* vol. 57 (summer), pp. 26-29.

Smith, K.R. and C.D. Zick (1994). Linked lives, dependent demise? survival analysis of husbands and wives. *Demography,* vol. 31, No. 1 (February), pp. 81-93.

Sorj, B. (2004). *Reconciling Work and Family: Issues and Policies in Brazil.* Conditions of Work and Employment Series, No. 8. Geneva: International Labour Office.

Spector, A. (2006). Fatherhood and depression: a review of risks, effects, and clinical application. *Issues in Mental Health Nursing,* vol. 27, No. 8 (October), pp. 867-883.

Spector, P.E., and others (2004). A cross-national comparative study of work-family stressors, working hours and well-being: China and Latin America versus the Anglo world. Personnel Psychology, vol. 57, No. 1 (March).

Sunderland, J. (2006). «Parenting» or «mothering»? The case of modern childcare magazines. *Discourse and Society,* vol. 17, No. 4, Conditions of Work and Employment Series, No. 8, pp. 503-527.

Swartz, S. and A. Bhana (2009). *Teenage Tata: Voices of Young Fathers in South Africa.* Cape Town: HSRC Press.

Tamis-LeMonda, C. and N. Cabrera, N. (1999). Perspectives on father involvement: research and policy. *Society for Research in Child Development,* vol. XIII, No. 2, pp. 1-32.

Taylor, S.E., and others (2000). Biobehavioral responses to stress in females: tend-and-befriend, not fight-or-flight. *Psychological Review,* vol. 107, No. 3, pp. 411-429.

Tepp, A.V. (1983). Divorced fathers: predictors of continued paternal involvement. *American Journal of Psychiatry,* vol. 140, pp. 1465-1469.

Toth, J.F. and X.I. Xu (1999). Ethnic and cultural diversity in fathers' involvement: a racial/ethnic comparison of African American, Hispanic, and White fathers. *Youth and Society,* vol. 31, No. 1 (September), pp. 76-99.

Townsend, L. and A. Dawes, A. (2004). Willingness to care for children orphaned by HIV/AIDS: a study of foster and adoptive parents. *African Journal of AIDS Research,* vol. 3, No. 1, pp. 69-80.

Townsend, N. (2002). Cultural contexts of father involvement. In *Handbook of Father Involvement: Multidisciplinary Perspectives,* C. Tamis-LeMonda and N.J. Cabrera, eds. pp. 249-277. Mahwah, New Jersey: Erlbaum.

Townsend, N.W. (1997). Men, migration, and households in Botswana: an Exploration of connections over time and space. *Journal of Southern African Studies,* vol. 23, No. 3 (September), pp. 405-420.

United Nations, ed. (2001). Part One: Report on the Technical Meeting on Population Ageing and Living Arrangements of Older Persons: Critical Issues and Policy Responses: Living Arrangements of Older Persons. *Population Bulletin of the United Nations:* Ageing and Living Arrangements of Older Persons: Critical Issues and Policy Responses, Special Issue, Nos. 43/43. United Nations publication, Sales No. E.01.XIII.16

_____ (2003). Major trends affecting families. New York: United Nations Programme on the Family, Division for Social Policy and Development, Department of Economic and Social Affairs.

_____ (2004). *World Youth Report 2003: The Global Situation of Young People.* Sales No. E-03.IV.7.

United States Census Bureau (2003). Children's living arrangements and characteristics: March 2002. Current Population Report, pp. 20-547. Washington D.C.: United States Department of Commerce, Economics and Statistics Administration.

van Onselen, C. (1976). *Chibaro: African Mine Labour in Southern Rhodesia 1910-1933.* London: Pluto Press.

Verhoef, H. (2005). A Child has Many Mothers: views of child fostering in northwestern Cameroon. *Childhood,* vol. 12, No. 3 (August), pp. 369-390.

Wall, G. and S. Arnold, S. (2007). How involved is involved fathering?: an exploration of the contemporary culture of fatherhood. *Gender and Society,* vol. 21, No. 4 (August), pp. 508-527.

Wenk, D., Hardesty, and others (1994). The influence of parental involvement on the well-being of sons and daughters. *Journal of Marriage and Family,* vol. 56, No. 1 (February), pp. 229-234.

Whittington, L. A. and H.E. Peters (1996). Economic incentives for financial and residential independence. *Demography,* vol. 33, No. 1 (February), pp. 82-97.

World Health Organization (2007). *Fatherhood and health outcomes in Europe: a summary report.* Copenhagen: WHO Regional Office for Europe.

World Bank (2010). Labor participation rate, female (% of female population ages 15+). Available from http://data.worldbank.org/indicators/SL.TFL.CACT.FE.ZS. Accessed 18 June 2010.

Winslow, S. (2005). Work-family conflict, gender, and parenthood, 1977-1997. *Journal of Family Issues,* vol. 26, No. 6 (September), pp. 727-755.

III

# Fathers in challenging family contexts: a need for engagement

Margaret O'Brien

## The author

Professor **Margaret O'Brien** (Ph.D., 1984, London School of Economics) co-directs the University of East Anglia Centre for Research on the Child and Family in the United Kingdom of Great Britain and Northern Ireland. She is a clinical psychologist with long-standing research interests in: fatherhood and work-family policy; and fathers, parenting and family life, in which areas she has published widely. Professor O'Brien serves on the editorial board of the *Journal of Fathering* and on several international and national advisory and government boards including: the Equality and Human Rights Commission Working Better Programme; the Caribbean Support Initiative Programme on Child-Rearing Research; the UNICEF international consultative group on child-friendly cities; and the International Network on Leave Policies and Research.

# Introduction

Over the last decade international social policy dialogue has begun to include consideration of fathers and other male kin in their caring as well as earning roles (Burgess and Russell, 2004). Historically, a rather narrow economics-oriented view of men's contribution to family life has been adopted by policymakers, resulting in men being viewed primarily through the lens of economic provisioning. As a consequence, men's personal family life experiences and the extent of their caring responsibilities and emotional obligations have not been a routine consideration in international mainstream policy developments or assessments. However, increasing awareness of the significance of what men "do" in and around their family for both children's well-being (Lamb, 2010) and gender equality (Haas and Hwang, 2008) has initiated a drive to explore polices for fathers (Lero, 2006). The main target of father-sensitive policy development has been in the area of work-family reconciliation, with the emergence of paternity and parental leave as specific measures designed to promote father involvement in the early years (see chap. I). Social and family policies focused on supporting specific groups of fathers, particularly the most vulnerable, and other issues such as the role of men in family violence are less well developed (Wall, Leitão and Ramos, 2010).

The aim of the present chapter is to examine issues and policy responses related to a range of problematic family environments facing contemporary men and related father figures in the lives of children and mothers. The issues have been selected to highlight sensitive and compromising family contexts for fathers. The first section of the chapter concentrates on circumstances in which fathers are separated from their children, whether it be through the increasingly common experiences of relationship fragility and breakdown or through the rarer occurrence of paternal imprisonment. Coltrane (2004) has characterized the simultaneous trends of greater father involvement and increased paternal marginality, especially through relationship breakdown, as constituting the "paradox of fatherhood" in modern times. A second focus of the chapter is the problematic family environment where, through domestic or child abuse, men create risks and dangers for the women and children with whom they live and to whom they are related. Fathers and male kin who fail their families through engagement in physical, emotional and sexual abuse are a source of global concern (World Health Organization, 2005), although the dimensions of the issue have still not been fully charted. The third section of the chapter, considers fatherhood in the contexts of youth, disability and older ages with a view to further examining cases where men's family care and earning capacities are at risk of being compromised or challenged.

Each section is organized into three parts: first, the demographic profile is reviewed; second, the main research messages are summarized; and third, policy and promising programmatic responses are highlighted. At the outset, the intention was to present a global perspective, with data from developing and developed countries; however, this goal was difficult to realize, as the critical mass of primary research on fathers and father-inclusive policy evaluations is concentrated in richer nations and, more generally, demographic data capture of men's parental status is still not a routine component in macrolevel multinational surveys of family life and problems. The chapter ends with a broader discussion of social policy implications for the United Nations, national Governments, local government, civil society and the research community.

# Fathers separated from their children

## Fathers separated from their children after marriage or when cohabitation ends

### Demographics

The increase in divorce and re-partnering towards the end of the last century has been a key demographic change shaping contemporary fatherhood. It has been a significant contributing factor to the growth in fathers living away from their children in different households (figure III .1). Since the 1970s, crude divorce rates have markedly risen across many developed countries (Organization for Economic Cooperation and Development, 2010) as part of the second demographic transition (see figure III.1). Although

Figure III.1

**Increasing crude divorce rates in all OECD countries from 1970 to 2006-2007**
(*number of divorces per 1000 population*)

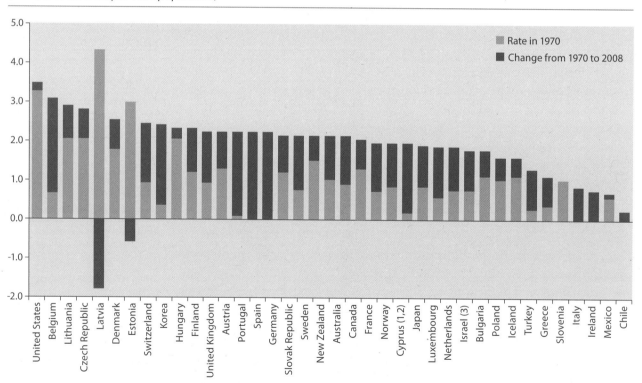

OECD Family Database www.oecd.org/els/social/family/database. OECD, Social Policy Division, Directorate of Employment, Labour and Social Affairs

**Sources:** Eurostat and United Nations Statistics Division.

**Note:** Data refer to 2005 for European Union countries except Germany and France; and to 2006 for Germany, France, Iceland, New Zealand, Turkey and the United States of America.

divorce rates have stabilized, and even declined, in several countries, linked to the decline in marriage, it is clear that increases in divorce, separation in consensual unions and re-partnering have changed the nature of fathers' families. Fathers are now more likely than in previous generations to experience more than one family type throughout their life course and in the process typically cease to reside with the children of their first relationship, thereby increasing the potential for marginalization in family life.

National rates of lone-mother households have been used as a demographic proxy for father absence through divorce and separation. Within Europe, 14 per cent of households with children are lone mother-headed representing, a doubling over 30 years (EU, 2008). However, actual father involvement with children in this family type can vary considerably; moreover, lone-mother households comprise more than just one family type, that of divorced mothers: the range is wider including, most importantly, never-married mothers. Notwithstanding these methodological problems, it is still clear that the global growth of lone-mother households (Organization for Economic Cooperation and Development, 2010, table III.1) increases the likelihood of lower levels of spousal and paternal assistance provided by men to women and children.

## Assessing levels of contact between separated non-residential fathers and their children

When fathers leave the family, household contact with children is less than when family members co-reside. Early research, often cross-sectional with small samples, suggested that for most divorced and separated fathers, contact with children declines over time (Pasley and Braver, 2004). More recent longitudinal research from the United States shows a more complex picture (Amato and Dorins, 2010; Cheadle, Amato and King, 2010). In a nationally representative sample, tracked over 12 years, only one group of separated fathers (23 per cent), displayed a clear pattern of declining contact (initial high involvement, which became lower). The largest group of separated fathers (38 per cent) maintained a high level of contact (at least weekly) over the 12 years and a further group (32 per cent) remained relatively uninvolved throughout. A minority (8 per cent) gradually increased their involvement over the time period. It is likely that these diverse patterns of separated-father contact will be exhibited when further cross-national studies are conducted. Generally, father-child contact was at higher levels when mothers were more educated and older at the birth of the child.

Where records are available, which is the case mostly in Australia, United States and Northern Europe, what has been seen is a notable decline in the proportion of "no contact" non-residential fathers, signalling a diminution in clean-break post-separation fathers. For example, in the United States no contact rates of non-residential fathers dropped from 37 per cent in 1976 to 29 per cent in 2002 (Amato, Meyers and Emery, 2009). Taken together, contact research findings (mainly from developed countries) also suggest more weekday than night caring of children by non-residential fathers, as well as the traditional patterns of alternate weekends and holiday visitation (Fabricus and others, 2010). For example, in a nationally representative sample of Australian children whose parents had separated within the last 28 months, 16 per cent experienced shared care parenting (defined as 35-65 per cent of nights in the care of each parent) (Kaspiew and others, 2009). Equal care time (48-52 per cent time with each parent) was found among 7 per cent of children. The researchers reported that shared care time was

Table III.1

**Distribution of children aged 0-14 by living arrangements, 2007[a]** (*percentage*)

| | Both father and mother are in the same household | Father and mother are not in the same household | Father of the young-ster is in the same household | Mother of the youngster is in the same household |
|---|---|---|---|---|
| Austria | 86.6 | 0.5 | 0.9 | 12.1 |
| Belgium | 65.0 | 4.4 | 11.0 | 19.5 |
| Bulgaria | 85.2 | 1.6 | 2.0 | 11.1 |
| Czech Republic | 80.8 | 0.6 | 1.2 | 17.4 |
| Cyprus [b,c] | | | | |
| Denmark[d] | 81.3 | 1.4 | 2.0 | 15.3 |
| Germany | 82.0 | 0.0 | 1.7 | 16.3 |
| Estonia | 66.8 | 6.7 | 1.1 | 25.4 |
| Finland | 95.2 | 0.2 | 0.4 | 4.1 |
| France | 79.5 | 0.6 | 2.9 | 17.0 |
| Greece | 93.6 | 0.2 | 0.8 | 5.4 |
| Hungary | 82.0 | 1.0 | 1.3 | 15.7 |
| Italy | 92.1 | 0.1 | 1.0 | 6.8 |
| Latvia | 64.9 | 2.7 | 2.2 | 30.2 |
| Lithuania | 72.4 | 2.0 | 4.7 | 21.0 |
| Luxembourg | 91.5 | 0.7 | 0.7 | 7.1 |
| Malta | 90.0 | 0.5 | 0.6 | 9.0 |
| Japan[d] | 87.7 | 0.0 | 1.7 | 10.6 |
| Mexico[d] | 87.1 | 0.0 | 1.6 | 11.3 |
| Netherlands | 87.4 | 0.1 | 1.3 | 11.2 |
| Poland | 82.0 | 1.1 | 1.0 | 15.8 |
| Portugal | 86.6 | 1.8 | 1.0 | 10.5 |
| Romania | 88.9 | 1.9 | 1.4 | 7.7 |
| Slovenia | 87.7 | 0.9 | 0.8 | 10.5 |
| Slovakia | 86.4 | 0.5 | 1.2 | 12.0 |
| Spain | 91.5 | 0.7 | 0.6 | 7.2 |
| Sweden[d] | 78.0 | 0.0 | 4.0 | 18.0 |
| Switzerland[d] | 84.7 | 0.1 | 2.3 | 12.9 |
| Turkey | 91.5 | 0.7 | 0.6 | 7.2 |
| United Kingdom | 68.9 | 1.1 | 2.4 | 27.6 |
| United States[d] | 70.7 | 3.5 | 3.2 | 22.6 |
| OECD–23 | 84.1 | 0.8 | 1.9 | 13.1 |

**Sources:** European Labour Force Statistics, 2007, except for Denmark, Japan, Sweden and Switzerland in which data were based on national responses to a separate OECD questionnaire; Mexico: Conteo de Poblacion y Vivienda, 2005 (INEGI); and United States: U.S. Census Bureau, Current Population Survey, 2007 Annual Social and Economic Supplement.

a Year 2000 for Switzerland; 2005 for Mexico and Sweden; 2007 for EU countries and the United States.

b Note provided by Turkey: The information in this table with reference to "Cyprus" relates to the southern part of the Island. There is no single authority representing both Turkish and Greek Cypriot people on the island. Turkey recognizes the Turkish Republic of Northern Cyprus (TRNC). Until a lasting and equitable solution is found within the context of the United Nations, Turkey shall preserve its position concerning the "Cyprus issue".

c Note provided by States members of the European Union that are members of the OECD and the European Commission: the Republic of Cyprus is recognized by all States members of the United Nations with the exception of Turkey. The information in this table relates to the area under the effective control of the Government of the Republic of Cyprus.

d Aged 0–17.

increasing in Australia generally for separated families but also in families where contact arrangements had been disputed between parents and finally determined through judicial review. However, the traditional care-time arrangement, of more nights with mother than with father, was generally more durable.

As regards developing countries, there is a huge academic gap in knowledge about the nature and quality of contact between fathers and their children after separation.

## Issues

### *Managing joint legal custody from a non-residential base*

Across the world, with its emphasis on mutual responsibility for the welfare of the child, there is a movement towards awarding joint legal custody to parents after divorce (see box III.1 for the case of England).

However, physical and residential custody orders are rarely joint and mothers assume physical and residential custody in a majority (68-88 per cent) of cases in developed countries, where international evidence is available (Fabricus and others, 2010). Currently, there is intense debate about whether a "shared care-time arrangement" should be introduced and formalized on the basis of a minimum of 30 per cent of the child's week time in order to give non-residential parents (typically fathers) a chance to maintain a relationship with their children (box III 2). Other scholars argue for, a more personalized case-by-case approach to ensure that the best interests of the child principle remains paramount.

### *Balancing best interests of the child principle and maintaining non-residential parental contact*

Under article 9.1 of the Convention on the Rights of the Child[1] (1989), the best interests of the child are deemed paramount in contact decisions over any concept of parental or gender rights to a child. However, the Convention also enshrines contact with parents as a basic human right for children. These principles are difficult to implement when there are conflicts about contact with a residential parent (usually the mother) versus that with a non-residential parent (typically the father). Fathers' lobbyists often complain that courts tend to underplay their childcare competencies whereas mothers' lobbyists decry fathers' desires for contact without responsibility.

1  United Nations Treaty Series, vol. 1577, No. 27531.

### *Supporting non-residential father contact and care of children*

Although lawyers may be involved, a majority of separating families organize post-separation custody and care arrangements without recourse to formal judicial decision-making. In post-separation environments, father involvement is higher when parents

---

Box III.1

**From fathers' rights to children's welfare: child custody in England**

**Before 1839**: Patria potestas: paternal power governed child custody decisions (legacy of Roman law)

1839  Infants Custody Act: discretion to allow mother custody of children under age 7

1873  Custody of Infants Act: discretion to allow mother custody extended to children up to age 16

1886  Guardianship of Infants Act: discretion to allow mother custody extended to children up to age 21

1925  Guardianship of Infants Act: welfare of children becomes the first and paramount consideration; neither parent's claim is superior

1973  Guardianship Act: equalization of parental rights of guardianship

are child-centred, cooperative, and flexible and this is when children's well-being is most supported (Kaspiew and others, 2009). Understandably, however, after a relationship breakdown, positive and constructive parenting can be difficult to sustain.

### Well-being of non-residential fathers

Non-residential fathers have poorer physical and emotional well-being (higher levels of depression and alcohol use) than divorced men without children and fathers in intact families (Eggebeen and Knoster, 2001). The well-being generally accrues from the status conferred by fatherhood but "once men step away from co-residence, the transforming power of fatherhood dissipates" (ibid. p. 391). It is not known whether the stressful experiences of non-residential fatherhood, as well as divorce, create these problems or if the non-residential fathers had pre-existing and enduring difficulties. For example, in a nationally representative Australian study of separated parents one half of the mothers and one third of the fathers indicated that mental health problems, the misuse of alcohol, drugs, gambling or other addictions had been apparent in the other partner before the separation (Kaspiew and others, 2009).

### High conflict contact cases

Estimates from developed countries indicate between 2 and 10 per cent of separating parents are involved in contested cases where contact arrangements are decided by judges (Fabricus and others, 2010) and about 14 per cent of separating couples report a highly conflictual relationship (Kaspiew and others, 2009). Conflicts about preferred post-separation care arrangements are a minority pattern but take up large amounts of legal time. Evidence is mixed about the quantity and type of parental conflict that children can tolerate in separated families (Lamb and Kelly, 2009). Where there are concerns about domestic violence and child abuse from non-residential fathers (relevant to a minority of high-vulnerability cases) there is consensus that supervised, limited or no father-child contact is in the best interests of the child (Kaspiew and others, 2009).

### Promoting non-residential father financial support (child support/maintenance of children)

Lone-mother households are at greater risk of poverty, although variations in income levels exist across the world. Countries have a range of mechanisms to ensure child support is enforced. Most child support programmes operate under the principle of the continuity of parental financial responsibility post-separation but disagreements do arise over the amounts non-residential fathers should pay.

## Policies and programmes

Policymakers have begun to focus on support for fathers who live apart from their children because of the increase in divorce and relationship breakdown. Separation and divorce programmes are wide-ranging and increasingly sensitive to non-residential fathering issues. Programmes include: advice services, dispute resolution, relationship support, mediation and parenting support. In many countries, there are active not-for profit organizations directly supporting separated fathers and practitioners working with fathers (for example, the Fatherhood Institute). Lobby groups agitating for separated fathers and fathers rights after divorce have also developed across the world (for example, Families need Fathers).

Box III.2
**The debate over shared parenting after separation**

"To maintain high-quality relationships with their children, parents need to have sufficiently extensive and regular interaction with them. Time- distribution arrangements that ensure the involvement of both parents in important aspects of their children's everyday lives and routines—including bedtime and waking rituals, transitions to and from school, extracurricular and recreational activities—are likely to keep non-residential parents playing psychologically important and central roles in the lives of their children."

(Lamb, Sternberg and Thompson, 1997, 400).

"A minimum of **one-third time** is necessary to achieve this criterion (a good- quality relationship) and that benefits continue to accrue as parenting time reaches equal (50–50) time" (Fabricius and others, 2010)

"The idea of a preferred arrangement conflicts with the **individualised approach** which is fundamental to the **welfare principle**" (Hunt, Masson and Trinder, 2009).

Innovation has occurred at national levels through changes in family law, such as those associated with Australia's Family Law Amendment (Shared Parental Responsibility) Act 2006 (SPR Act 2006), which represents an attempt to affect a systemic cultural change in the management of parental separation away from litigation and towards cooperative parenting (see box III.3). Early intervention family relationship

Box III.3
**A new shared parenting policy and programme in Australia**

The policy objectives of the Family Law Amendment (Shared Parental Responsibility) Act 2006 were to:

Help build strong healthy relationships and prevent separation.

Encourage greater involvement by both parents in their children's lives after separation, and also protect children from violence and abuse.

Help separated parents agree on what was best for their children (rather than litigate), through the provision of useful information and advice, and effective dispute resolution services.

Establish a highly visible entry point which would operate as a doorway to other services and help families access those services.

Changes to the programmes and service delivery system included the establishment of 65 family relationship centres (FRCs) throughout Australia, the family relationship advice line (FRAL) and family relationships online (FRO).

Legislative changes comprised four main objectives:

Requiring parents to attend family dispute resolution (FDR) before filing a court application, except in certain circumstances, including those where there were concerns about family violence and child abuse.

Placing increased emphasis on the need for both parents to be involved in their children's lives after separation through a range of provisions, including the introduction of a presumption in favour of equal shared parental responsibility.

Placing greater emphasis on the need to protect children from exposure to family violence and child abuse.

Introducing legislative support for less adversarial court processes in respect of matters relating to children.

**Sources:** Parkinson (2010) and Kaspiew and others (2009).

centres have been central to the process of helping parents reorder post-separation family life in the immediate aftermath of relationship breakdown. Preventative relationship education is also provided in the centres. A further bold element of the legislation has been the introduction of mandatory mediation (non-court "family dispute resolution" (FDR)) before an application for a parenting order may be filed. Exceptions can be made in cases of child abuse or family violence. The new and expanded services in Australia have been welcomed by parents and early evaluation suggests family relationship centres and the use of family dispute resolution have helped reduce litigation and facilitated more constructive parental dialogue about relationships, contact and care of children (Kaspiew and others, 2009). There is also evidence that fathers and mothers are being more creative about engaging fathers in children's everyday routines across two households. However, the importance of managing contact with high risk non-residential fathers is heightened in an environment where care time by fathers becomes normative. In such cases, greater investment in identification of high-risk parents is essential to ensuring that child safety and well-being are paramount.

High-conflict divorces, where there is violence, necessitate investment in supervised family contact centres which have developed in several countries. During visitation, trained professionals are present to ensure child safety. Residential parents are not required to have face-to-face contact with their partner and can drop off children in advance of visitation time.

Australia has also demonstrated innovation through a new child support programme (operational from July 2008) which represents an established attempt to modernize its approach and adapt to new post-separation parenting roles. Under the "income shares" and "care share" approach the amount of care given (and its cost) by non-residential fathers (and mothers) is included in the model for calculating financial support transfers (Parkinson, 2010). Further:

The essential feature of the proposed new scheme, based on the income shares approach, is that the costs of children are first worked out as a percentage of the parents' combined income, with those costs then distributed between the mother and the father in accordance with their respective shares of that combined income and levels of care (ibid. p. 607).

Levels of care are carefully defined: under "regular care", children are cared for 14-34 per cent of nights per year and under "shared care" each parent spends at least 35 per cent of nights caring for the child. The new formula is transparent and perceived to be fair to non-residential parents, usually fathers. This approach has helped more fathers accommodate their children over night, but in its early stages has been taken up only by about 10 per cent of non-residential Australian fathers.

In general, formal child support payments can operate to decrease child poverty in mother-headed households (Bradshaw, 2006) and are associated with better outcomes for children. For developing countries the lack of an adult male "breadwinner" after separation can cause considerable distress for lone-mother families; and research suggests that, despite the existence of family codes, there is weak enforcement of maintenance payments by non-residential fathers, especially among the poor (Chant, 2007).

A body of evidence shows that child support is strongly associated with higher levels of non-residential father contact with children, although the direction of causation is unclear (Amato and Dorius 2010). In order for child support enforcement approaches to be effective they need to mesh with the local cultural norms concerning family life and gender roles, as well as operate within the framework of national tax and welfare models.

## Unmarried non-resident fathers who are separated from their children

### Demographics

Precise demographic data on the proportion of fathers separated from their children in non-marital unions are not available, as information on informal couple unions, although thought to be common throughout the world, is rarely captured by demographic administrative systems. However, the proportion of non-marital births is a useful proxy for this statistically invisible group of fathers and that figure is collected by many countries. Measure of trends show that in a majority of, but by no means all, OECD countries, the number of parents who were not married at the time of the birth of their first child has increased since the 1970s, but absolute levels vary (Organization for Economic Cooperation and Development, 2010). For example, in France and most Nordic countries 50 per cent or more children are born outside of marriage, whereas the proportion is less than 10 per cent in Greece, Japan, the Republic of Korea and Mexico (Organization for Economic Cooperation and Development, 2010d). However, the proportion of non-resident fathers in these unions remains unknown.

Recent cohort and birth studies are providing insights into the profile of unmarried non-resident fathers (Kiernan, 2006; Carlson and McLanahan, 2010). For example, United Kingdom millennium birth cohort data show that, in comparison with fathers in cohabiting and married contexts, non-residential fathers are: younger (37 per cent under 24 years in contrast to 22 per cent of cohabitating fathers and 4 per cent of married fathers) and more likely to be living in economically disadvantaged neighbourhoods (55 per cent in comparison with 43 per cent in cohabiting partnerships and 26 per cent in married partnerships) (Kiernan, 2006). Sole mothers in non-marital unions are also significantly more likely to be under age 20, to have no educational qualifications and to be Afro-Caribbean British and poor. Similar demographic trends have been found in the United States (Carlson and McLanahan, 2010). In other parts of the world (for instance in some Caribbean countries, where non-marital visiting fatherhood is more common), men's demographic profile is more varied (Brown and Chevannes, 1998).

### Issues

Unmarried non-resident fathers are not a homogeneous group. While some men may not be aware of, or deny, their paternity, others remain connected to the mother and are involved with the child. Children born out of wedlock and cohabitation are often unplanned.

### *Under-reporting of children by fathers*

Demographers suggest that men are more likely than women to under-report children with whom they are not living. Children's existence may be unknown, concealed or denied, although the extent of under-reporting is hard to establish estimates suggest 5 per cent of children may be unreported by fathers (Clarke, Joshi and Di Salvo, 2000).

### Significance of presence at childbirth and name on birth certificate

Unmarried non-resident fathers who both attend childbirth and are named on the birth certificate are significantly more likely to continue to be on friendly terms with the mother, visit the child and show interest in the child (Kiernan, 2006). However, some fathers are **permanently lost to their children.** Records indicate about 31 per cent of unmarried non-resident fathers have no contact with their child at one year after birth (Kiernan, 2006) with the proportion rising slightly by age 5 (Carlson and McLanahan, 2010). Visitation arrangements of fathers in less developed countries are not widely recorded.

### Fragile fathering

Contrary to expectations the majority of unwed non-resident fathers are involved with their children (Cabrera and others, 2004), but involvement is difficult to sustain if it is not supported by birth mothers and drops over time and after relationships end. Two thirds of fathers have at least monthly visits at one year (Kiernan, 2006; Carlson and McLanahan, 2010). A minority move in with the mother on a full-time or part-time basis for a period of time when fathering is more engaged.

### Quality of couple relationship

Even when the romantic relationship has terminated, the ability of the couple to cooperate and avoid conflict is a key predictor of stability in father involvement.

### Unmarried non-resident father involvement and child wellbeing

Evidence is mixed on the benefits of unmarried non-residential father involvement on child well-being. Fathers in this group, who have antisocial or abusive personal histories, can be harmful to child well-being whereas those who can serve as authoritative figures and practice child-centred parenting can be an asset (Fagan and Palkovitz, 2007)

### Low financial resources

The fact that the unmarried non-residential fathers have disadvantaged backgrounds means, that they have few financial resources to transfer to mother and child. They are less likely than divorced fathers to pay formal child support (Lerman and Sorenson, 2000) but a significant minority do make some informal or formal financial contribution. Data from the United Kingdom indicate that by nine months after birth, one third had contributed some maintenance or child support, increasing to 50 per cent for fathers who had been named and present at the birth (Kiernan, 2006).

### Child Support enhances child wellbeing

The amount of child support paid to children by unmarried non-resident fathers is positively associated with educational attainment and psychological well-being (Tamis-Lemonda and McFadden, 2010).

## Policies and programmes

As unmarried non-resident fathers separated from their children tend to be poor, policy approaches are closely linked to country-level welfare systems, with some countries compensating for lack of paternal income. However, since the mid-1990s, as the number of children born out of wedlock has increased, Governments across the world have been pursuing more vigorous child support polices focusing on encouraging and enforcing paternal financial contribution. Since unmarried non-resident fathers are hard to reach, particularly if the father's name is not recorded at the birth, a policy focus has been on paternity registration at birth (Mincy, Garfinkel and Nepomnyaschy, 2005).

*Establishment of policies on paternity*

*The child shall be registered immediately after birth and shall have the right from birth to a name, the right to acquire a nationality and, as far as possible, the right to know and be cared for by his or her parents* (Convention on the Rights of the Child, article 7).

The paternity recognition principle is encapsulated in the Convention on the Rights of the Child but has not always been enforced by administrative bodies. Mothers may avoid including a father's name in order to optimize formal public benefits and retain informal private benefits (Curran, 2003).

Notably, poor countries with a high number of children without named fathers have started to pursue "presumed fathers" through legislation (for example, the Law for Responsible Paternity, (*Ley de Paternidad Responsable)* 2001, Costa Rica (see box III.4). New acts of enforcements are designed to ensure the rights of children to paternal recognition and economic assistance, and also to reduce the financial and social burdens of lone parenthood on women (Chant, 2007).

---

Box III.4
**Law for responsible paternity**
(*Ley de Paternidad Responsable)*, **Costa Rica, 2001**

Of the 78,526 births in Costa Rica reported in 1999, 51.5 per cent were of children conceived out of wedlock. Of these, 23,845 births were from unregistered fathers (that is, the children had only their mother's last name).

The primary purposes of the Law for Responsible Paternity are to strengthen the protection of girls and boys, and to promote the participation of fathers, together with mothers, in the upbringing of their children.

According to the principle change effected by the Law, a child born out of wedlock and not acknowledged voluntarily by his or her father, may report (through the mother) the name of the presumed father. This declaration should be made by the mother before an officer of the Civil Registry at the hospital where the child was born or at the offices of the Registry of Births, Marriages and Deaths. The child should be registered provisionally with the mother's last name. After receiving this notice, the presumptive father is given 10 working days within which to respond regarding whether or not he acknowledges paternity.

If the presumptive father acknowledges paternity, the child is registered with the father's and mother's last names. If the presumptive father does not accept paternity, the Registry of Births, Marriages and Deaths Registry requests a genetic markers (DNA) test.

A failure by the presumptive father to appear for the test or his refusal to take the test will be considered malicious conduct and the mother's statement shall be assumed to be true. In such cases, the child shall be registered with the presumptive father's last name and the mother shall be entitled to paid alimony (including part of the pregnancy and maternity expenses, as well as her child's food expenses for 12 months after birth).

Source: "Law for Responsible Paternity, No. 8101", La Gaceta (official newspaper), 2000.

The "golden opportunity" moment of birth has been utilized as the basis for "in-hospital paternity establishment registration programmes", the number of which has been growing (see box III.5 for an example from Richmond, Virginia). These programmes have been successful in increasing paternity recognition, child support and ensuring children's entitlements to a range of public benefits in the United States (Mincy, Garfinkel and Nepomnyaschy, 2005).

The programmes have less relevance in countries with more greatly enhanced arrangements for public financial support of children (funded through taxation or social insurance schemes), like the Nordic and other Northern European countries. In those countries, children's basic health, educational and social entitlements are not solely dependent on the private income of parents. Instead, all citizens contribute to children's welfare and support through taxation and insurance systems.

In an increasing number of developed countries, jointly registered unmarried fathers (cohabiting and non-resident) are more likely to be formally recognized as a "legitimate and responsible parent", an arrangement that is protective in case of couple dissolution. Patterns in developing countries, on the other hand, remain uncharted.

## Fathers in prison
### Demographics

The increasing male prison population worldwide creates yet another context in which fathers are separated from their children (Walmsley, 2005). Although parental status is rarely recorded for male prisoners, it is estimated that the vast majority, about 92 per cent, of imprisoned parents are men. In most countries, imprisoned fathers are more likely than the general population to be young, poorly educated, economically and socially disadvantaged and from minority groups (Day and others, 2005). In a national survey in the United States, of fathers in state prisons, 88 per cent had at least one child living with the child's mother, 13 per cent with the child's grandparent, 5 per cent with other relatives, 2 per cent in foster care, and 2 per cent with friends or others (Glaze and Maruschak, 2008).

### Issues

Imprisonment represents one extreme case where fathers live away and apart from children, often for an indeterminate period which is out of their control, unlike intermittent absences through marital or work-related separations.

#### Invisibility of parental status

In many countries, parental status is rarely considered as regards fathers at sentencing. Information about fatherhood and family responsibilities is not routinely recorded.

#### Father-child and partner contact

Through not "being there" for children, father imprisonment negatively affects paternal identity and family life (Clarke and others, 2005). Spouses or partners face serious financial strains, social isolation and stigma, loneliness and negative emotions such as anger and resentment, with couple relationships often breaking down in consequence (Bahr and others, 2005).

Box III.5
**Information for unmarried parents as provided by the
paternity establishment programme in Richmond, Virginia**

IT'S IMPORTANT!! Help your Baby, put the Father's Name on the Birth Certificate! After a baby is born, an unmarried mother and biological father may sign a form that will place the father's name on the birth certificate. He will then be a legal father. This form is called *Voluntary Acknowledgment of Paternity*. Unmarried parents cannot put the father's name on their child's birth certificate until the biological father acknowledges paternity. IT'S SIMPLE!! Unmarried parents can acknowledge the paternity of their child by filling out a simple form and signing under oath. You will get this form from the hospital when your baby is born. You may also get the form by asking your local child support agency, your midwife or local Department of Health. IT'S FREE!! Hospital staff will help parents complete the form at the time of the child's birth at no cost to the parents.

You should have the Voluntary Acknowledgment of Paternity form witnessed. You each must sign the form in front of a witness at the hospital. There is no fee when the form is sent from the hospital with the birth certificate.

How does this help your baby?

Regardless if the father is young or old, rich or poor, he is the only birth father your baby has. A child whose parents are both named on the birth certificate has the same rights as a child born to a married couple. Here are just a few examples:

- Health Insurance
- Inheritance Rights
- Social Security Benefits (if the father dies or becomes disabled)
- Access to the father's family's health history (by the child's doctor). This is important for hereditary conditions such as diabetes and sickle cell.

Source: Richmond, Virginia, Department of Health website.

*Reappraisal of fathering role*

For some fathers being in prison creates an opportunity for life re-appraisal and reconnection with family members through letters and phone calls (Clarke and others. 2005)

*Resettlement*

Fathers who have been in prison have a legacy of problems which limit their ability to be successful at resettlement including substance abuse, mental illness, low educational attainment and poor employment histories (Boswell and Wedge, 2002).

*Effects on children*

Children of imprisoned fathers may experience numerous life stressors, including caregiver changes, increased poverty, and involvement with the child welfare system, in addition to the strain of paternal separation. These events have been linked to increased rates of anxiety, depression, learning problems and aggression, although the impact of maternal imprisonment is thought to be greater (Murray and Murray, 2010).

*Fathers' rights in prison*

Less attention may be given to imprisoned fathers' entitlements in contested divorce, contact or adoption procedures (Brooks-Gordon, 2003).

## Policies and programmes

There is considerable variability in policy approaches to imprisoned fathers across the world. Some countries have begun to incorporate fathers into family preservation and prison-based parenting programmes (Dowling and Gardner, 2005; Day and others, 2005, see box III.6). This approach is part of a wider effort to integrate in-prison treatment with post-prison resettlement. The growing body of evidence showing that links with the family can be a protective factor against male re-offending (Hairston, 1995) gives some support to the movement aimed at establishing family strengthening programmes, where contact with spouse and kin is encouraged. However, in other countries an alternative "deep break" between the outside and life inside prison is the norm (Nurse, 2002) and within this penal environment, fathering identities and the family responsibilities of inmates tend to remain invisible.

Enhanced father-child contact during imprisonment (in addition to letters and telephone calls) is facilitated by family-friendly visiting arrangements (for example, visiting rooms with toys for children). Typically, these contact provisions are facilitated through the efforts of volunteers or non-for profit groups connected to prisons, such as, prison visitors and action groups for prisoners and their families (for example, The Ormiston Trust, Action for Prisoners Families). Such groups provide leaflets and storybooks that discuss the problems faced when fathers and mothers are in prison (see for example, Watson and Rice, 2003).

## When fathers hurt or do not help: domestic violence, drug and alcohol dependency and other problems related to men in families

### Demographics

#### Domestic violence

Abuse and violence in families, particularly against women and girls, constitute a widespread problem persisting across the world. A recent study by the World Health Organization (2005), of mainly developing countries, reported high levels of intimate-partner violence towards women. For example, the proportion of women who had ever suffered physical violence by a male partner ranged from 61 per cent in rural Peru to 13 per cent in Japan. Sexual violence was less frequent than physical violence in most countries, apart from (rural) Bangladesh, Ethopia and Thailand. This research suggests that intimate-partner violence is found more consistently in rural populations where women's legal and social status is low. In OECD countries lifetime prevalence rates for physical and/or sexual violence against women by an intimate partner are also high, ranging from 10 per cent (Switzerland) to almost 40 per cent (the Czech Republic) (Organization for Economic Cooperation and Development, 2010e).

There is little evidence regarding the prevalence of intimate-partner violence against men, as so few studies have examined family violence for both genders (Wall, Leitão and Ramos, 2010). The 2005 WHO study had originally included a plan to interview men as well as women but financial resources did not allow. In the very small number of countries where information is available, rates are lower for men than

Box III.6
**Responsible Fatherhood Program for Incarcerated Dads, Fairfax County, Virginia**

**Aim:** to educate incarcerated fathers about child development, responsible fathering and to rekindle child-father relationships. .

**Curriculum or programme model:** The Responsible Fatherhood Program comprised weekly sessions over 10 weeks. Each session ran for about an hour and a half.

The curriculum covered:

- Demographics on fatherhood and parenting
- Understanding child development
- Co-parenting
- Responsible manhood,
- Conflict resolution and moving on.

Each lesson had homework components that often required interaction with the prisoners' children. Participants were also required to maintain a journal of reflections on classes and interactions with their children.

**Evaluation** Two groups of prisoners, a treatment group and a control group, were drawn from a population of inmates just beginning their sentence or just about to leave the prison system by the Director of Community Corrections. Differences in key outcome measures were shown between fathers who had participated in at least four program sessions and those in the control group. Fathers in the treatment group exhibited a significant increase in frequency of contact with their children, knowledge about fatherhood and understanding of the justice system.

**Source:** Bronte-Tinkew and others (2007).

for women; for example, in the United Kingdom lifetime prevalence of intimate partner physical violence were reported by 11 per cent of men and 19 per cent of women (Organization for Economic Cooperation and Development, 2010e, see table III.2).

The assessment of the full extent of men's role in family violence presents a challenge, as many countries do not have the administrative infrastructure or cultural impetus to record incidents and, when they do, full information on the sex and age

Table III.2
**Prevalence rates of intimate partner violence against women and men, Canada, United Kingdom and United States, 1995-1996, 2004 and 2004-2005**

| Lifetime rate | Year | Physical Violence | Sexual Violence | Physical and/or Sexual Violence | One-year rate Physical Violence | One-year rate Sexual Violence | One-year rate Physical and/or Sexual Violence |
|---|---|---|---|---|---|---|---|
| **Women** | | | | | | | |
| Canada | 2004 | .. | .. | .. | .. | .. | 2 |
| UK | 2004/2005 | 19 | 6 | .. | 3 | 1 | .. |
| USA | 1995-1996 | 22 | 8 | 26 | 1 | 0 | 2 |
| **Men** | | | | | | | |
| Canada | 2004 | .. | .. | .. | .. | .. | 2 |
| UK | 2004-2005 | 11 | 1 | .. | 2 | 1 | .. |
| USA | 1995-1996 | 7 | 0 | 8 | 1 | .. | 1 |

**Sources:** Data in OECD table derived from the following sources: OECD Family Database (www.oecd.org/els/social/family/database), OECD–Social Policy Division—Directorate of Employment, Labour and Social Affairs, Canada, General Social Survey (2004), British Crime Survey (2004), USA, National Violence against Women Survey.

**Note:** Canada: population aged 18 years or over; United Kingdom: population aged 16-59; United States: population aged 18 years or over.

(..) signify that data are unavailable

of the victim or perpetrator can be missing (United Nations, 2006). Similarly physical and sexual assault of women and men in war zones and armed conflicts are rarely systematically recorded.

### Child maltreatment

Standardized global prevalence data on maltreatment of children in families is also very difficult to collect (Butchart and others, 2006) and the available international comparative literature suggests significant underreporting (Gilbert and others 2009). Cultural practices, normative in some communities, such as circumcision of infant boys, genital mutilation of young females, and recruitment of children in armies are rarely included in estimates, testifying to the complexity of conceptualization and subsequent record-keeping on child maltreatment (United Nations, 2006; United Nations Children's Fund, 2007).

Estimates from high-income countries (Gilbert and others, 2009) indicate that about 4–16 per cent of children are physically abused and 1 in 10 is neglected or psychologically abused during childhood. Reported rates of sexual abuse are lower. Parents are implicated in the majority (over 80 per cent) of child maltreatment incidents (physical, sexual, neglect, and emotional abuse) with fathers overrepresented in physical and sexual abuse (Gilbert and others, 2009; Holden and Barker, 2004). However, the parent's gender is "inextricably clustered" with other risk factors within a culture, community, and family (Gilbert and others 2009, p. 72). Common factors such as poverty, living in high-crime neighbourhoods, mental health problems, low educational achievement, alcohol and drug misuse, and exposure to maltreatment as a child are strongly associated with mistreatment of their children by fathers and mothers. Many national-level studies report a co-occurrence of intimate-partner violence and physical maltreatment of a child by fathers.

In terms of consequences, exposure to abuse, both as an adult and as a child, has huge physical and emotional impacts, and international evidence show associations with increased mortality, morbidity and psychological problems (ibid. 2009).

## Issues

Although most men do not abuse children or their partners, there is surprisingly little systematic study of the minority of fathers and male partners who do (Holden and Barker, 2004). Nevertheless, understanding of a range of factors is evolving which in turn is enlarging the understanding of male perspectives on family violence.

### Mental health of fathers

Historically, the mental health of fathers has rarely been discussed explicitly or tracked in the clinical and medical literature; however, since the late 1990s, there has been an emergence of research on paternal mental health, particularly in the post-partum period (Ramchandani and others, 2005). For example, it has been found that about 3-6 per cent of men in developed countries suffer from clinical depression (half the female rate) but that male rates are nearly doubled after childbirth. Paternal depression is associated with childhood behavioural problems but has not been found to predict abusive or violent behaviour in either children or for adult men themselves (Flouri, 2010). In general, paternal mental health remains an underresearched public health issue.

## Paternal substance abuse

Alcohol abuse prevalence ranges from 4-14 per cent of adult males across the developed world, with lower rates for substance abuse 1-5 per cent (Ramchandani and Psychogioul, 2009). Globally, alcohol and substance abuse rates are higher in males than females. There is growing evidence that substance-abusing fathers, especially those using cocaine and opiates, may represent a higher risk to their children than alcohol abusing fathers although problems occur for this latter group too (Fals-Stewart and others, 2004). Cocaine and opiate-abusing fathers have been found to practise harsher disciplining and laxer monitoring and to be more physically aggressive with intimate partners than fathers in comparison groups.

## Unrelated males and social fathers

There has been considerable debate about whether biological paternal relatedness offers some protection against child maltreatment (Holden and Barker, 2004). For instance, Canadian research has shown significantly higher child homicide rates during the first two years of life for children living with stepfathers in contrast with genetic fathers (Daly and Wilson, 1996) and a greater risk of sexual abuse in stepfather families (Marsiglio and Hinojosa, 2010). Similarly, presence of unrelated males and co-resident social fathers has been found to elevate children's risk of physical abuse and neglect in low-income United States households (Fragile Families and Child Wellbeing Study, 2010). These patterns have been explained by the tendency for unrelated males and new social fathers to have less enduring emotional and economic investment in non-biological children.

A growing body of research demonstrating the value of stepfathers to mothers and stepchildren (Marsiglio and Hinojosa, 2010) highlights the importance of differentiating among the diverse types of social fathers in children's lives.

## Men who experience domestic abuse and violence

Abuse and violence against men by women constitutes a neglected global issue but the subject has recently begun to be openly discussed by men's lobby groups in developed countries (for example, Mankind). Research suggests that prevailing gender norms emphasizing male power and strength make it difficult for men to admit to being victims of female violence and to report spousal violence to the police (Wall, Leitão and Ramos, 2010). A meta-analysis of sex differences in respect of aggression between heterosexual partners in rich nations has suggested that although men were more likely than women to inflict a severe injury on their partner, women were slightly more likely than men to use frequent ongoing mild physical aggression (Archer, 2002). Policy development for the purpose of understanding domestic violence against males in families and supporting those males is embryonic.

## Professionals' response to abusive fathers and men in families

There is a substantive body of research highlighting the marked failure of health and social care professionals to engage with fathers and men in cases of child protection and domestic abuse (for example, Scourfield, 2006; Stega and others, 2008; Phares and others, 2010). The researchers argue that the neglect of fathers and male instigators of family violence can lead to a culture of "mother and female blaming". According to

Stega and others, (2008, p. 706) "When physical abuse is the problem, workers focus on mothers and ignore fathers and father-figures, even when they were the source of the family's difficulties". Practitioners can be fearful of men, leading to avoidance, exclusion in treatment (Scourfield, 2006) and even "clouded professional judgement" (Brandon and others, 2009). In consequence, overlooked fathers may be lost to the public social care system and go on to establish new relationships with women and mothers of young children within which they repeat previous patterns of abusive behaviour.

## Policies and programmes

2   See General Assembly resolution 48/104.

Since the solemn proclamation by the United Nations General Assembly on 20 December 1993 of the Declaration on the Elimination of Violence against Women,[2] there has been a tremendous global effort to identify and combat violence against women. More recently, there has been a growing understanding that effective legal, social and psychological interventions need to engage men in violence prevention programmes at macrolevels in order to confront social norms that legitimize male power and use of violence (United Nations Development Fund for Women).

There is also increasing awareness that the so-called unidirectional model, which assesses violence only against women, may not be broad enough to confront the complex nature of gender violence or contribute to a fuller understanding of men's role as both instigator and victim of violence (Wall, Leitão and Ramos, 2010).

In terms of specific programmes and initiatives, there has been a notable expansion of organizations from around the world that work with men and boys to promote gender equality and end violence against women and girls (World Health Organization, 2007). Systematic independent evaluation of most of these initiatives is rare but the World Health Organization's review of evidence from 58 programmes (some of which focused on men and family violence) showed: decreased self-reported use of physical, sexual and psychological violence in intimate relationships in 2 of the programmes (the Stepping Stones programme in South Africa and the Safe Dates Programme in the United States). The World Health Organization (ibid) also noted that preventative programmes involving men and boys (for example, an initiative in South Africa, Soul City) had helped change discriminatory community perceptions of domestic violence and convey the importance of citizens' taking action against it.

The Internet has been helpful in disseminating good practice and information sharing. For example, MenEngage, a global alliance of 400 non-governmental organizations and United Nations organizations (across sub-Saharan Africa, Latin America and the Caribbean, North America, Asia and Europe) has a website displaying resources associated with projects that engage boys and men in gender-equality and violence reduction programmes.

In richer countries, the effectiveness of individual, couple and group therapies with violent men are being investigated. For example, Morrel and others (2003) examined the relative efficacy of cognitive-behavioural group therapy (CBT) and supportive group therapy (ST) for partner-violent men at a community agency. The investigators found that both approaches helped men reduce physical assault, psychological aggression, and injuries, and resulted in significant increases in self-esteem and self-efficacy arising from their having abstained from partner aggression. Three years later, both approaches were found to be associated with reductions in partner reports of criminal recidivism. These programmes highlight the importance of group therapy where experiences of effective violence reduction strategies can be shared and reviewed.

In terms of child maltreatment issues, there is strong evidence that intensive home-based support of vulnerable parents pre- and post-natally as exemplified by the Nurse–Family Partnership, (NFP) has the strongest preventative impact (Olds and others, 1997; Macmillan, 2009). The Nurse-Family Partnership, developed in the United States by Olds, is an evidence-based home-visiting nurse programme designed to improve the health, well-being and self-sufficiency of young first-time parents and their children. It involves weekly or fortnightly structured home visits by a specially trained nurse from early pregnancy until children are 24 months old. The curriculum is well specified and detailed with a plan for the number, timing and content of visits. The heart of the programme is the formation of a strong therapeutic relationship between nurse and mother which has a mandate to engage the infant's father or mother's main partner throughout.

## Fathering issues related to major social groups

## Young fathers

### Demographics

Although teenage birth rates vary considerably across the world, it is estimated that globally about 10 per cent of all births are to an adolescent mother, aged 15-19 (United Nations, 2009). A father's age at birth is not regularly recorded but it is likely that the rates for men are similar or even higher owing to boys' earlier age of sexual initiation (United Nations Population Fund, 2005) and general under-reporting of fatherhood by men (Clarke, Joshi and Di Salvo, 2000). In some regions, up to 35 per cent of males report sexual initiation before their fifteenth birthday.

Early parenthood has become less normative in developed and richer countries. For example, among OECD countries, the mean age of women at the birth of their first child varies from 21.3 years of age (in Mexico) to 29.8 years of age (in the United Kingdom) (OECD 2010f).

### Issues

#### Invisibility

There is still little research on young fatherhood compared with the enormous amount of information available on young motherhood. The research that does exist tends to come from developed and richer countries where young fatherhood is less condoned socially, although in some countries it is still common. A historical emphasis on the irresponsibility and ignorance of youthful fatherhood is being supplemented by greater sensitivity to the vulnerabilities of boys and men who become fathers at an early age (Marsiglio and Cohan, 1997).

#### Legacy of emotionally and economically fragile families of origin

Young fathers are more likely than childless peers to have family histories of: youthful mothers, low levels of parental education, family breakdown, financial hardship, and parental substance abuse (Bunting and McAuley, 2004; Pears and others, 2005).

*Limited socio-economic and educational resources*

As young fathers may still be in school or seeking employment, their socio-economic resources are low. Most research shows that just like young mothers, young fathers are less educated and have low employment prospects (Vinnerljung, Franzén and Danielsson, 2007).

*Young fatherhood: a risk*

The experience of young fatherhood can itself heighten boys' risk of psychosocial problems, antisocial behaviour and low self-esteem (Sigle-Rushton, 2005). Young fatherhood is associated with several risk behaviours including crime (Weinman, Buzi and Smith, 2005). In the majority of cases pregnancies are unplanned and is reported as having been a surprise to young man.. Knowledge about infant development needs may be minimal.

*Youngest fathers least likely to sustain involvement with child*

Research focusing on the nine months after birth suggests that younger men (under age 17) are least likely to be involved with the child (Quinton, Pollock and Anderson, 2002). In most of these cases, the mother, also young, continues living with her parents.

*Quality of relationship with the mother is significant*

While romantic relations can be short-lived, the quality of young men's relationship with their partner during pregnancy, and not an adverse family and social background, is the most important predictive factor for men's post-natal involvement with infants. A good-quality relationship with the baby's mother can promote active paternal involvement (ibid.)

*Young father partner support can improve outcomes*

Although evidence is mixed, emotional and practical support from low-risk young fathers can be associated with stronger maternal well-being and better child outcomes (Roye and Balk, 1996).

*Kin links can be protective*

In developed countries, prospective grandparents are rarely positive about adolescent fatherhood, but many young men may be co-resident with their own or maternal kin, who can provide material and emotional support (Quinton, Pollock and Anderson, 2002).

*A new positive status*

When male fertility is valued a fatherhood status can to create a new identity for young men, with marginal interpersonal peer benefits (Marsiglio and Cohan, 1997).

*Young fathers slipping through the support gap*

Young fathers can feel excluded from antenatal and post-natal care; for their part, health and social care professionals report lack of skills in engaging with young fathers. Opportunities to provide contraceptive, educational and employment advice to young men can therefore be missed.

## Policies and programmes

Many rich and developed countries have adopted a preventative policy approach to teenage parenthood. Although programmes vary in detail, two general measures are common: comprehensive information, advice and support, from parents, schools and other professionals, combined with accessible, young people-friendly sexual and reproductive health services. National campaigns target young people and parents with the facts about teenage pregnancy and parenthood, advice on how to deal with pressures to have sex, and focus on the importance of using contraception if they do have sex. For example, in the Netherlands, a country with the lowest teen pregnancy rate in the world, all children are taught in school about the «Double Dutch» responsible contraceptive method developed to protect against unplanned pregnancy and sexually transmitted diseases. Youth-based educational guidance suggests that two forms of protection be used each time young people have sex: the female always uses the pill and the male always uses a condom.

Such methods have proved effective in reducing teen pregnancies rates but are not culturally acceptable in many developing countries of the world or in richer nations such as the United States, where abstention programmes have been tested, with teen pregnancy rates remaining relatively high.

As regards youthful fatherhood, most professional support for adolescent parents, particularly from health services, has been concentrated on adolescent mothers, although this pattern has started to shift, after decades of critique. Across the world, fathers are beginning to be included in some teen parenting assessment and family support packages, although developments are still patchy (Cabrera, 2010). A key ingredient of effective holistic support to the family of which the father is a part is early identification and a needs assessment of both parents in the antenatal period (Olds and others, 1997) and dedicated, sustained support throughout the post-natal period which draws in specialist services as needed. This intensive approach is expensive, however, and rarely used.

Instead, a range of post hoc initiatives with varied goals tend to be adopted with some aimed at promoting the well-being of young fathers in both their couple and parenting roles; others focused on education and training and tailored to support young fathers in prison environments. Evidence is emerging on effective approaches to practice in working with teenage fathers, notably in United States populations (Bronte-Tinkew, Burkhauser and Metz, 2008).

Bronte-Tinkew and others (ibid.) in their recent systematic review of 18 fatherhood programmes for teen fathers for the National Responsible Fatherhood Clearinghouse, identified one of them as a «model» programme and three as «promising».

### Model programme

*The Young Dads*—Transition to Fatherhood for Young Fathers Programme (New York) was identified as the model programme (see box III.7).

### Promising programmes

- Prenatal Education Intervention—prenatal classes for young fathers
- Respecting and Protecting Our Relationships—an HIV prevention program for inner-city Latino adolescent parenting couples (Los Angeles)
- STEP-UP: Mentoring for Young Fathers—a self-sufficiency programme for young fathers (Phoenix, Arizona)

For the 4 programmes reported above 10 features were identified as good practice (Child Trends, 2009). Although based on the United States context, several of these features have already been reported to be associated with success in other national contexts; and they could be explored further in future trials.

*Promising teen fatherhood programmes: initial evidence lessons from the National Responsible Fatherhood Clearinghouse*

Based on the systematic analysis of features in the four programmes, evidence showed that the more effective teen fatherhood programmes:

1. Partnered with community organizations such as schools, prenatal clinics and programmes for teen mothers to facilitate recruitment and engagement of teen fathers.
2. Had programme staff develop one-on-one relationships with teen fathers, in small groups, through individual case management, or through mentoring services.
3. Offered a comprehensive array of services to teen fathers which went beyond parenting information alone.
4. Began with a theoretical programme model and used theories of change or logic models which were effective with adolescent parents.
5. Delivered services in engaging and interactive ways.
6. Conducted needs assessments and/or used participant feedback to provide teen fathers with the services they wanted.

---

Box III.7

**Evaluation of the Transition to Fatherhood for Young Fathers Program (New York)**

**Target population and aim:** African American adolescent fathers. Aim was to help them become more confident and responsible fathers. The fathers were contacted through the adolescent mother programmes conducted in a local hospital, for their child's mother. The mothers of the participants' children were receiving services through a teen mothers' support programme or were in a mother-baby group residence. The mean age of their children was nine months. Couples had known each other for almost a year before the women became pregnant.

**Programme:** Once enrolled, the fathers were asked to list areas in their lives where they needed assistance. The male staff members (social workers) served as positive parenting role models and focused on:

- individual and group counseling
- education/vocational referrals and placements
- medical care and referral
- housing and legal advocacy
- cultural and recreational activities
- parenting skills training.

**Staff-participant ratio:** Two social workers, a parenting instructor, and an educational-vocational counsellor were assigned to 30 fathers.

Compared with members of a randomly assigned control group, teen fathers who had received the treatment showed statistically significant follow-up improvements in: employment rates, vocational plans, perceptions of current relationships with their children, perceptions of the quality of the future relationship with their children, frequency of contraceptive use, and the availability of persons with whom a problem could be discussed.

**Source:** Mazza (2002); and Bronte-Tinkew, Burkhauser and Metz (2007).

7.  Hired professionals who were experienced, empathic, enthusiastic, well connected in the community and carefully matched to participants.
8.  Incorporated teaching methods and materials that were appropriate for teen fathers and for their culture and age.
9.  Used incentives with teen fathers and their families.
10. Mentored teen fathers.

## Fathering and disabilities

### Demographics

Currently, about 10 per cent of the total population of the world, or roughly 650 million people, live with a disability (UN, 2009). Disabilities span a wide continuum in respect of their severity with conditions including learning or intellectual difficulties and physical and sensory impairments, and are classified according to international diagnostic systems (for example, the International Classification of Diseases and the Diagnostic and Statistical Manual of Mental Disorders). In relation to this issue, there have been more studies, albeit still limited, of fathers without disabilities caring for children with disabilities (Macdonald and Hastings, 2010) than on the experience of being a disabled father (Kilkey and Clarke, 2010). Demographic records of both "hidden populations" do not exist.

### Issues

#### *Marginal and marginalized fathers in disability*

Historically, there has been considerable interest in the mothers rather than in the fathers of children with disabilities; similarly, fathers with disabilities have remained shadowy or peripheral figures in research, practice and policy. Men's "caring" or "need for care" roles in these disability contexts are relatively hidden. For example, practitioners are often mother-focused and do not recognize that fathers may experience intense emotions in response to the birth and diagnosis of their disabled child. The effect of impairment on disabled men's capacity to engage in daily caring and earning activities can be underestimated by professionals (Kilkey and Clarke, 2010).

#### *Stress and stigma*

Fathers of children with disabilities report daily stress, poor sleep quality, physical health problems, depression and coping problems; however, on balance, the effects are less negative than for mothers (Pottie and Ingram, 2008). Research suggests that men in disability contexts are less enthusiastic about reaching out for professional support, relying more on kin and spousal relations (Macdonald and Hastings, 2010). The capacity of a parenting couple to support each other is important for both parents, but the fact that this is particularly so for fathers can put an extra strain on mothers.

Being in paid work protects the well-being of parents of children with disabilities and disabled parents (Olsson and Hwang, 2006). However, with disability, there are considerable challenges in respect of sustaining employment and family responsibilities (Rigg, 2005).

## Policies and programmes

The fact that across the world, the personal rights and needs of adults and children with disabilities have become more visible and openly discussed has been helping to move countries away from an institutionalization policy approach (Waldschmitdt, 2009; Olsson and Hwang, 2003). A range of health, educational, and social public services have been developed, although many disabled adults and children are mainly dependent on personal care from family and kin.

Research suggests that within the household, mothers of children with disabilities typically seek outside help from external sources, whereas fathers are more likely to look towards the couple relationship and rely on the support of their partner (Saloviita, Italinna and Leinonen, 2003). Approaches have focused on meeting the needs of fathers by working towards strengthening the parental dyad and keeping the lines of communication open between the parents (Crowley and Taylor, 1994). However, in terms of men's parenting, it is also important to develop strategies designed to increase the confidence of disabled men and fathers of disabled children.

At the national level in richer and more developed countries, there have been investments in career strategy programmes to support parents with caring roles through: respite care (short breaks); personal health checks; parenting information and family-employment reconciliation measures (see box III.8). Similarly, national-level programmes have been developed to improve the coordination of medical, educational, and social support of disabled children and their families (for example, Aiming High for Disabled Children programme and Better Support for Families, 2007). Programmes can claim to be gender-neutral but they often implicitly assume the presence of a main home-based career, typically a mother, who is not engaged in the labour market. Calls for greater recognition of fathers in their caring or need-for-care roles within these disability contexts are beginning to be heard (see for example, Towers, 2009). However, there is still some way to go before a father-inclusive approach towards supporting parents of disabled children and disabled parents themselves is fully established.

## Older fathers, grandfathers and intergenerational aspects of fathering

### Demographics

Increased longevity and lower mortality rates in many parts of the world have extended men's reproductive and caring lives and provide a further dimension for understanding fathering. More fathers will live long enough to become grandfathers and even great-grandfathers. Ageing effects will increase the potential for more generations to coexist for longer periods (Bengston, 2001). For example, demographic estimates suggest that in Europe future parent-child relationships may last from six to seven decades and grandparent- grandchild relations from three to four decades (Hagestad and Herlofson, 2007). Ageing trends are expressed in different ways globally, with multigenerational families coexisting for shorter periods in poorer countries and grandparenthood dissociated from old age in early-fertility countries (Lloyd-Sherlock, ed., 2004). While there may be more generations coexisting, the tendency towards having fewer children will

**Box III.8**
**The right to flexible working arrangements**

Starting in April 2003, British employers were required to commence carrying out their legal "duty to consider" requests for "flexible working time arrangements" from employees who were parents with responsibility for children under age 6 (or under age 18 in the case of disabled children) and who had worked for an organization for six months or more.

Options included flexi-time for hospital appointments, flexibility with regard to starting and finishing hours, working from home, part-time work, and school-term hours of employment. There have been discussions in the European Parliament on disseminating these ideas among the 27 European Union (EU) members.

reduce kin numbers within each generation, signalling the move towards a thinner and longer "beanpole" family structure (Grundy, Murphy and Shelton, 1999).

There is a further significant demographic trend: men are having children at later ages in developed countries. For instance, nearly half of all English babies born in 2008 (47 per cent) had mothers aged 30 years or over, but nearly two thirds of babies (63 per cent) were fathered by men in this age group (United Kingdom, Office for Natural Statistics, 2009). This demographic trend is mainly related to later first fatherhood for an increasing majority of men in rich countries and additional births at a later age for those men in new partnerships after separation and divorce. However, in the English case less than 5 per cent of babies born in 2008 had fathers 45 years of age or over.

## Issues

### Neglect of older men, male kin and grandfathers

Despite early research (for example, Cunningham-Burley, 1984; Arber and Gilbert 1989), there has been a low critical mass of academic and policy research on older men, male kin and grandfathers. Since the turn of the decade a notable increase in scholarship has been apparent (for example, Mann, 2007).

### Diversity of male kin activities in later life

As the later life course becomes more extended, varied and complex, men may begin to have overlapping multiple opportunities and obligations with respect to family and work. For example, grandfathering may coexist with employment, and the active parenting of a new set of children. Older men will face challenges in confronting earning and care responsibilities on multiple fronts, resulting in an expansion of the category "double front" family (Kröger and Sipila, 2005).

### Men's intergenerational financial transfers

In wealthier countries and high-income families, financial transfers between generations are extensive (Snarey, 1993) but in poorer countries and vulnerable kin groups, there is little for men to transfer (Saraceno and Keck, 2008). In some developing countries, old-age pension systems are quite expansive, especially for men, and there is evidence that these benefits are partly shared with younger household members (Schwartzer and Querino, 2002; Moller and Ferreira, 2003).

*Conflicting norms about intergenerational obligations*

In most societies mixed expectations about the scale and nature of intergenerational obligations coexist. For example, in Latin America, research offers evidence for both the weakening and resilience of elder care and support norms (Lloyd-Sherlock and Locke, 2008). Younger generations can create stress and vulnerability for elders (when they go "off the rails") as well as serve as a resource for them.

*From the deficit male kin carer to the generative male role model*

The deficit male kin carer model legacy exists (Thompson, 2006) but new models of masculinities are offering socially valued nurturing and engaged roles for men as they age (see for example, Palkovitz, 2002; Sorensen and Cooper, 2010).

*Grandfather care of younger generations*

Grandmothers generally provide more care than grandfathers to grandchildren. For example, cross-national European survey research showed that 26 per cent of grandfathers provided childcare almost weekly or more in the last year in contrast to 34 per cent of grandmothers (Hank and Buber 2009). Grandparent care is most common in areas where co-residence rates are high. Grandfathers are more involved when their spouses are involved and grandsons aged 12 years or over are more likely to choose the maternal grandfather as the favoured grandparent in some Societies (Mann, Kahn and Leeson, 2009).

*Older men caring for partners*

Mutual spousal care is normative in many cultures. Research suggests that levels of care provided by older male partners in couple households are similar to that given by females: 42 per cent of men were cared for by wives and 40 per cent by husbands (Arber and Gilbert, 1989).

*Older men living alone*

Throughout the world more older men are living alone which can exacerbate mental and physical health problems when there are socio-economic disadvantages and low kin support (United Nations Department of Economic and Social Affairs, Population Division, 2005).

*Older Fathers*

Antenatal and post-natal support groups can be insensitive to the challenges faced by "second time around" fathers who have multiple obligations to two families.

## Policies and programmes

As men's longevity increases, a wide range of intergenerational obligations and work commitments will coexist. Accordingly, a range of policy approaches and programmes sensitive to older males will need to be developed. It is clear that policymakers are only just becoming aware of the complex heterogeneity of older men lives and their kin and employment obligations. Recent reviews (for example, Hagestad and Herlofson, 2007) are calling for greater coordination between developments in social care polices for older people and family and gender policy approaches. "Family policy" usually refers to young families and much of the discussion is carried out under the heading of "work-family interface". Writings on adult generations of parents and children carry headings such as "ageing policies", "long-term care policies" or "caregiver burden" (Kuronen, Jokinen and Kröger, 2010: 38). However, the initial focus of this more holistic perspective appears relatively female-focused, centring on how women reconcile informal care for elders with their employment responsibilities.

The contribution of men to, and the needs of older men for, informal and home care will become heightened as many developed countries move towards home care, private provision of professional formal care and cash transfers in care for older people (Simonazzi, 2009). In terms of supporting vulnerable older men living alone, service design may need to be more "outreach"-focused, as research suggests this group of men may be more reluctant to engage in formal organizational activities (Davidson, Daly and Arber, 2003).

In respect of developing countries, the role of male carers, and grandfathers in particular, has been hugely neglected. This gendered pattern is reflected in research studies: a large portion of the literature is devoted to the subject of the role of grandmothers, particularly with reference to caring for AIDS orphans (see Chapter V). Knodel and Saengtienchai (2004) observe that in Thailand, grandmothers are significantly more likely than the grandfathers to be the main home-based caregivers for children with AIDS than are grandfathers. However, they report little difference between the sexes in terms of instrumental support provided outside the household (such as help with transportation, shopping or arranging for welfare benefits).

## Policy recommendations

This chapter has highlighted the developing evidence base of social research on men and fathers in vulnerable or challenging family contexts. Across the world, there is an increasing appreciation of both the importance and the diversity of fatherhood. Cultural models of fatherhood are in flux as commentators stress either its demise or its renaissance. Caring-father ideals are challenged by views emphasizing "fatherhood in crisis", a condition where men are thought to be unable to either care or provide cash for their families. The chapter has offered evidence for both depictions of fatherhood in the context of men's hidden and untapped potential for contributing to family life, for instance through their being more available to care because of increased life expectancy, and of the strain they face in their negotiation of parenting in insecure settings such as divorce. There are a range of policy approaches that international, national and local bodies have currently adopted to deal with selected social problems and the new challenges of fatherhood and approaches to specific issues have been reviewed in the appropriate sections. In the present section, general policy implications and recommendations are highlighted. The recommendations draw on the evidence gathered and highlight the positive role that significant stakeholders can play in relation to promoting active involvement by fathers in family life.

### Improving demographic data about fathers

A key challenge in responding to the needs of vulnerable fathers and men in vulnerable family contexts is the lack of comprehensive and systematic data collection on fathers.

Basic demographic information on the parental status of men, male fertility and family formation is not routinely collected in many countries. WHO world statistics has no information on fatherhood. When men are admitted into public institutions such as prisons or mental health centres there is typically no registration of parental status or parenting responsibilities. Countries and institutions are unable to plan strategically without adequate and reliable information on the current situation, needs and profiles of vulnerable fathers and fathers in vulnerable families.

The United Nations should establish an expert group to consider how to improve demographic data on men's family characteristics. The group could build on the protocols developed in the project entitled "Nurturing Fatherhood: Improving Data and Research on Male Fertility, Family Formation and Fatherhood" (Federal Inter-Agency Forum on Child and Family Statistics, 1998).

## Father inclusive international research networks

The evidence base for critical aspects of fathers' experiences and their emotional and economic investments in family life is extremely fragile, particularly in developing countries. Increased resources are needed to build the capacity of research organizations in developing countries to carry out timely studies about men's perspectives on family life and caring. Networks across developing and richer nations should be fostered by the United Nations. Well-established international organizations working on gender, the child, employment and family welfare need to become more "father-inclusive" in their research design and strategies.

## Paternity establishment initiatives

Paternity establishment initiatives (formal registration of the biological father at the time of a child's birth) can serve to encourage greater economic and emotional investment in children by non-residential fathers. An increasing number of developing countries are enforcing paternity establishment orders. More international research is needed to track the impact of voluntary and enforced paternity establishment orders on income transfers from father to mother and child and on subsequent non-residential father involvement with the child.

## Promoting non-residential fathers' contribution to the care of children

As divorce rates rise there needs to be greater expectations that, after relationship breakdown, non-residential fathers will make formal contributions (for example, child support payments) and informal contributions (for example, through caregiving and overnight stays) to their children—and greater appreciation of those potential contributions. Governments should share good practices in parenting programmes, such as mediation and dispute resolution, and child income support regimes, and in the development of gender-sensitive legal custody and contact frameworks. More longitudinal research is needed to track the child well-being outcomes for children living in countries where "shared care" post-divorce arrangements can be implemented.

Increasingly, scholars are aware that if research is focused only on fathers who are co-resident, married and presumed biological, theory and concepts will not reflect the diversity of fathers and father figures in contemporary society.

## Engaging fathers and male kin in the care of children so as to prevent institutionalization

More research is needed on how to engage male kin and fathers in caregiving and child protection so as to prevent unnecessary institutionalization and inappropriate alternative care placement. An active fatherhood task force (see below) should collaborate with the Better Care Network in coordinating national and international efforts to improve the care and protection of children without adequate parental care, and in promoting networking and information sharing on the potential of male kin and fathers under the Guidelines for the Alternative Care of Children (United Nations, 2009a).

## Invisible fathers and a fathering support deficit

Evidence has revealed how vulnerable fathers, male carers and fathers in vulnerable family contexts tend to be excluded from support services as it is assumed that they do not have family support needs. In many countries, men's "caring" or "need for care" roles are relatively hidden, with more attention and responsibilities given to women and mothers. The support deficit is a reflection of the consistent underplaying of men's caring responsibilities and obligations to children and partners.

One recommendation is that governments and local service providers need to ensure greater inclusion and enhanced visibility of men's parenting and care responsibilities throughout the life course. Including fathers can also lead to an increase in support to mothers, by affirming joint responsibility for children's well-being and underpinning the principle that mothers should not be expected "to do it all".

In addition more research, programme development and discussion is needed to improve the means by which social systems care for and protect fathers with disabilities, fathers in prison, substance- and alcohol-abusing fathers, young fathers and non-residential fathers so that they can continue to care for their families and support them economically where appropriate.

## Men, child maltreatment and family violence

Even in child protection cases, where fathers or unrelated males may be implicated, evidence shows they are often omitted from the most basic public service accountability procedures, such as name capture, case assessments and planning. Omissions are more common when fathers do not share the same household as the primary caregiver. Research has highlighted that the presence of unrelated males is indicative of greater risk for child maltreatment. It is essential that more research, programme development, and discussion be conducted regarding the challenges of engaging and working with men in cases of child maltreatment (including prevention and intervention work).

The feasibility of an international multicountry study on domestic violence against men should be discussed by the appropriate international organization and piloted, so as to improve the effectiveness of preventative services and deepen understanding of male perspectives on family violence.

## Pre-retirement coaching for older men

Pre-retirement coaching and educational programmes (and other innovative measures) should be initiated in countries where men are living longer, in order to increase the supply of intergenerational care and support to others in these societies.

## United Nations active fatherhood taskforce (ACT)

Coordination of policies and programmes relating to the contribution fathers and male carers can make to family life requires political will, leadership, and creative thinking from Government. Research on and development of family policies for fathers have gained momentum, particularly in developed countries, but their dissemination world-wide is still uneven. A special United Nations active fatherhood task force could provide a major impetus to these developments. A crucial objective of the task force would be to encourage dialogue about fatherhood between family policy, gender equality and child welfare specialists with representatives of organizations of fathers, mothers, women and children and gender-equality organizations. It could build on good models of global and national knowledge transfer initiated by the International Fatherhood Summit 2003 (organized by Fathers Direct with the financial support of the Bernard van Leer Foundation) and the Father Involvement Research Alliance (2006, Canada). The United Nations active fatherhood task force would coordinate international initiatives such as creating an index of the best place to be a father (mirroring the "best place to be a mother index). Consideration should be given to the proclamation of an international year of fathers and father figures.

# References

Amato, P. and C. Dorius (2010). Fathers, Children and Divorce. In *The Role of the Father in Child Development*, 5th ed., M.E. Lamb, ed. Hoboken, New Jersey: John Wiley and Sons.

Arber, S. and N. Gilbert (1989). Men: the forgotten carers. *Sociology,* vol. 23, No.1 (February), pp. 111-118.

Archer, J. (2002). Sex differences in aggression between heterosexual partners: a meta-analytic review". *Psychological Bulletin*, vol. 126, No. 5 (September), pp. 651–681.

Barker, G., C. Ricardo and M. Nascimento (2007). Engaging Men and Boys in Changing Gender-based Inequity in Health: *Evidence from Programme Intervention*. Geneva: World Health Organization.

Amato, P., C. Meyers and. R. Emery (2009). Changes in nonresident father-child contact from 1976 to 2002. *Family Relations,* (February) vol. 58, No. 1, pp. 41-53.

Bahr, S.J., and others (2005). The reentry process: how parolees adjust to release from prison. *Fathering*, vol. 3, No. 3, pp. 221-241.

Bengtson, V. L. (2001). Beyond the nuclear family: the increasing importance of multigenerational bonds, *Journal of Marriage and Family*, vol. 63, No. 1. (February), pp. 1-16.

Boswell, G. and P. Wedge (2002. *Imprisoned Fathers and Their Children*. London: Jessica Kingsley.

Bradshaw, J. (2006). *Child Support.* York, UK: Joseph Rowntree Foundation

Brandon, M., and others (2009). *Understanding Serious Case Reviews and their Impact: A Biennial Analysis of Serious Case Reviews 2005-07.* Research Report DCSF-RR129. London: Department for Children, Schools and Families.

Bronte-Tinkew, J., and others. Elements of promising practice for fatherhood programs: evidence-based research findings on programs for fathers. Gaithersburg, Maryland: National Responsible Fatherhood Clearinghouse. Available from www.fatherhood.gov.

Bronte-Tinkew, J., M. Burkhauserand A. Metz (2008). Elements of promising practice in teen fatherhood programs: evidence-based and evidence-informed research findings on what worked. Report available from www.fatherhood.gov.

Brooks-Gordon, B. (2003). Contact in containment. In *Children and Their Families: Contact, Rights and Welfare.* A. Bainham and others, eds. Oxford, UK: Hart.

Brown, J. and B. Chevannes (1998). Why man stay so: an examination of gender socialization in the Caribbean. Kingston: University of the West Indies.

Bunting L. and C. McAuley (2004). Research review: teenage pregnancy and parenthood–the role of fathers. *Child and Family Social Work*, vol. 9, No. 3 (August), pp. 295-303.

Burgess, A. and G. Russell (2004). Fatherhood and public policy. In *Supporting fathers: contributions from the International Fatherhood Summit* 2003. Early Childhood Development: Practice and Reflections No 20. The Hague: Bernard van Leer Foundation.

Butchart A. and others (2006). *Preventing child maltreatment: a Guide to Taking Action and Generating Evidence.* Geneva: WHO and International Society for the Prevention of Child Abuse and Neglect.

Cabrera, N. (2010). Father involvement and public policies. In *The Role of the Father in Child Development,* 5th ed., M.E. Lamb, ed. Hoboken, New Jersey: John Wiley and Sons.

Cabrera, N., J. Fagan and D. Farrie (2008). Explaining the long reach of fathers' prenatal involvement on later paternal engagement. *Journal of Marriage and the Family* vol. 70, No. 5 (December), pp. 1094-1107.

Cabrera, N. J., and others (2004). Low-income fathers' involvement in their toddlers' lives: biological fathers from the Early Head Start Research and Evaluation Study. *Journal of Fathering*, vol. 2, pp. 5–30.

Carlson, M. and S. McLanahan (2010). Fathers in fragile families. In *The Role of the Father in Child Development.* 5th ed., M.E. Lamb, ed. Hoboken, New Jersey: John Wiley and Sons.

Chant, S. (2007). Children in female headed households: interrogating the concept of intergenerational transmission of disadvantage with particular reference to the Gambia, Philippines and Costa Rica and new *Working Paper*, Series 19. London: London School of Economics, Gender Institute.

Cheadle, J., P. Amato and V. King (2010). Patterns of nonresident father contact. *Demography,* vol. 47, No. 1 (February), pp. 205-225.

Child Trends (2009).Ten promising practices in teen fatherhood programs. E-newsletter 28 January. Available from www.childtrends.org.

Clarke, L., H. Joshi and P. Di Salvo (2000). Children's family change: reports and records of mothers, fathers and children compared. *Population Trends*, vol. 102, pp. 24-33. London: Office National Statistics

Clarke, L., and others (2005). Fathering behind bars in English prisons: imprisoned fathers' identity and contact with their children. *Fathering*; *A Journal of Theory, Research and Practice about Men as Fathers,* vol. 3, No. 3 (fall), pp. 221-241.

Coltrane, S. (2004). The paradox of fatherhood: predicting the future of men's family involvement. In *Vision 2003: contemporary family issues.* Minneapolis, Minnesota: National Council on Family Relations.

Crowley, S.L. and M. Taylor (1994). Mothers' and fathers' perception of family functioning in families having children with disabilities. *Early Education and Development,* vol. 5, No. 3, pp. 213–225.

Cunningham-Burley, S. (1984). "We don't talk about it ...": issues of gender and method in the portrayal of grandfatherhood. *Sociology,* vol. 18, No. 3, pp. 325-338.

Curran, C. (2003). Social work and fathers: child support and fathering programs. *Social Work.* vol. 48, No. 2 (1 April), pp. 219-227.

Davidson, K., T. Daly and S. Arber (2003). Older men, social integration and organizational activities. *Social Policy and Society,* vol. 2, No. 2, pp. 81-89.

Daly, M. and M. Wilson (1996). Violence against step children. *Current Directions in Psychological Science,* vol. 5, No. 3 (June), pp. 77-81

Day, R.D. and others (2005). Incarcerated fathers returning home to children and families: introduction to the special issue and a primer on doing research with men in prison. *Fathering: A Journal of Theory, Research and Practice about Men as Fathers,* vol. 3, No. 3 (fall), pp. 83-200.

Dowling, S. and F. Gardner (2005). Parenting programmes for improving the parenting skills and outcomes for incarcerated parents and their children. Protocol. The Cochrane Database of Systematic Reviews. See also http://www.mrw.interscience.wiley.com/cochrane/clsysrev/articles/CD00555 7/frame.html.

Eggebeen, D. J. and C. Knoester (2001). Does fatherhood matter for men? *Journal of Marriage and Family,* vol. 63, No. 2 (May), pp. 381-393.

European Commission (2008). Demography report: meeting social needs in an ageing society. (2008) SEC (2009) (2911). Luxembourg: Office for Official Publications of the European Communities.

Fabricius, W., and others (2010). Custody and parenting time: links to family relationships and well-being after divorce. In *The Role of the Father in Child Development.,* 5th ed. M. E. Lamb (ed.) Hoboken, New Jersey: John Wiley and Sons.

Fagan, J. and R. Palkovitz (2007). Unmarried, non-resident fathers' involvement with their infants: a risk and resilience perspective. *Journal of Family Psychology,* vol. 21, No. 3, pp. 479-489.

Fals-Stewart and others (2004). Emotional and behavioural problems with drug-abusing fathers: comparisons with children living with alcohol-abusing and non-substance abusing fathers. *Journal of Family Psychology,* vol. 18, No. 2, pp. 319-330.

Federal Interagency Forum on Child and Family Statistics (1998). *Nurturing fatherhood: improving data and research on male fertility, family formation and fatherhood.* Washington DC.

Flouri, E. (2010). Fathers' behaviors and children's psychopathology. *Clinical Psychology Review,* vol. 30, No. 3, (April), pp. 363-369.

Fragile Families and Child Wellbeing Study (2007). Fathers' risk factors and their implications for healthy relationships and father involvement. *Fragile Families Research Brief* No. 37 (February). Princeton, New Jersey: Princeton University, Center for Research on Child Wellbeing. Available from http://www.fragilefamilies.princeton.edu.

Fragile Families Research Brief (2010). CPS Involvement in families with Social Fathers. *Fragile Families Research Brief* No. 46. Princeton, New Jersey: Center for Research on Child Wellbeing, Princeton University; Available from http://www.fragilefamilies.princeton.edu.

Gilbert, R. and others (2009). Burden and consequences of child maltreatment in high-income countries, *The Lancet,* vol. 373, No. 9657, pp. 68-81.

Glaze, L.E., and L.M. Maruschak (2008). *Parents in prison and their minor children.* Bureau of Justice Statistics Special report. Washington, DC. US Department of Justice Office of Justice Programs.

Grundy, E., M. Murphy and N. Shelton (1999). Looking beyond the household: intergenerational perspectives on living kin and contacts with kin in Great Britain. *Population Trends*, vol. 97 (autumn), pp. 19-27.

Haas, L. and P.C. Hwang. (2008). The impact of taking parental leave on fathers' participation in childcare and relationships with children: lessons form Sweden. *Community, Work and Family*, vol. 11, No. 1, pp. 85-104.

Hagestad, G. and K. Herlofson (2007). Micro and macro perspectives on intergenerational relations and transfers in Europe. In "United Nations Expert Group Meeting on Social and Economic Implications of Changing Population Age Structures. Mexico City, 31 August-2 September 2005," ESA/P/WP.201, pp. 339-358. New York: Department of Economic and Social Affairs.

Hairston, C.F. (1995). Fathers in prison. In *Children of Incarcerated Parents*, K. Gabel and D. Johnston, eds. New York: LexingtonBooks.

Hank, K. and I. Buber (2009). Grandparents caring for their grandchildren: findings from the 2004 Survey of Health, Ageing, and Retirement in Europe. *Journal of Family Issues*, vol. 30, No. 1, pp. 53-73.

Holden, G.W., and T. Barker (2004). Fathers in violent homes. In *The Role of the Father in Child Development,* 3rd ed. M.E. Lamb ed., New York: John Wiley and Sons.

Hunt, J. Masson, J. and L. Trinder (2009). Shared parenting: the law, the evidence and guidance from Families Need Fathers. *Family Law*, vol. 39, (September), pp. 831-835.

Kaspiew, R. and others (2009). *Evaluation of the 2006 Family Law Reforms.* Melbourne, Australia: Australian Institute of Family Studies. Available from http://www.aifs.gov.au/institute/pubs/fle/index.html

Kiernan, K. (2006). Non-residential fatherhood and child involvement; evidence from the Millennium Cohort Study. *Journal of Social Policy,* vol. 35, pp. 651-669.

Kilkey, M. and Clarke (2010). Disabled men and fathering: opportunities and constraints. *Community Work and Family,* vol. 13, No. 2, pp. 127-146.

Knodel, J. and C. Saengtienchai (2004). AIDS and older persons: the view from Thailand. In *Living Longer, Ageing, Development and Social Protection*, P. Lloyd-Sherlock, ed. London: Zed Books/United Nations Research Institute for Social Development,

Kröger, T. and J. Sipilä, eds. (2005). *Overstretched. European Families up Against the Demands of Work and Care.* Oxford: Blackwell.

Kuronen, M., K. Jokinen and T. Kröger (2010). *Social care and social services*: Working report 7. Family Platform Research for Families and Family Policies, European Union's 7th Framework Programme.

La Gaceta (2000), Responsible Paternity Law No. 8101. No. 166, 30 August, www.inamu.go.cr/publicaciones/responsible_paternity_law.pdf

Lamb, M.E., ed. (2010). *The Role of the Father in Child Development*, 5th ed. Hoboken, New Jersey: John Wiley and Sons.

_____ and J.B. Kelly (2009). Improving the quality of parent-child contact in separating families with infants and young children: empirical research foundations. In *The Scientific Basis of Child Custody Decisions,* 2nd. ed. R. M. Galatzer-Levy, L. Kraus, and J. Galatzer-Levy, eds. Hoboken, New Jersey: Wiley.

_____ and K.J. Sternberg. and R.A. Thompson (1997). The effects of divorce and custody arrangements on children's behavior, development, and adjustment. *Family and Conciliation Courts Review*, 35, No. 5 (October), pp. 393–404.

Lerman, R. and E. Sorenson (2000). Father involvement with their nonmarital children: patterns, determinants, and effects on their earnings. *Marriage and Family Review*, vol. 29, pp. 137–158.

Lero, D. (2006). Introduction: fatherhood and family policy. In *Inventory of Policies and Policy Areas Influencing Father Involvement*, D. Lerg, L. Asbourne and D. Whitehead, eds. Guelph, Ontario: Centre for Families, Work and Well-being, Father Involvement Research Alliance. Available from www.fira.uoguelph.ca.

Lloyd-Sherlock, P., ed. (2004) *Living Longer: Ageing, Development and Social Protection.* United Nations Research Institute for Social Development Report, Zed Books, London.

_____ and C. Locke (2008). Vulnerable relations: lifecourse, wellbeing and social exclusion in Buenos Aires, Argentina. *Ageing and Society,* vol. 28, pp. 1177–1201.

Macdonald, E. and R. Hastings (2010). Fathers of children with developmental disabilities. In *The Role of the Father in Child Development,* 5th ed., M.E. Lamb, ed. Hoboken, New Jersey: John Wiley and Sons.

Mann, R. (2007). Out of the shadows? grandfatherhood, age and masculinities. *Journal of Aging Studies*, vol. 21, No. 4, pp. 281-291.

Mann, R., Kahn, H. and G. Leeson (2009). Age and gender differences in grandchildren's relations with their maternal grandfathers and grandmothers Oxford Institute of Ageing Working Papers, No. 209. Available from www.ageing.ox.ac.uk.

Marsiglio, W. and M. Cohan (1997). Young fathers and child development. In *The role of the father in child development.* M. E. Lamb ed., 3rd ed. New York: John Wiley and Sons.

Marsiglio, W. and R. Hinojosa (2010). Stepfathers' lives: exploring social context and interpersonal complexity. In *The Role of the Father in Child Development,* 5th ed. M.E. Lamb, ed. Hoboken, New Jersey: John Wiley and Sons.

Mazza, C. (2002). Young dads: the effects of a parenting program on urban African American adolescent fathers. *Adolescence*, vol. 37, No. 148, pp. 681-693

Mincy, R., I. Garfinkel and L. Nepomnyaschy (2005). In-hospital paternity establishment and father involvement in fragile families. *Journal of Marriage and Family*, vol. 67, No. 3 (August), pp. 611–626.

Moller, V. and M. Ferreira (2003). *Getting by:* Benefits of non-contributory pension income for older South African households. Cape Town and Grahamstown: Institute of Ageing in Africa, University of Cape Town.

Morrel, T. M. and others (2003). Cognitive behavioral and supportive group treatments for partner-violent men. *Behavior Therapy,* vol. 34, No. 1 (winter), pp. 77-95.

Murray, J. and L. Murray (2010). Parental incarceration, attachment and child psychopathology. *Attachment and Human Development,* vol. 12, No. 4, (July), pp. 289–309.

Nurse, A.M. (2002). *Fatherhood Arrested: Parenting from Within the Juvenile Prison System.* Nashville, Tennessee: Vanderbilt University Press.

Organization for Economic Cooperation and Development (2010a). OECD Family Database. Supplement SF3.1: Marriage and divorce rates. OECD–Social Policy Division—Directorate of Employment, Labour and Social Affairs. www.oecd.org/els/social/family/database.

_____ (2010b) OECD Family Database Supplement SF1.3: Further information on living arrangements of children. OECD–Social Policy Division—Directorate of Employment, Labour and Social Affairs. www.oecd.org/els/social/family/database

_____ (2010c) Chart SF2.4.B: Changes in the proportion of out-of-wedlock births since the 1970. OECD Family Database. OECD–Social Policy Division—Directorate of Employment, Labour and Social Affairs. www.oecd.org/els/social/family/database

_____ (2010d) Chart SF2.4.A: Proportion of births outside marriage, 2007 or most recent. OECD Family Database–Social Policy Division–Directorate of Employment, Labour and Social Affairs. www.oecd.org/els/social/family/database

_____ (2010e) A and B: Table SF3.4: Family violence. OECD Family Database. OECD–Social Policy Division–Directorate of Employment, Labour and Social Affairs. Available from www.oecd.org/els/social/family/database

_____ (2010f ) OECD Family Database. Table SF2.3: Mean age of mother at first childbirth. OECD–Social Policy Division–Directorate of Employment, Labour and Social Affairs. Available from www.oecd.org/els/social/family/database

Olds, D.L. (2006). The Nurse-Family Partnership: an evidence-based preventive intervention. *Infant Mental Health Journal*, vol. 27, No.1, pp. 5-25.

_____ and others (1997). Long-term effects of home visitation on maternal life course and child abuse and neglect: fifteen-year follow-up of a randomized trial. *JAMA,* vol. 278, No. 8, pp. 637-643.

Olsson, M. B. and C. P. Hwang (2003). Influence of macrostructure of society on the life situation of families with a child with intellectual disability: Sweden as an example. *Journal of Intellectual Disability Research*, vol. 47, Nos. 4-5, pp. 328–341.

_____ (2006). Well-being, involvement in paid work and division of child-care in parents of children with intellectual disabilities in Sweden. *Journal of Intellectual Disability Research*, vol. 50, No. 12 (December), pp. 963–969.

Palkovitz, R. (2002). *Involved Fathering and Men's Adult Development*. Mahwah, New Jersey: Lawrence Erlbaum Associates.

Parkinson, P. (2010). Changing policies regarding separated fathers in Australia. In *The Role of the Father in Child Development*, (5th ed., M.E. Lamb (ed.) Hoboken, New Jersey: John Wiley and Sons.

Pasley, K. and S. Braver (2004). Measuring father involvement in divorced, non-resident fathers. *Conceptualising and measuring father involvement*, R. Day and M.E. Lamb, eds. Mahwah, New Jersey: Lawrence Erlbaum Associates.

Pears and others (2005). The timing of entry into fatherhood in young, at-risk men. *Journal of Marriage and the Family*, vol. 67, No. 2 (May), pp. 429-447.

Peterselia, J. (2003) *When Prisoners Come Home: Parole and Prisoner Re-entry*. Oxford: Oxford University Press.

Phares, V. and others (2010). Including fathers in clinical interventions for children and adolescents. In *The Role of the Father in Child Development*, 5th ed., M.E. Lamb, ed. Hoboken, New Jersey: John Wiley and Sons.

Pottie, C.G., and K.M. Ingram (2008). Daily stress, coping and well-being in parents of children with autism: a multilevel modelling approach. *Journal of Family Psychology,* vol. 22, No. 6 (December), pp. 855–864.

Quinton, D.S. Pollock, and P. Anderson. (2002). The Transition to fatherhood in young men: influences on commitment–summary of key findings. Bristol, UK: School for Policy Studies, University of Bristol.

Ramchandani, P.G. and others (2005). Paternal depression in the postnatal period and child development: a prospective population study. *The Lancet*, vol. 365, No. 9478 (25 June-July), pp. 2201-2205.

Ramchandani, P.G. and L. Psychogiou (2009). Paternal psychiatric disorders and children's psychosocial development. *The Lancet,* vol. 374, No. 9690, pp. 646-653.

Rigg, J. (2005). Labour Market Disadvantage amongst disabled people: a longitudinal perspective. CASE paper no. 103. London: London School of Economics, Centre for Analysis of Social Exclusion.

Roye, C. and J. Balk (1996). The relationship of partner support to outcomes for teenage mothers and children. *Journal of Adolescent Health*, vol. 19, No. 2 (August), pp. 87-93.

Saloviita, T., M. Italinna, and E. Leinonen (2003). Explaining the parental stress of fathers and mothers caring for a child with intellectual disability: a Double ABAX Model. *Journal of Intellectual Disability Research*, vol. 47, Nos. 4-5 (May-June), pp. 300–312.

Saraceno, C. and W. Keck (2008). The institutional framework of intergenerational family obligations in Europe: A conceptual and methodological overview. Multilinks project funded by the European Commission under the 7th framework programme. Available from www.multilinks-project.eu.

Schwartzer, H. and V. Querino (2002*). Non-contributory pensions in Brazil: The Impact on Poverty Reduction.* Extension of Social Security, Paper 11. Geneva: International Labour Office, Social Security Policy and Development Branch.

Scourfield, J. (2006). The challenge of engaging fathers in the child protection process. *Critical Social Policy*, vol. 25, No. 2 (May), pp. 440-449.

Sigle-Rushton, W. (2005). Young fatherhood and subsequent disadvantage in the United Kingdom. *Journal of Marriage and Family*, vol. 67, No. 3, pp. 735-753.

Simonazzi, A. (2009). Care regimes and national employment models. *Cambridge Journal of Economics*, vol. 33, No. 2, pp. 211–232.

Snarey, J. (1993). *How Fathers Care for the Next Generation: A Four Decade Study.* Cambridge, Massachusetts: Harvard University Press

Sorensen, P. and N.J. Cooper (2010). Reshaping the family man: a grounded theory study of the meaning of grandfatherhood. *Journal of Men's Studies,* vol. 18, No. 2 (April), pp. 117-136.

Stega, S. and others (2008). Connecting father absence and mother blame in child welfare polices and practice. *Children and Youth Services Review*, vol. 30 (July), No. 7, pp. 705-716.

Tamis-Lemonda, C. and K. McFadden (2010). Fathers from low-income backgrounds: myths and evidence. In *The Role of the Father in Child Development*, 5th ed., M. E. Lamb, ed., Hoboken, New Jersey: John Wiley and Sons.

Thompson, E. (2006). Images of old men's masculinity: still a man? *Sex Roles,* vol. 55, Nos. 9-10, pp. 633-648.

Towers, C. (2009). Recognizing fathers: a national survey of fathers who have children with learning difficulties. London: Foundation for People with Learning Difficulties.

United Kingdom, Office for National Statistics (ONS) (2009). Who's Having the Babies? Her Majesty's Stationery Office (HMSO), London.

United Nations (2006). *The World's Women 2005: Progress in Statistics.* Sales No. E.05 XVII.7.

United Nations (2009) *World Survey on the Role of Women in Development*. Department of Economic and Social Affairs. New York

_____ (2009). Guidelines for the alternative care of children, 2009. General Assembly resolution 64/142, annex, 18 December. Available from http://ap.ohchr.org/documents/).

_____ (2008). Economic and Social Council (2008). Note by the Secretariat on mainstreaming disability in the development agenda. 23 November. E/CN.5/2008/6.

United Nations, Department of Economic and Social Affairs, Population Division (2005). *Living Arrangements of Older Persons Around the World.* Sales No. E.05. XIII. 9.

United Nations, Statistics Division (2009). Statistics and indicators on women and men. Table 5g: Maternity leave benefits. Updated December 2009. Available from unstats.un.org/unsd/demographic/products/indwm/tab5g.htm.

United Nations Children's Fund (2007). The State of the World's Children 2007. New York.

United Nations Development Fund for Women (forthcoming). Knowledge asset on partnering with men and boys to prevent violence against women and girls developed by Men Engage/Instituto Promundo/Alessandra Guedes. New York

United Nations Population Fund (2005). *State of World Population,* 2005: *The Promise of Equality—Gender Equity, Reproductive Health ad the Millennium Development Goals.* New York. Available from www.unfpa.org.

Vinnerljung B, E. Franzén, M. Danielsson (2007). Teenage parenthood among child welfare clients: a Swedish national cohort study of prevalence and odds. *Journal of Adolescence*, vol. 30, No. 1 (February), pp. 97-116.

Waldschmitdt, A. (2009). Disability policy of the European Union: The supranational level. *ALTER European Journal of Disability Research* vol. 3, No. 1 (January-March), pp. 8-23.

Wall, K., M. Leitão and V. Ramos (2010). Report on social inequality and diversity of families. Social Platform Research for Families and Family Policies: European Union's 7th Framework Programme.

Walmsley, R. (2005). World Prison population List, 7th ed. London: King's College—School of Law, International Centre for Prison Studies.

Watson, S. and S. Rice (2003). *Daddy's Working Away: A Guide to Being a Dad in Prison.* Cardiff: Care for the Family.

Weinman, M.L. and Buzi, R.S. and P.B. Smith (2005). Addressing risk behaviours, service needs and mental health issues in programs for young fathers. *Families in Society*, vol. 86, No. 2, pp. 261-266.

World Health Organization (2005). *Multi-country Study on Women's Health and Domestic Violence against Women*. Geneva.

IV

# Migration, families and men in families

Mary Haour-Knipe

## The Author

**Mary Haour-Knipe** has extensive experience in the fields of migration and families, and of migration and health, in particular migration and HIV/AIDS. She is currently working as an independent adviser; her work in that capacity includes providing scientific guidance to the European Centre for Disease Control project on "Improving HIV data comparability in migrant populations and ethnic minorities in the EU/EEA/EFTA countries", advising on migration-related elements for the survey of "Behavioural surveillance related to HIV and STI in Europe", writing a review of "Migration, families and AIDS" for the Joint Learning Initiative on Children and AIDS, and researching and writing a paper on "Return migration of nurses" for the International Centre on Nurse Migration. She previously served as senior Advisor on Migration and HIV/AIDS at the International Organization for Migration, carried out several evaluation studies of Swiss HIV prevention programmes for migrant communities and others, and led a European Union working group assessing AIDS prevention activities for migrants and travellers in European countries, and has worked as a researcher and teacher. She is the author or editor of four books, including *Mobility, Sexuality and AIDS* (Routledge, 2010) and *Moving Families: Expatriation, Stress and Coping* (Routledge, 2001), as well as of numerous reports, book chapters and journal articles.

An essential part of the identity of countless families throughout Africa, the Americas, Asia, Europe and Oceania is bound up with their being migrants, or having an ancestor who was a migrant. The present chapter traces patterns of international migration and some of the demographic and social factors that increase population movement and examines the complex relationships between migration and families. It zooms in on men, who have traditionally turned to migration as a way of fulfilling their roles as breadwinners; today, however, women are migrating for the same reasons, and in numbers that are now more or less equal to those of male labour migrants. This "feminization of migration" has been the object of a great deal of attention in the migration literature, in which men—ironically—have now become far less visible.

The main purposes of the chapter are thus to draw attention to the situation of migrant families and, particularly, to bring attention back to men in the context of migration and families, while focusing primarily on migration that is "voluntary". Some of the possible implications of such migration for couples and for fathering are teased out, and the implications for policy are considered.

## World migration and population mobility

Today some 214 million individuals, or approximately 3 per cent of the world population, are international migrants. Migration patterns have become more complex over the past two to three decades, making most countries simultaneously countries of origin, transit and destination as well as of return. Most population movement worldwide remains within regions, and a great deal of population movement is temporary. As for permanent settlement, the United States of America has long been, and still is, the world's major migration receiving country, along with Canada and Australia. By continent, European countries are increasingly becoming migration destination countries; however, and Asia is seeing increasingly important labour migration. Countries of Latin America and the Caribbean countries tend to see more outmigration than in-migration, as is also the case for Africa, although population movement between countries within the region is also substantial (International Organization for Migration, 2008).

Three key factors tended to increase worldwide population movement (UN Development Programme 2009):

- An increase in income inequalities between most developing and developed regions. People who migrate can expect a 15-fold increase in income. They are also able to enrol twice as many of their children in school, and people from countries with a low human development index (HDI) experience 16 times less child mortality subsequent to migration.
- Population pressures. Between 1960 and 2010, there were an additional 2.8 billion working-age people in the world, 9 out of 10 of whom were in developing countries.
- Significantly decreased transport and communications costs. The real price of air travel fell by three fifths between 1970 and 2000; and with the advent of

Internet telephony, the cost of communications fell to practically zero. People who migrate can travel to their destinations, or home for regular visits, relatively reasonably. They can also keep in contact by mobile phone and the Internet while they are away.

Migration and human development are related in important ways. Migration tends to be highest in middle-income situations, a phenomenon referred to as "the migration hump". Except when war or natural catastrophes lead to destitution and hence to "survival migration" under the worst conditions, absolute poverty is a barrier to migration: the very poorest are simply unable to gather the necessary resources (Castles, 1999). Incipient development provides families with the financial resources needed to buy transport, and also the social resources and skills necessary to be able to go where jobs may be more available and incomes higher. At the same time, massive asymmetries exist between the legal migration opportunities open to those from more affluent nations and the opportunities open to those from poorer countries (Davidson and Farrow, 2007); receiving countries' entry policies are increasingly selective, oriented towards those of working age and the most productive and highly skilled (International Organization for Migration, 2008).

Other and quite different forms of population mobility also exist. Some 16 million people were refugees or asylum seekers as of 2008 (UN High Commissioner for Refugees, 2009) and an additional 26 million had been displaced within their countries (Internal Displacement Monitoring Centre/Norwegian Refugee Council, 2009), fleeing political instability, conflict, environmental degradation and natural disasters. An additional 740 million people worldwide move within the same country, as internal migrants: seasonal migration has long been part of life in many parts of the world, but the development of modern transportation systems is making it increasingly easier for members of farming families to commute to urban centres for part-time work throughout Asia (Hugo, 1994; Jones and Pardthaisong, 2000) and Africa (Tienda, and others, 2008), for example. Both within and between countries, undocumented migrants continue to be in considerable demand as inexpensive and easily controllable labourers (Salt, 2001; International Organization for Migration, 2008). Many other men and women—cross-border commuters, short-term labourers and petty traders, for example—regularly move from place to place in pursuit of livelihoods.

Finally, although return and circular migration have always existed, they are increasingly important today: decreased transportation costs mean that it is easier for migrants to go back to their home countries, both for visits and for permanent return after periods of living and working in other countries (Ghosh, 2000; Cassarino, 2004; Long and Oxfeld, 2004). In other forms of circular migration people working abroad return home after one short-term contract only to migrate again under another, or migrants based in one country regularly travel to another to run a business (Tiemoko, 2003).

## Migration, gender and marriage

According to what was long assumed to be the typical pattern for migration, a young single man would go abroad to work, marry a woman (most likely from the country of origin), have children, perhaps bring over other family members, and settle the family in the destination country for future generations. This pattern still exists, but the patterns of temporary and circular migration just mentioned have now altered this "traditional" model. It is physically, if not administratively, easier to travel between home and destination countries, and thus to envisage working abroad for a few years, while maintaining contact with home through frequent visits and telephone calls, and then returning, instead of settling permanently. The other major shift is in the gender of the person who goes abroad to work. About half of today's labour migrants are women, who migrate independently and as main income-earners, instead of following male relatives as they had in previous generations. Women now account for the majority of the migrants living in most European countries and Oceania, and for about half of the migrants in Latin America and the Caribbean and North America (UN Economic and Social Affairs, Population Division, 2010). Women's share in total immigration in Organization for Economic Cooperation and Development (OECD) countries is shown in figure IV.1.

The proportion of women among immigrants rose between 1990 and 2000 in practically all OECD countries. Proportions were highest in Poland and Portugal at about 55–60 per cent in 2000, and lowest in Germany and Iceland, at some 40–45 per cent (Docquier, Lowell and Marfouk, 2007). The number of women migrating had surpassed that of males in some countries in Asia by the mid-1990s, as had also been the case in the Caribbean in the 1950s. Further, in 2005 47 per cent of Africa's

**Figure IV.1**
**Women's share in total immigration, OECD countries, 1990 and 2000**

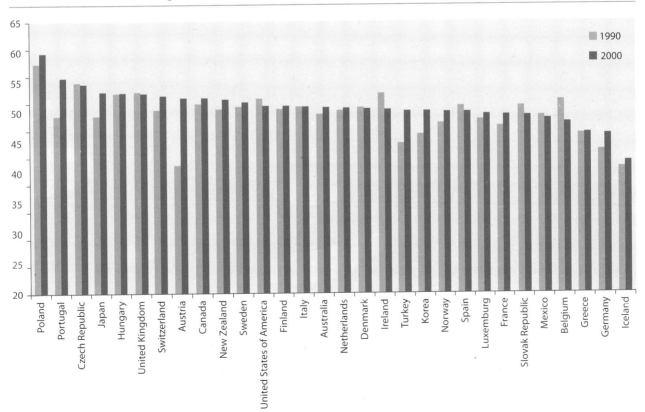

**Source:** Docquier, Lowell and Marfouk (2007).

17 million immigrants were women, up from 42 per cent in 1960 (United Nations Population Fund, 2006).

There are several possible reasons for the shift, one being, quite simply, that attention is finally being paid to a phenomenon that has always existed. Analysts have pointed out that until roughly the 1980s, migration research, although seemingly gender-neutral, was in fact driven by models based on the experiences of men; women, when their presence was acknowledged at all, were almost always treated as dependants who had migrated to be with family members, while any economic or social contributions they might have made went unseen (Kofman, 2000, as cited in United Nations, 2005). Other, more tangible reasons for an increase in female labour migration include changing gender relations in countries of origin, changes in immigration legislation, and (especially) gender-selective demand for foreign labour, with women's specific skills and traditional roles now being prioritized in the global demand for migrant labour. Employers may prefer female labourers, based on a stereotype that women will be more docile, desperate for jobs, hardworking and compliant (Carling, 2005) but women's share in skilled immigration has also risen significantly. At all skill levels, though, most women who migrate remain within traditional feminine occupations, especially in the domestic and caring sectors (Dumont, Martin and Spielvogel, 2007).

A few studies have examined the interactions among gender, migration and marriage. In Ghana, for example, careful life history event analysis of a representative sample of 2,505 adults has shown that among the more educated, women are more likely than their male counterparts to move, particularly to urban areas. Interestingly, in this country where migration for work or trade has a long history, and where it is culturally acceptable for both men and women to migrate in order to support their families, being married or in union appears to have little effect on migration probabilities for either men or women (Reed, Andrzejewski and White, 2010). In South Africa, on the other hand, the possibility of migration—in interaction with social and economic factors—is profoundly affecting both marriage and gender relations (see box IV.3). A combination of rising unemployment, dramatically reduced rates of marriage, and the reorganization of rural households as geographically flexible institutions within which women engage in circular migration to urban areas, has led to new forms of relationships and profoundly influenced sexual and other exchanges. Sharp increases in male unemployment have made it difficult for men to act as dependable "providers" in a marriage, and the new forms of exchange render some men marginal (Hunter, 2007). In Asia, a qualitative study in Sarawak, Malaysia, showed quite different motivations behind migration, as well as different family ramifications. The reasons women gave for their migration were partly economic, but at the same time a major motivation was the desire "to become modern". The women interviewed rarely complained about their repetitive, dirty, "dead-end" work: their main aim was to live in the city, to be independent, and to send money home, and employment in restaurants or hotels, or as domestic workers, was simply a means to accomplish this. The young women's new economic independence had modified the way they saw marriage: getting married become one option among others and, as such, could be postponed or even rejected; moreover, husband selection could now be approached quite pragmatically (Hew, 2003).

Box IV.1
**Types of family migration**

There are several formal types of family migration:

**Family reunification**, in which migrants who have obtained residence status in a new country are permitted to bring immediate family members such as children or spouses, and sometimes parents and others.

**Family formation** or migration for marriage.

**Family migration**, in which an entire family migrates to a new country.

Family migration used to be encouraged by receiving States on the assumption that it would facilitate integration, but it has become much less common in recent years. In fact, many countries are enhancing border controls and making migration policies more strict, including by limiting the possibilities for family members to accompany entering migrants (Kofman and Meeton, 2008). Several more precarious types of family-related migration also occur, including that of children and young people who migrate alone, and clandestine migration (Kofman, 2004). Families of irregular migrants often take great risks when they cross borders, and live in extremely insecure circumstances at destination. They have very little protection, and their rights, including to education and health care, are very few.

# Families and migration

Most of the research dealing with migration and families has been carried out in developed receiving countries. A complete review of the literature would be an ambitious endeavour, and was far beyond the scope of this chapter, but the following sections focus on some of the studies and reviews that have been carried out, concentrating on those from developing countries. We begin with migration as the outcome of a pre-departure family decision, then go on to discuss its effects in destination countries and its impact on transnational families living across countries (see box IV.2) and on families who remain in the countries of origin.

## Pre-migration: family decisions

It is very often the needs of an entire family rather than those of an individual that motivate migration. Economic theorists have suggested that families send members abroad in order to increase the material well-being of the entire unit: the migration is a "family project", for which resources are pooled; and the outcomes will be for all its members, including descendants (Stark and Taylor, 1989; Nauck & Settles, 2001). The benefits include the wealth generated by migrants, but they also come in less tangible forms such as an increase in the family's status, education and access to health services (Collinson and others, 2006). Decisions about which family member will move are determined by cultural norms (Adepoju, 1997; Hugo, 1994; Asis, 2003), but are also based on particular skills and attributes: households deliberately choose those who are to migrate from among the family members most likely to provide net income gains. In some instances, in fact, specific children may be deliberately educated with migration in mind: for example, sons and daughters may be trained as health professionals since doctors and nurses can easily find employment abroad (Redfoot and Houser, 2005).

Other theorists postulate that families may use migration as a sort of insurance, that is, as a way of diversifying their activities so as to minimize risk. In rural areas, for example, migration of one or more family members allows households to protect themselves against crop failure or other unanticipated drops in income by spreading their sources of income across different locations and sectors of the economy (Zourkaléini and Piché, 2007; Findley, 1997). Temporary deployment of family members to distant locations also allows a family to make maximum use of labour when there are periodic lulls in the home area, and to take advantage of needs at destination (Hugo, 1994; Massey, 2006). Another form of risk insurance is driven by labour market insecurity: in countries as widely separated as South Africa (Posel, 2006), Barbados (Chamberlain, 1998), Jamaica (Thomas-Hope, 1999) and Thailand (Hugo, 1998; Rende Taylor, 2005), job insecurity in the home country encourages families to spread their risks by maintaining households both in communities of destination and in communities of origin.

In still other instances migration is enabled and encouraged by social and family structures: migration is the norm, is prized per se, and may carry potent symbolic value. In the Caribbean, for example, detailed exploration of family histories shows that underpinning what may appear to be an individual's economic motive for migration there may well be a family history of social and geographical mobility (Chamberlain, 1998). In addition, in numerous places throughout the world, temporary migration is a part of growing up, a rite of passage that marks a young person's transition from childhood to adulthood (United Nations Population Fund 2007, Monsutti, 2007).

## Post-migration

Studies of family effects of migration reveal a decidedly mixed picture. In the best of cases, migration brings improvement in a family's economic well-being, an improvement that affects schooling and health, among other factors. Capacities are built and independence is increased for the individuals and families that migrate, as well as for those who remain behind. In the worst of cases, migration leads to destitution, leaving family members with little means for survival; partners and families grow apart, and children experience a range of behavioural and emotional problems that they blame, rightly or not, on their parents' abandonment. The present section describes studies of families in destination countries, then in countries of origin.

### Families living together in destination countries

As has already been noted, certain levels of social and economic resources are necessary in order for people to be able to migrate in the first place. Thus, there exist the "healthy migrant effect"–the good level of health of recent immigrants—which has been established in countries as different as the United States (Singh and Siahpush, 2001), Canada (Gushulak and others, 2010), Germany (Razum and others, 1998) and Costa Rica (Herring and others, 2010). The effect extends to their children. Studies in the major migration receiving countries increasingly report good physical and mental health among youth whose families have recently immigrated: the health of such young people in fact tends to be better than that of their peers from the destination country. Their advantages later tend to fade, however: "second generation" immigrant young people are reported to be less healthy and to engage in more risk behaviours, and by the third and later generations, rates of most such behaviours approach or exceed those of native-born ethnic majority adolescents (cf. Hernandez and others, 1998; Gfroerer and Tan, 2003; Brindis and others, 1995 for the United States; and McKay, Macintyre and Ellaway, 2003, for a review of the international literature). Structural factors help explain the slippage: children of some immigrants encounter social contexts in host country schools and neighbourhoods that may lead to "downward assimilation", exemplified, inter alia, by dropping out of school, joining youth gangs, and using and selling drugs (Portes and Rumbaut, 2005). For some, lack of skills, poverty and a context of hostile reception accumulate and grow into difficulties that are insurmountable, whereas for others intellectual, material, and social resources build on each other and this leads to increasing advantages within and across generations (Portes, Fernandez-Kelly and Haller, 2005).

An extremely important factor influencing the impact that migration will have on a family is its legal status in the destination country: regulations about family reunification, and also labour migration policies, determine whether or not families can remain together when some of their members migrate (Glick, 2010). This also influences whether or not they can obtain proper medical care and send their children to school, whether or not they can live in a particular neighbourhoods and even whether or not they can feel safe going outside their homes on the simplest of errands. Socio-economic factors are also critical: in many areas today, low wages, poor employment conditions and limited space restrict migrant workers ability to live with their families. Farm workers in Zimbabwe (Gwaunza, 1998), Kenya (Ondimu, 2010), Papua New Guinea (Wardlow, 2010) and the United States (Holmes, 2007) are examples of migrants so restricted. In addition, in countries throughout the world migrants are hired to take the jobs that locals do not want. Migrant workers are thus often to be found in dangerous industries, and in hazardous jobs and tasks in such areas as food processing, construction, manufacturing, and low-wage service jobs. Such workers, especially those with irregular legal status, are vulnerable to coercion, abuse and exploitation, and may find it difficult to support their families on the wages they receive (Benach and others, 2010) and that relegate them to the kind of inner-city neighbourhoods mentioned above.

As regards family functioning, for migrant families who live together in the host country, the new environment provides opportunities and constraints, new conditions which may change the balance of authority within the family, and new sets of values, beliefs and standards, which they must use to create syntheses of the old and the new cultures (Foner, 1997). Strier and Roer-Strier (2010) have carried out an ambitious review of the literature on migration and fatherhood, one that is highly pertinent for our purposes and also introduces a welcome degree of theorization. They classify existing research on the basis of two different theoretical approaches to the study of immigrant families: the deficit perspective and the resiliency perspective. From the "**deficit perspective**", immigration is predominantly a source of stress, and a risk factor for families. Migration challenges the stability of roles, identities and well-being, and is associated with "culture shock", with psychological and somatic problems, and with deterioration in health. The difficulties associated with adjusting to a new home, social environment, language, culture and work environment may include a decrease in self-esteem due to unemployment, poverty, loss of social status, and lack of social support. The adjustments also entail changes in roles for all family members, and thus in family relationships. The most frequently noted problems—for fathers as well as for mothers–are sadness, guilt and anxiety over separation; threats to the parents' self-image when their children adapt to the new culture and language faster than they do; increased dependency on others to effect even minimal contact with people in the host society; undermining of capacity to perform parenting roles because of difficulties related to immigration; difficulties in reasserting control over the children when families are reunited; feelings of grief, loss, guilt, isolation and marginalization; and alcohol abuse and domestic violence (Strier and Roer-Strier, 2010). Other tensions in the destination country stem from, inter alia, trying to make ends meet in a hostile environment, and worrying about children who are growing up in a racist context, where they are at risk of adopting the negative and destructive values of marginalized subcultures. In the face of such worries and uncertainties, parents sometimes fall back on traditional and conservative family practices, such as imposing strict gender and generational norms and values, a position quite likely only to exacerbate conflicts with their children (Goulbourne, 2010; United Nations, 2005).

From "**resilience perspective**", on the other hand, immigration can be positively related to family functioning. Resilience is the ability to rebound from crisis and overcome life challenges. It involves building strengths under stress, and achieving positive transformation and growth as a result; and it may be forged through crisis and prolonged adversity (Walsh, 2006). Important components of a family's resilience are its cohesiveness, flexibility and effective communication, and also the meanings that it constructs around a particular event (Patterson, 2002). Strier and Roer-Strier review a number of studies that, in line with many of the studies mentioned at the beginning of this section, have shown no significant differences between the mental health of immigrant children and that of their counterparts, or that have shown—in addition to higher income—fewer risk behaviours, higher educational achievement, and stronger family ties for children of migrants. They note that families are capable of giving lasting and significant emotional and practical support to their members, and that rather than leading to disintegration, migration can give rise to family patterns that are strengthened by a mix of old and new cultures and practices. What seems to make the difference at the level of the family is the feeling of being relatively in charge of what is happening; the ability to define clearly the difficulties and the choices available; and the ability to function together as a unit, with a strongly developed sense of the family group and the feeling that whatever affects one of them affects them all (Haour-Knipe, 2001).

## Family members that remain in countries of origin

Parents from numerous countries feel that they can best care for their children from afar, by working abroad to increase the family's economic well-being (Ehrenreich and Hochschild, 2003; Hew, 2003; Jolly and Reeves, 2005; Labib, 1997; Orellana and others, 2001). When the migration project is successful, in fact, increased resources are consistently found to be one of the most positive aspects of family migration (Rajan, 2007; Chamberlain, 1998; Sorensen and Guarnizo, 2007; United Nations Development Programme, 2009). Studies concerning children who have remained at home while their parents went abroad to work tend to concur: in the Maghreb, for example, the physical health of children of migrants is reported to be better than that of children of more stationary parents (Charbit and Bertrand, 1985); and in the Philippines, Indo-

Box IV.2
**Transnational families living in between**

A blossoming literature deals with "transnational families" whose members live between two or more cultures, feel at home in several different places, and may in fact hold several different nationalities (Sorensen and Guarnizo, 2007; Levitt and Jaworsky, 2007). Such arrangements are maintained for several reasons, including countries' restrictions on immigration of family members and underlying family tensions which migration makes it possible to circumvent in a socially acceptable way (Martin, 2005; CARAM Asia, 2004). Other reasons are cultural, some of which have been long-existing. For example, parents who migrate may leave their children at home, or send them back, to shield them from the cultural influences of the host society. Many parents in Brazzaville, Congo, for example, are convinced that children cannot grow up "properly" outside their ancestral homeland, and—in a culture where fostering of children is perfectly usual—they send their children to be raised by uncles, aunts, grandparents or others in the home communities while they are working abroad (Whitehouse, 2008).

Other cultural factors underlying the development of transnational families are new and are driven by previous migration. One example concerns the British-born children and grandchildren of Pakistani migrants to the UK, who are increasingly wishing to return to their cultural roots by marrying partners from their country of origin rather than those born and raised in Britain. In recent years, almost half of such marriages have concerned men who came from Pakistan to join fiancées in the UK. The young men experience a number of social, economic and cultural difficulties for which they were not prepared, such as downward occupational mobility when their credentials are not recognized, and those that arise from living in culturally atypical proximity to their wife's family. The tensions that result—which are made worse by stereotypes about dependent and subservient sons-in-law, and "scroungers"–can give rise to violence, abuse and desertion (Charsley, 2005).

Studies of migrant men like those described directly above are rare indeed. A more usual approach has been to look at children, who, indeed have been described as "pivotal points" or "linchpins" for households that span national borders (Orellana and others, 2001). Another has been to look at entire family systems, as did one study of transnational families living partly in the UK and partly in the Caribbean, Italy and India. This study found strong participation in family rituals in such families, and the maintaining of extensive contact with widely dispersed family members, a function usually carried out by women. Male kin were more likely to provide financial assistance in the form of remittances; they sent money to purchase or renovate properties, or to help pay for repairs, goods or other services, or they sent presents or make contributions in the form of social remittances, that is, new ideas or expertise provided during returns home (Goulbourne, 2010).

nesia and Thailand, a major review of the literature comparing the health of children of overseas workers with that of the children of non-migrants found either essentially no differences, or better health for the former (Bryant, 2005). In common with many others, both of these studies note the role played by increased economic resources in the children's well-being: poverty is a potent source of family problems, and migration is usually an effective way of alleviating poverty.

Numerous studies have shown that roles within families shift after migration, especially when only one parent migrates. While husbands and fathers who migrate to work maintain their role as breadwinners in their families, even if at a distance, the women and children who remain behind usually adjust rapidly, even in precarious social and economic situations. They often see the adoption of their new roles and responsibilities as making for a learning experience (Martin, 2005), and take over the tasks traditionally performed by the absent family members, as studies have shown in the Maghreb (Mélika, 1997), sub-Saharan Africa (Adepoju, 1997; Gwaunza, 1998), the Americas (Hirsch, 2002), and Asia (Hugo, 1994; Asis, 2003). There is reason to question whether profoundly anchored gender roles are really transformed, however, especially when men maintain their roles as breadwinners and primary decision makers by going abroad to support their families (Menjívar and Agadjanian, 2007).

Several authors have argued that migration causes problems for the families—and especially for the children—left behind (cf. CARAM Asia, 2004). One of the most negative pictures was that painted by the United Nations Special Rapporteur on the human rights of migrants who, after a visit to the Philippines to enquire into the situation of migrant workers, expressed serious concerns about the social costs of such migration. She noted that rates of divorce and separation were particularly high among migrant women (although it is difficult to know whether the marital breakdowns were a result or a cause of the migration, especially in a country in which divorce is otherwise difficult). Some of the difficulties included the fact that husbands were poorly prepared to take over their wives' responsibilities when the latter went abroad to work; over-dependency on migrant workers' incomes; emotional distance which compounds physical distance; new relationships established in the absence of a spouse; arguments over guardianship of the children and control of property in the case of break-up; and new businesses set up on return that failed because of lack of planning, training and information (United Nations, Commission on Human Rights, 2002a).

There are number of studies that have examined the effects of migration on the children involved, including a series from the Philippines, whose conclusions are in marked contrast to the above and buttress the resilience perspective discussed in the previous section. One such survey, carried out, among 1443 children aged 10-12 with one or both parents working abroad, found that the children of migrants were taller and heavier than their classmates, reported somewhat fewer minor health problems, and less abuse or violence, and performed well in school. The children perceived the main reason for migration as having been economic. Family relationships were close, maintained by constant telephone and text-message communication, and the overseas parents were consulted about important decisions, including discipline. The mother cared for the children when the father was abroad, and other family members (often the grandmother) did so when the mother had migrated. There were very few differences by caretaker in any of the outcomes, except that those whose mothers were working abroad had done somewhat less well in school than the others. Reflecting on the generally positive results, which were in contrast with those provided by previous studies, the authors noted that migration of parents is a cultural norm in the Philippines, that religion and spirituality were important sources of support to the children studied, that these families were otherwise relatively stable, and that, in addition, the improved economic situation of such children led to other advantages, such as being able to attend better schools. Many of the migrants' children were already thinking about migrating to work abroad, and planning for careers they knew would be marketable abroad (Scalabrini Migration Center, 2003). Another study from the Philippines among slightly older children who had also grown up in a situation where one or both parents worked abroad confirmed these observations: the young people reported that the emotional hardships of separation were buffered by support from extended families and communities, as well as by the emotional guidance that their mothers, in particular, had been able to provide from afar. The young people saw migration as a survival strategy that required sacrifices from both children and parents, and some even observed that such sacrifices could provide good training for later life (Parrenas, 2003). Similarly, studies of early adolescents from China, Central America, the Dominican Republic, Haiti, and Mexico living in the United States (Suarez-Orozco, Yodorova and Louise, 2002), and also of former migrants from seven Asian countries who had returned home after working in the Middle East (Gunatilleke, 1991), found that although there might have been difficulties during the period of separation, most young people thought that migration had had a positive effect on their families. Economic well-being had been improved, but this was not the only positive effect: awareness of the value of family relationships was heightened, as was the need for closer communication.

Studies of parents with migrant children abroad are beginning to appear, and to report that elderly parents are not necessarily abandoned. As in the Filipino families just discussed, family relations (between adult migrant workers in cities and their parents in rural communities in Thailand, for example) were tightly maintained by mobile telephones, and many of the elderly parents had travelled to the cities to visit their children. Remittances and other gifts made most of the parents much better off than they would otherwise have been. Parents also helped their adult children, for example when problems arose, or by taking care of grandchildren (Knodel and Saengtienchai, 2007). Extended families have also been found to provide both practical and emotional support to migrants working in Canada (Creese, Dyck and McLaren, 2008), and in the United States. In fact, elderly parents of migrants from less developed countries may establish a pattern of seasonal migration to help their grown children through efforts that may even challenge traditional gender roles, as in the case where older men take up kitchen chores (Treas and Mazumdar, 2004).

## Men, fatherhood and migration

As already discussed, according to classical models, migrants who are fathers either immigrate accompanied by their families, or–if they migrate alone–send later for their wife and children. An alternative was for a man to send remittances home to the family, then return once goals had been achieved. In other, unfortunate–but also classical–cases, some men return home without having achieved their goals, and others abandon their families in the home country without support, and without returning. As has been discussed at length here, the classical models are still present, but migration patterns have significantly changed over past decades: fathers may increasingly stay behind with their children while their wives go abroad to work. In addition, and as discussed in chapter I, families have also changed very significantly throughout the world over the past generation: more fathers are divorced or separated and have children who live with their mother somewhere else, or they live with the biological children of a new partner, or in a mixed "recomposed" family. In the case of migrant fathers, in addition, and regardless of marital status, such men may well be responsible for children in two or more countries. Calculating the numbers of fathers and children involved would be a difficult endeavour, but there does exist a small but growing theoretically and qualitatively oriented literature on fatherhood and migration. The present section takes a look at that literature.

Immigration may affect fathers' roles and practices in numerous ways that have already been discussed. First and foremost, when it is the fathers who migrate, their employment abroad often offers them better social and economic conditions in which to perform their paternal roles: fathers may see supporting their families as the main component of their paternal role. A subtle analysis of the experiences of Mexican mothers and fathers residing in the United States, for example, finds that although the parents behave in similar ways when they are separated from their children (both parents keep in contact through phone calls made at similar intervals and discuss similar matters during the calls, and both send money home about twice a month), their emotional responses to separation differ in ways that are tied to notions of roles. Specifically, if mothers' relationships are highly dependent on demonstrating emotional intimacy from a distance, fathers roles are bound up with their economic success as migrant workers, and also with being able to show children how to act honourably in the face of adversity. Fathers can earn more in the United States, migration is a means to honourably provide for their families, and leaving their children is rarely a source of guilt as it is for women. Leaving does not require a complex explanation. In fact, some fathers said they left home without saying goodbye, because they did not want to upset their children. As migration is often seasonal, they can visit their children regularly. In another variant, temporary migration was a family project: fathers started out alone in the United States, then sent for their wives, while leaving the children behind while they worked hard to save money for a few years. The decision to leave the children was a practical one: border crossing is dangerous and expensive for children whose papers are not in order, and in addition they felt the children would be well cared for at home. Some of the fathers admitted to having had marital problems prior to leaving, in which case migration provided an alternative that permitted the marriage to remain intact. Others reported marital problems post-migration, and strains on their marriages. The author observed, however, that when fathers grow distant from their children, it is generally when they cannot send money home—in other words, when they believe they are unable to fulfil their role as provider of the family. As long as they are able to send money home, their symbolic position as father remains intact. When migrant fathers were economically successful they tended to maintain stable and regular relationships with their absent children regardless of marital status: indeed, some described more extensive efforts to cultivate relationships with their children after a divorce (Dreby, 2006).

A number of studies have shown that fathers may modify certain traditional roles after immigration, for example, by becoming more engaged in childcare. Others have focused on the way in which immigration affects father-child relations. Many of these have been centred on the cultural misunderstandings and conflicts that can arise, for example, between family and school (Strier and Roer-Strier, 2010). A study of immigrant fathers from several different cultures living in Canada and Israel gives some indications of how such problems may develop: one of the factors that made fathering difficult was the loss of control and authority that occurred when a child spoke the new language more fluently than his or her father, and when the father could not communicate directly with the school. More generally, fathers' lack of understanding of the system exacerbated their loss of authority. In discussing their feelings about fatherhood, men talked about taking responsibility for providing for their children, but also about the importance of serving as a role model, and of guiding and teaching their children so as to prepare them for the future. They all faced structural barriers which eroded their authority as well as their ability to serve as a role model for their children, however. The most important obstacle was lack of employment, or employment in a job that did not make good use of the man's education and skills: as one father put it, he was not able to be a man of whom his children would be proud. Other systemic barriers included racism and discrimination, which precipitated the devaluation of the paternal figure, and seriously damaged another traditional role, that of taking responsibility for preserving the honour and pride of the family and of the cultural community. Excluded by the system and insulted by racism, the father figure inevitably lost stature (Roer-Strier and others, 2005).

On the other hand, immigrant fathers may feel that they need to protect their children from risks not present in their home communities. The example of parents who feel it is safer to leave their children in the community and culture of origin has already been discussed. Another example is that of Mexican fathers living in United States, who felt they had to protect their school-age children from drugs. These fathers also reported being concerned that cultural adaptation would make their children lose respect for authority, and for their elders, and that they had in fact become stricter because of the risks: they felt they had to discipline more to protect their children from the new standards with which they disagreed, such as excessive freedom, detachment from family, and disobedience. They also reported being especially protective of their daughters (Behnke, Taylor and Parra-Cardona, 2008).

The review of the literature on migrant fathers already cited at length has explored the way in which immigration may affect fathers' identities, and has pointed out that fathers may view immigration as a "cultural identity project", offering an opportunity to attach new meanings to traditional roles, to reinterpret previous definitions of fatherhood, and to "reinvent oneself as a father and as a man". The difficulties involved can lead to growth, for example when strength is gained from overcoming fears of the unknown, from learning, and from confronting prejudice. The outcome will depend on such factors as how long ago the migration took place, and on whether or not immigration was common in the father's country of origin. It will also depend on the contextual factors just mentioned, such as racism and unemployment or underemployment, which may undermine fathers' self-perceptions as breadwinners and heads of families, and also change wives and children's perceptions of their status and success (Strier and Roer-Strier, 2010). This brings us to the primary reason why people migrate to work abroad, which is to earn money.

# Remittances

The importance of remittances–the money that people working abroad send back to their families—has been a substantial theme in the migration literature over the past few years. Such funds link countries of origin and countries of destination, and can have an important impact on households, families, communities and even on the overall development of countries. According to World Bank tracking, officially recorded remittance flows to developing countries have risen steeply since 1990, reaching $316 billion in 2009.[1] Although this means remittances were down 6 per cent from 2008

1  Actual remittance exchanges are even greater than those reflected in official statistics: very significant amounts of money are also transferred through informal channels, or in the form of goods and cash taken back when migrants return home to settle or for visits.

when the figure was $336 billion, remittance flows to developing countries are expected to increase by 6.2 per cent in 2010 and by 7.1 per cent in 2011. This represents a faster pace of recovery than had previously been forecast, as remittances were more resilient than expected during the financial crisis. Their resiliency has highlighted the importance of such funds to the countries receiving them, and has also increased awareness of overseas diasporas as potential sources of capital (Ratha, Mohapatra and Silwal, 2010). A World Bank study of Filipino migration patterns during the global recession reveals that deployment of overseas foreign workers actually accelerated during the crisis, and as a result remittances are projected to grow by 8 per cent in 2010 in that country. Males, especially those engaged in construction, were among the workers most affected in the Philippines. By contrast, females, services workers, seafarers and rehires proved resilient to the crisis, or even benefited from it: for example, the demand for Filipino seafarers—who account for almost one quarter of that country's overseas workers—expanded sharply in spite of contraction in the shipping industry (World Bank, 2010). Human Development Report 2009 (UNDP, 2009) maps the flow of remittances in 2006 and 2007 as follows:

As might be expected, remittance flows reflect rather closely the migration patterns described in the first section of this chapter. Such funds remain largely within the regions in which they were earned, but figure IV.2 also describes a busy crisscross of patterns as funds are transferred between continents. Remittances have had direct positive effects on household welfare, nutrition, food, health and living conditions, and have been shown to reduce poverty in a number of countries and communities. Less direct economic effects include local employment generated by remittance spending (for example, when houses are built or businesses established or expanded) and creation of a store of capital that can be spent in ways that will lead to further improvements such as in schooling–effects that can take place over the very long term. To these must be added social remittances—the new ideas, practices, identities and social capital that migrants take back to their communities of origin, and that may substantially modify the lives of those who remain behind, affecting class and race identity, and family relations and gender roles.

## Remittances, men and gender relations

It is difficult to identify simple and clear-cut effects where migration is concerned given the large number of variables involved, and even more difficult to identify gender effects among possibly quite different situations. Thus, very few studies have attempted to specifically examine differences in the remitting behaviour of female and male migrants across countries. One exception is an unpublished report (cited with permission) to the World Bank describing random surveys of formal remittance senders from 18 different countries in Latin America, the Caribbean, and West Africa who were residing in the United States, Germany, and the United Kingdom. The pooled findings by sex are presented in table IV.1.

Detailed examination suggests several differences between male and female migrants. First, as shown in the table, men from most countries remit greater amounts than women. Second, men increase the amount of the remittances only when sending to their spouse, while women remit more monies than men to people other than their

Figure IV. 2
**Flows of international remittances primarily from developed to developing countries, 2006-2007**

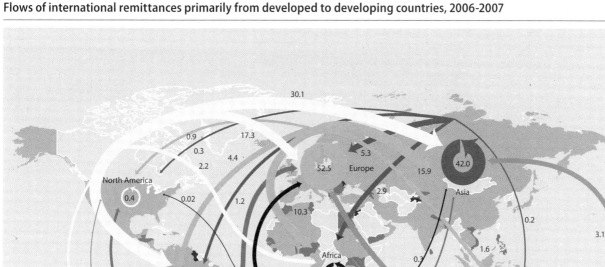

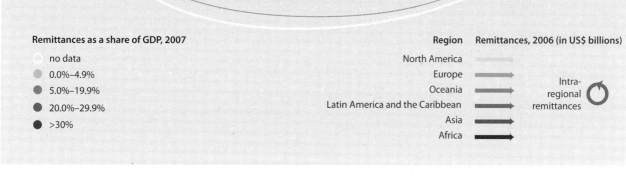

**Source:**  United Nations Development Programme, (2009), p. 73.

spouse, especially more distant family members. In general, typically lone-migrant men remit to sustain their unemployed wife at home who, in turn, spends those monies on the household; female migrants are likely either to migrate with their husbands, or, if they are lone migrants, to have families in need back home. Third, both men and women remit more the longer they have been sending remittances, but over time women remit more than men. The money that women send is more often used for basic expenditures on food or clothing, and less often for expenditures on business or loans. The authors remark that women are a greater resource during times of crisis and for distributing remittances across the sending community: their remittances may be more counter-cyclical than men's, and they may generate less inequality between households in their home communities (Orozco, Lowell and Schneider, 2006).

Studies carried out at country levels tend to concur and may go into more detail, especially about how children and family relationships are factored in. Examination of

Table IV.1

**Average remittances sent by males and females per year,
by sending country and receiving region**

| Sending Country | Gender | Receiving Region | | | | |
|---|---|---|---|---|---|---|
| | | South America | Central America | Caribbean | Africa | Total |
| Germany | Male | | | | 1793.2 | 1793.2 |
| | Female | | | | 1391.4 | 1391.4 |
| United Kingdom | Male | | | | 2458.5 | 2458.5 |
| | Female | | | | 2138.8 | 2138.8 |
| United States | Male | 3756.4 | 3750.8 | 2583.3 | 4781.2 | 3630.0 |
| | Female | 2744.1 | 2475.6 | 2986.7 | 4487.1 | 2983.6 |
| **Total** | | **3251.8** | **3333.6** | **2744.9** | **3259.5** | **3179.0** |

**Source:** Orozco, Lowell and Schneider (2006), table 3.

socio-economic panel data in Germany, for example, shows that female migrants in that country tend to support their children first and foremost, while male migrants tend to support a wider network of more distant family members and friends (Holst, Schafer and Schrooten, 2008). Excellent qualitative work with Salvadoran immigrants in the United States and El Salvador goes a step further, demonstrating that the gender of migrant parents strongly affects how well their families fare: although immigrant mothers were more likely to be structurally disadvantaged (with improper working conditions, fewer legal protections and lower wages), they invariably remitted higher proportions of their earnings, and more consistently, than did immigrant fathers, and their families at home were more often judged to be thriving economically. There are two key mechanisms behind the paradox. First, fathers were less restricted by stringent social expectations, and seemed to approach parenting more loosely. The mothers, in contrast, were driven by social expectations that they would place their children's well-being above their own, and were therefore willing to make extreme sacrifices in order to be able to send their children money consistently. Second, mothers remained committed to their children even if their relationship status changed: they continued to send money if they joined with a new partner, and some explained that new relationships actually allowed them to send more, since they now shared household expenses abroad. Fathers, on the other hand, often associated fathering with marital responsibilities: when partnerships ended they were likely to loosen ties with children as well. They stopped remitting when their partners began

Box IV.3

**Migration, gender and remittances**

A series of studies launched by the United Nations International Research and Training Institute for the Advancement of Women (INSTRAW) is particularly interesting for our purposes. The studies analyse the gender dimensions of sending, use and impact of remittances in countries with different histories, cultures, migration patterns and levels of economic development, on three different continents. They were carried out with women and development in mind, but a great deal can be extracted from them about family relationships, and men in families.

The study of migrants from **Senegal to France**, for example, deals with "older" migration, in which migrants are more permanently installed at destination. Sending remittances is nevertheless still extremely important: such funds, which are almost always sent monthly, represent 15-65 per cent of the revenue of the migrant sending them, and 30-80 per cent of the budget of the households that receive them in Senegal. Remittances are the only source of income for 65 per cent of the women, who receive them, compared with 31 per cent of the men who do so. The funds are used for health, food and lodging, ceremonies (marriages, funerals, birth or religious festivals) with only subtle gender differences in priorities. Most migrants also invest in such social projects at home as building mosques, morgues, health centres, schools and post offices—projects that also provide employment in the home communities. As for changes in gender norms as a result of migration, the study notes that these are minimal in this traditional and patriarchal society. A woman in the community of origin may take more responsibility when her male partner is away, but remains within the control of the extended family. As for the destination community, tensions, conflicts and sometimes violence arise when women start to adopt the new norms—when, for example, they go out to do their own shopping, or to work or to study or when they wish to choose their own partners. In turn, such changes raise numerous questions about the children of the migrants in the destination country, the so-called "second generation".

The studies of migrants from **Albania to Greece** and from **Morocco to Spain** both deal with "newer" migration. In these cases, the traditional model, in which low-skilled male workers from rural areas migrate first, to be followed later by their wives and children, is shifting towards encompassing female migration, but not quickly. In the case of Albania, women migrating alone as principle economic migrants remain rare, and are not particularly well regarded. At the household level, remittances have been crucial to economic survival and poverty alleviation, and have ensured a necessary supply of capital for small businesses. In the case of Albania, men send the majority of remittance funds and gender norms had changed little at the time of the study. If women reported a certain increase in standard of living, they also spoke of several negative aspects, including emotional costs of separation, increased responsibility for maintaining households, and lack of decision-making power with regard to how to spend the funds. In the case of Morocco, 70 per cent of Moroccan women in Spain arrived under formal or informal family reunification processes, compared with only 20 per cent of men. In contrast, 70 per cent of males and only 20 per cent of females reported that they had migrated with the intention of working, although 49 per cent of the migrant women now did so (a 22 per cent increase). As elsewhere, both men and women tended to work in low-skilled industries. One particular concern is migration of women for work on farms, a phenomenon that emerged several years previously when agricultural companies initiated temporary migration programmes that gave priority to female labourers—one way to assure that workers would indeed return home was to hire women who were mothers, and not allow them to bring their children (United Nations International Research and Training Institute for the Advancement of Women; and United Nations Development Programme, 2010). As for remittances, only 40 per cent of Moroccan immigrants send remittances home, of whom 80 per cent are men. More than three-fourths send remittances to their parents, and 15 per cent to their spouse. With the exception of wives, the majority of recipients are males. The funds are used to cover household needs such as food, housing, health and education, to attend to the needs of dependent family members such as elder parents or other dependants, or to pay for construction or renovation of a home. The studies from Morocco find that migration is causing domestic problems, especially since women's absence from their communities is not considered socially acceptable: there is a sense of shame incurred when women must work outside of the home to help sustain the household. Other changes are occurring in the communities of origin. For example, it is increasingly difficult for young men to find work at home, and their international migration is giving rise to a lack of available men of marriageable age, causing a gradual delay in the age of marriage. Gender roles are beginning to change slowly as a result of the migration process, but the repercussions for men and for families have not yet been explored

Box IV.3
**Migration, gender and remittances** (*continued*)

In the case of migrants from the **Dominican Republic going abroad to work in Spain**, the majority were similarly women: they migrated when the economic situation had made it increasingly difficult for men to maintain employment at home, and since there was a job market for women abroad. In this case, the study's authors note that men's contributions to households have become less and less important over the years, and their role has become increasingly secondary and marginal. The vast majority of the Dominican woman who went abroad to work left their households in the charge of another woman, a mother or a sister, or a Haitian woman hired to help out; men did not take on more tasks at home when their wives migrated, nor were they expected to do so. In the vast majority of cases, women working abroad sent remittance funds to be managed by other women (usually to a mother or a sister); women had remitted money to their husbands when migratory flows first began, but many of the husbands were reported to have used the money unwisely, considering it a personal asset rather than one for the collective good. The authors note that when men migrate and send money home, they are seen as fulfilling their paternal responsibility, which is to provide for their families, and their absence is not perceived as traumatizing for the children. When women migrate, on the other hand, their contribution may be admired, but at the same time they are blamed for not respecting traditional gender norms and fulfilling traditional maternal roles. Their absence is perceived as an abandonment of their families, an abandonment that may well result in the disintegration of the home and have catastrophic effects on the children. Indeed, several problems were evoked among the children involved, including low educational achievement, school abandonment, early pregnancy, and drug use (Garcia and Paiewonsky, 2006).

In **Lesotho**, migration patterns are also in transition. The country has a long history of male migration for work in goldmines in South Africa, but recently female migration has also increased, driven by a decrease in work available for men in mines and agricultural decline. A high prevalence of HIV, in addition, has meant that women whose partners fell ill or died have needed to find other means of support. Both male and female migrants send money home to their families, but significant gender differences emerge: male migrants, especially those who are still employed in the mining industry, usually send more than twice as much as female migrants, who receive far lower and less reliable incomes as informal traders or domestic workers. Remittances are crucial to the survival of the recipient households: the greatest portion has been spent on basic necessities such as food, fuel, clothes, transportation and medical expenses. As for family repercussions of migration, hardly any of the survey respondents recognized any positive aspects; instead, they mentioned loneliness and separation from spouses or from parents and children. Men's migration, especially to the mines in South Africa, used to be temporary: it was regarded as a rite of passage and also as a means for a young man to earn money to marry. A major shift began in the 1980s, however, when mine jobs became more scarce. Those who could get such jobs kept them, making working in the mines more of a long-term career. Migrant men spent less and less time at home, and repeated separations strained relationships. The authors of the report note that mine retrenchments—combined with agricultural decline–are giving rise to a fundamental reworking of gender relations and ideologies in this highly patriarchal society. In particular, female migrant workers are in demand, and labour migration of women is increasingly common. However, it still represents a departure from what is regarded as proper behaviour, and is perceived as a "'last resort" and a source of shame and embarrassment to the household, especially if it is related to a man's perceived failure to earn a living for his family. The report refers to an increase in domestic violence in contexts of male loss of employment, and also damage to men's sense of identity, masculinity and self-esteem. These effects may be exacerbated when women take over the role of family breadwinner, inducing feelings of envy, resentment and failure in their male partners (Crush and others, 2010).

(or were rumoured to have begun) new relationships. Some said they were uncomfortable sending money to a household that now included another male, and others justified their remittance behaviour as a response to the women's moral character (Abrego, 2009).

Box IV.3 discusses a particularly interesting set of studies that closely examine gender and remittance behaviour.

In a critical review of the literature on remittances and gender, Carling (2008) made several observations that help explain the differences uncovered in the studies sketched in box IV.3. He found that although gender differences in remittance behaviour are not always statistically significant, when they are, men with some exceptions are generally more likely to remit, and to remit larger amounts, although women may remit a substantially larger proportion of their wages. He noted that such differences must be understood in the context of family migration histories (involving such factors as whether one or both spouses are abroad, time since migration and family structure) and household structures (that is, remittances tend to be positively associated with household size at the origin and negatively associated with household size at the destination). In addition, households headed by women tend to be more likely to receive remittances than those that are headed by men, a finding that, usually, simply reflects the nature of separation through migration (i.e., men remit to their wives left in the home country. Carling notes that keeping in contact with the community of origin is also related to sending remittances, and, conversely, that not having remitted—for whatever reason—can be a strong disincentive to visiting or returning and facing the non-recipients. On the other hand, many such financial transfers (for example, to children or elderly parents) would have taken place between the same individuals even without migration. In sum, gender differences in remittance behaviour vary according to:

- The nature of families and households: Remittance behaviour is not the same in places with patriarchal or traditional family structures (for example, Mexico) as that in places where conjugal relations are more unstable and male attachment to families is relatively low (for example, the Dominican Republic);
- The normative settings: Moral values play an important role in migrants' transnational activities, including remittance sending. In some settings, migrants experience substantial pressure to remit and relatives at home feel entitled to receive support;
- The migration context: Differences in migration patterns are obviously responsible for much of the variation in remittance behaviour. For one thing, more attention is usually paid to money sent internationally. More importantly, remittance behaviour in circumstances where migration is to be temporary (that is, when the migrant intends to return and maintains a firm home base in country of origin) is quite different from remittance behaviour in a context where the migrant is permanently settled in the new country, and sends money mainly to elderly parents (Carling, 2008).

## Policies and programmes: what can be done?

This chapter has focused on families and men in the context of labour migration, in other words of "voluntary" migration engaged in to improve one's livelihood, and also—in the best of circumstances—out of a sense of curiosity or adventure, or simply because it is traditional to live away from home for an interval. The chapter has sketched the way in which migration patterns have become increasingly complex over the past generation, with notable increases in short-term and circular migration, migration of skilled workers, and of female labour migration. It has also stressed that such migration is usually a family affair: families organize to send one or more of their promising members abroad on behalf of the entire group.

Some of the men and women who go abroad to work have families of their own. Many move with their partners and children, while many others leave them behind, usually because they feel their families will be better cared for in the home community. Studies from many different countries report that the mother usually takes care of the children when a man becomes a labour migrant; but when it is a woman who migrates, the children are most often cared for by other family members, such as grandparents, or by another woman hired to do so. Today, families with one or more of their members working abroad often maintain close contact, helped by increased ease of travel and of communication. Indeed, "transnational families" have arisen, in which members remain closely connected while living in places geographically quite separated.

The chapter has sketched the ways in which migration can lead to significantly increased economic and social well-being for families and communities, and may also bring about subtle and not-so-subtle changes in family relations. Such changes have been studied to some extent for children, and also for women. They have been much less studied for men. In fact, one observation running through the chapter is that migrant men have increasingly been left out—they have quite literally been left behind in home communities as the international market privileges female labour migrants, and also left out of research, of programmes, and of policy discussions. The following section formulates recommendations for policies and programmes concerning development, emigration and immigration, conditions for migrant workers and their families in destination countries, and strengthening resilience of families and the men in them. It starts, however, with the need for improving data.

## Improving migration data, and recognizing families and men

"Today it is possible to systematically measure cross-border movements of toys and textiles, of debt, equity, and other forms of capital, but not cross-border movements of people. Our patchy statistics on international migration amount to an enormous blind spot." (Center for Global Development, 2009, p. v).

Difficulties with respect to migration data include lack of agreement on definitions, failure to collect, tabulate or publish information on people who enter countries and especially on those who depart, and inadequacy of information on gender, age and family status of those who do enter and depart. Numerous calls have been made for better migration data, ever since the 1890s, in fact, whose deficit precipitated the creation of a blue-ribbon expert panel to formulate specific, simple and feasible recommendations for improving general migration data. Countries have, inter alia, been requested to ask about country of citizenship, country of birth, and country of previous residence during every population census and then publish cross-tabulations of this information by age and sex. They have also been asked to better exploit administrative data sources and surveys containing migration data. Important backup roles have been assigned to specific United Nations organizations with respect to setting standards, providing capacity-building, coordinating and also funding census projects (Center for Global Development, 2009). Better data will help better ground policy discussions, and are also essential to correcting popular beliefs and misconceptions and to building public knowledge and understanding of the economic, social and cultural impacts of migration (Organization for Economic Cooperation and Development, 2010).

Related to the need for better data is that of recognizing families and men in relation to the migration process within research and knowledge-production, as in policy dialogue. In the individualistic societies from which most research and policy dialogue originate, the extent to which migration is very often a family affair has generally not been adequately recognized. In addition, the fact that migrant workers often have partners and children, either left behind in the country of origin or living with them in the country of destination—regularly or irregularly—is very often quite simply ignored. As regards men in the context of migration, after a period in which they were the unique focus in migration discussions, followed by an interval in which the importance of women in migration was at last rightly recognized, it has become apparent that men have rather systematically faded from the picture. In addition to Governments and international organizations whose roles were just mentioned, researchers and academics also have an important role to play: they must conceptualize and generate data and carry out specific studies that take families and men into account. Non-government organizations, in addition, must also advocate for, request and generate better data.

## Including migration, and the gender aspects thereof, in development discourse and policy

Several of the very basic themes of this chapter come under the heading of development, and have already been the object of extensive discussion elsewhere. One such theme is poverty reduction and support of families: migration should be an option that a family chooses freely, to improve its livelihood, rather than simply to make a livelihood possible. Men and women should not have to seek work in other countries simply so that their families at home will have enough to eat (United Nations Development Programme, 2009). Similarly, migration should not have to be undertaken in order to secure basic social services that are offered by well-functioning States, such as unemployment, retirement, education and decent health care.

Other themes from development discussions that were invoked in this chapter include the migration of the highly skilled, and the question whether or not such migration may drain resources in the countries of origin (cf. Global Commission on International Migration, 2005; International Organization for Migration, 2008; Dumont, Martin and Spielvogel, 2007), as well as that of global care chains, that is, the market for women from poorer communities hired to take care of the children of professionally active women in richer communities. The point made by this chapter is that each of these development issues must also be viewed in the context of its repercussions for men and for families. Many of the policy implications are complex, and many of the possible repercussions are the result of individual decisions, but there are nevertheless measures that can be taken to increase the likelihood that labour migration will lead to increased well-being for men and for families. Box IV.4 presents some relevant recommendations, made in 2009.

Box IV.4
**Reforming migration policy to maximize its impact on human development**

Several of the expert recommendations recently formulated for reforming migration policy so as to maximize its impact on human development, while at the same time recognizing the underlying challenges and constraints, have implications for families. The recommendations are directed at destination-country Governments, as well as those of countries of origin and at other key actors such as the private sector, unions, non-governmental organizations and individual migrants themselves. They include liberalizing and **simplifying regular channels that allow people to seek work abroad, ensuring basic rights for migrants, and addressing discrimination and xenophobia.**

For example, while recognizing that countries have the sovereign right to determine who is to enter their territory, the *Human Development Report 2009* (United Nations Development Programme, 2009) proposes that regular channels of entry into countries be opened up in two major ways, by expanding schemes for truly seasonal work in sectors such as agriculture and tourism (an intervention that should involve unions and employers, as well as destination- and source-country Governments) and by increasing the number of visas for low-skilled people. Mechanisms for deciding desired numbers of entrants, based on employer demand and economic conditions in destination countries, should be transparent and public. Establishing fair and clear-cut mechanisms ensuring that migrants have the right to enter and to leave countries freely would facilitate the establishment not only of their right to work abroad, but also of their right to travel home to visit their families while doing so.

As for ensuring basic rights for migrants, the report calls for Governments to ensure that migrants have, inter alia, right to equal pay for equal work, to decent working conditions and to collective organization. It also calls for Governments to act quickly to stamp out discrimination and, in this regard, it points out that while some situations will require active efforts to combat discrimination, address social tensions and prevent outbreaks of violence against immigrants, civil society and Governments do have a wide range of positive experiences upon which to draw as models for such efforts (United Nations Development Programme, 2009).

A more general but particularly important point to be emphasized in these discussions is that policy and scholarly discourses celebrating migration, remittances and transnational engagement as embodiments of self-help development "from below" must not distract attention from the structural constraints involved and the limited albeit real ability of individuals to overcome such constraints. States must continue to play a role in shaping the general conditions favourable for the achievement of human development (de Haas, 2010); and international organizations and civil society must play a significant role when the welfare of the groups in question involves the responsibilities of several States, as is the case with migrants.

## Making emigration and immigration more friendly to families

Some **sending countries**, such as the Philippines, have deliberately promoted emigration as a way of improving their economies. Since its inception in 1974, indeed, the Overseas Employment Programme has been instrumental in lifting many Filipino households out of poverty, and providing steady employment even during times of economic crisis (World Bank, 2010). The Philippines is often regarded as having created a prototype for "sending country" migration policies inasmuch as overseas employment is regulated by legislation, there is widespread acknowledgement of and respect for the social contribution of migrant workers, and migrant workers receive a number of very tangible benefits and services, such as access to special "express lanes" and lounges in airports and favourable rates on bank loans. The Government, non-governmental organizations and the private sector share responsibilities for recruiting and providing information to potential migrant workers and for supporting their families, as described in box IV.5.

As for **destination countries**, immigration policy determines which members of a family can enter the country, in what order, and, to some extent, their living conditions, especially in the case of irregular migrants (Glick, 2010). Regulations on entry of persons into countries–and on how they are treated and protected once they get there–have generally not, however, kept pace with the recent changes in migration patterns (Global Commission on International Migration, 2005). Would-be migrants are currently confronted with growing legal and administrative barriers, established in the light both of fears that migrants will take jobs from nationals in a context of economic crisis, and of countries' fears concerning possible links between migration and security. Such barriers feed clandestine migration, a phenomenon that leaves the door open to abuses, and can have the very negative effects on families discussed throughout this chapter, such as when their irregular status prevents migrant workers from visiting their families, or prevents their children from going to school.

Thus, as proposed in box IV.4, measures to facilitate regular migration–the formulation of clear and transparent criteria that would allow labour migrants and their families to live and work abroad more easily–would benefit families in addition to providing other benefits. Other issues concerning family reunification are discussed in box IV.6.

On the other hand, it would be naïve not to recognize the darker sides of migration, which also bring out some of the complex policy issues. In addition to the very positive aspects of increasing economic wellbeing and reuniting separated families, migration may also encompass such abuses as trafficking in persons and exploitation of migrant workers and children. Any measures that Governments institute for facilitating temporary migration, or promoting family reunification, must also ensure that the workers involved and their families are protected, and that policies are not abusive (an example of one such policy, that of separating female agricultural workers from their children to ensure that the workers will return home, was mentioned in box IV.3). A strong role exists for non-governmental organizations and for international organizations in identifying and advocating against cruel policies, and abuses. At the level of the individual migrant, and as has also been discussed in this chapter, some men and women decide to migrate not only because they wish to improve the well-being of their families, but also to increase distance in troubled relationships. Others may feel that conditions for their partners and children are better at home than in the destination community. Thus any policy promoting family reunification must navigate among numerous options, some of which imply delicate issues about which those involved may prefer not to speak.

Other complex policy issues are raised in the case of transnational families, when members of the same nuclear family may live in several different countries; different family members may have different nationalities, thus different rights in the countries

Box IV.5
## Policies and programmes of the Philippines for departing migrant workers

The Philippines currently sends over 1.5 million contract workers abroad each year to nearly all countries (World Bank, 2010). Subsequent to the documentation of abuses (UN, Commission on Human Rights, 2002b, 2002b), and after advocacy by non-governmental organizations and migrants' associations, the Filipino Government enacted legislation to protect migrants at home and abroad, and established specific programmes for such workers and their families.

The relevant Government institutions include two agencies specifically created to develop overseas labour markets, regulate and monitor recruitment, ensure the well-being of workers, and provide welfare assistance to registered overseas workers and their families. These operate in collaboration and critical dialogue with several other key actors: non-governmental organizations (including church groups, unions and migrants' associations which have been particularly active in advocating for and shaping policy changes), the private sector (for example, recruitment agencies and banks which provide information and practical support) and international organizations (for example, the International Labour Organization (ILO), which has campaigned for decent work, and helped design and implement assessments of the impacts of programmes and policies; and the International Organization for Migration (IOM) which has produced audio-visual aids, films and theatre pieces on labour migration and trafficking).

There have been many efforts to disseminate information about the risks and opportunities of international migration in the Philippines. Examples include, inter alia, a mass audience awareness-raising campaign which targets young people; inclusion of migration issues in the curricula of elementary and secondary schools; public service advertisements and radio programmes; face-to-face meetings; pamphlets, comics, cartoons and posters; country-specific cards listing numbers to call in case of emergency; and up-to-date information websites. In destination countries, embassies and resource centres make themselves available to overseas workers, a 24-hour helpline is maintained, and Filipino migrants have created associations that use the media (including text- messaging on mobile phones) to help overseas workers keep in contact with home, and also share their experiences.

The Philippines has established itself as a pioneer in pre-departure orientation and training programmes run by the Government, non-governmental organizations and the private sector. All departing migrants are required to attend a pre-departure orientation seminar, a 4 ½ hour region-specific session which covers travel tips, learning how to understand an employment contract, dos and don'ts in the destination country, values, HIV/AIDS, how to remit money through banks, plans for reintegration, and what to do in a crisis. Workers who have been identified as especially vulnerable or who have special needs (for example, domestic workers, entertainers, those travelling to particular countries, and workers who have not gone through recruitment agents) attend special sessions. There are also special sessions for those engaged in seafaring, a profession said to enjoy model recruitment, training and handling as a result of strong union presence. Filipinos migrating as fiancé(e)s or spouses of foreign nationals are also required to attend guidance and counselling programmes which discuss migration laws affecting emigrants, welfare and support services available abroad, the rights of migrants overseas, and how to cope with problematic domestic situations. The trainers in such programmes, many of whom were formerly welfare officers abroad, have been trained and accredited by the Government, and are periodically assessed.

Many non-governmental organizations also provide training programmes of their own, for example, to migrants and their families, community leaders, and local government officials. One example is a programme for returning migrants on reintegration and entrepreneurship. Some recruitment agencies also offer short training courses. One such course is a "pre-application briefing", designed to give prospective migrants a realistic idea of what they will be expected to do, and to help, weed out those who are not suited for migration, or who do not really want to go (Siddiqui, Rashid and Zeitlyn, 2008).

## Box IV.6
### Family reunification conundrums

Family reunification, which refers to the process of reuniting immediate family members with the primary migrant in the country of destination, is supported by international human rights law.[a] People who have been accepted as refugees normally have the right to family reunification, a measure that is essential to the mental health of families separated as they flee conflict and violence. Other family members usually have to wait for a given period and then satisfy certain conditions, for example that of demonstrating that housing and income are adequate to support them (International Organization for Migration, 2008). Over the past few years, changes in family reunification policies have increasingly tended to involve the imposition of restrictive criteria, including the use of language or civics tests as a precondition for family reunification (Organization for Economic Co-operation and Development, 2010).

The regulations and determinations regarding which family members may be admitted under family reunification vary between countries. In Canada, to take just one example, a Canadian citizen or permanent resident who is at least 18 years of age is allowed, subject to certain conditions, to sponsor for permanent residence: spouse, common-law partner, or conjugal partner aged 16 years or over, parents and grandparents, a dependent child, a child whom the sponsor intends to adopt, orphaned brothers, sisters, nieces, or grandchildren under age 18 and who are not married or living in a common-law relationship (Wikipedia posting on "family reunification", as of 19 September 2010). Specifications and regulations are under discussion in a great many migration receiving countries, and shifting, hence the usefulness of such up-to-date general sources as the one just cited.

The subject of family reunification intersects with two intricate subject areas: international law and definitions of family. Migration is a highly complex area of international law, since exit and entry are governed both by national rules and by international regulations. Family reunification introduces the added difficulty arising from the fact that there are conflicting legal norms relating to the family—and no authoritative legal definition of the term "family". Family may be defined quite variously based on marriage, genetic and biological criteria, or dependency (a criterion that may be just, but that can be difficult to establish, especially over time). In sum, family reunification must grapple with conflicting definitions of the family, as well as with different national jurisdictions, and also with international law (Staver, 2008).

a Article 16(3) of the Universal Declaration of Human Rights states that "the family is the natural and fundamental group unit of society and is entitled to protection by the society and the State".

concerned, and also different attachments to those countries. Measures for increasing well-being for transnational families would include lowering such barriers as limits on dual nationality and extremely restrictive eligibility criteria for acquiring the nationality of the host country. Such measures would help improve immigrants' labour-market outcomes (Organization for Economic Cooperation and Development, 2010), facilitate travel between countries of origin and of destination, and clear up some of the policy conundrums just mentioned. The relevant actors for such reforms include not only Governments which determine migration and welfare policies for their own countries, but also international organizations and non-governmental organizations (with respect to facilitating cross-border discussions and advocating) as well as employers (with respect to recruitment and formulating or repealing policies such as those for single-sex labour migration). The complexity of the issues involved reinforces the need to include representatives of the migrant men and women in the discussions.

## At destination: conditions for migrant workers and their families

Another of the main arguments of this chapter has been that structural conditions—the inadequate social and working conditions often experienced by migrant workers in destination communities–have negative effects on their families. Such conditions affect the jobs migrant workers can do, the neighbourhoods in which they live, and even their self-images. One potentially important mechanism for addressing such conditions is the International Convention on the Protection of the Rights of All Migrant Workers and Members of Their Families, discussed in box IV.7. Respect for the Convention's contents—along with its more extensive ratification, especially by countries that receive migrants—would help immeasurably in improving the situation of migrants, including that of migrant men.

Another extremely important measure–described in the Human Development Report 2009 as possibly the single most important reform for improving human development outcomes for migrants–would be to allow people to work. As the Report points out, access to the labour market is vital not just because of the associated economic gains but also because employment greatly increases the prospects for social inclusion (United Nations Development Programme, 2009, p. 104). After allowing regularly admitted migrants to work, the next step would be to assure decent and safe conditions once they began to do so. These would include both the employment conditions under which they were hired, and the working conditions that would protect their health and safety. Some examples of measures through which this might be achieved were described in box IV.5, which discussed the measures implemented by the Government of the Philippines to protect Filipino workers abroad. Such protection requires joint efforts on the part of Governments, employers and unions as well as non-government organizations and migrant workers themselves.

As regards inadequate social conditions, another major theme of this chapter, these are reinforced by the security concerns mentioned above, which then combine with economic concerns to produce what can become vicious circles: immigrants'

---

**Box IV.7**

**The International Convention on the Protection of the Rights of All Migrant Workers and Members of Their Families**

a  United Nations Treaty Series, vol. 2220; No. 39481.

b  General Assembly resolution 217A(iii).

c  See General Assembly resolution 2200 A (XXI), annex.

d  Ibid.

The International Convention on the Protection of the Rights of All Migrant Workers and Members of Their Families[a] explicitly applies the rights elaborated in the International Bill of Rights (the Universal Declaration on Human Rights[b] and the 1966 International Covenants on Political and Civil Rights[c] and Economic, Social and Cultural Rights[d]) to the specific situation of migrant workers and members of their families. The Convention, and the complementary ILO Conventions, provide a comprehensive normative framework for defining national and international migration policy under the rule of law. They outline a rights-based approach, and also set parameters for a wide range of national policy and regulatory concerns, delineating the agenda for inter-State consultation and cooperation on such issues as information exchange, combating irregular migration, smuggling of migrants and trafficking in persons, pre-departure orientation, and orderly return and reintegration in home countries.

As of 30 March 2009, the Convention had 41 accessions or ratifications, and another 15 States had signed it, thus signalling a general disposition towards compliance. There are very few migration receiving countries either among those States that acceded or ratified or among those that signed, however (International Steering Committee for the Campaign for Ratification of the Migrants Rights Convention, 2009).

labour-market disadvantage and unemployment, social exclusion, and relegation to unsafe neighbourhoods can give rise to antisocial or criminal behaviour which then confirms security-related fears (United Nations Development Programme, 2009). This downward spiral has direct repercussions for migrant families, and particularly the men in such families, who are subject to discrimination and abuse, along with racism and xenophobia, in forms that can be violent. The structural changes needed to address such conditions would extend very far beyond migration; however, there are migration-related measures that *can* be implemented. These include identifying the issues, gathering the data for documentation purposes, and discussing the results, as well as ensuring migrants' regular and safe entry into countries to live and work, and protection once they have done so. Another measure would be to ensure decent living conditions, including housing (discussed in box IV.8).

Roles do exist in this area, as in the area discussed in the previous section, for international organizations (in promoting needs), Governments, non-governmental organizations and employers and others from the private sector.

---

Box IV.8
**Housing migrant workers and their families**

---

The literature contains numerous descriptions of the housing problems of migrant workers. Such workers usually do not have access to the same means of identifying and paying for housing as do locals in the destination community. They often find themselves living in poor-quality lodging, and paying exploitive rents. It is not unusual for migrant workers who wish to keep expenses down to share housing or even to take turns using sleeping spaces. In numerous instances male migrant workers live with other migrant men when they first arrive, then move to larger quarters once their family members can join them (Parrado, Flippen and Uribe, 2010). There have been graphic descriptions of situations in migrant labour hostels of South Africa (Ramphele, 1993), tea plantations in Kenya (Ondimu, 2010) and palm oil plantations in Papua New Guinea (Wardlow, 2010), to take just some examples, where family members join migrant workers in housing that was originally built for single male workers. When a wife and children attempt to settle into a space meant for a single man the result is overcrowding, noise and promiscuity, not to mention the problems centred around cooking places and toilets, and, the risks for women and children which, in turn, increase family tensions.

These issues have been addressed in a number of reviews and accords over the years (cf. Lean and Hoong, 1983; Van Parys and Verbruggen, 2004), as well as on the website of the Centre on Housing Rights and Evictions[a] although it is very difficult to find vetted practical examples of potentially good practice in this realm. One interesting example of such good practice comes from China, where a recent study has examined the emergence of purely private sector housing for migrant workers in the city of Shenzhen. Faced with loss of their agricultural land as a result of rapid urban growth, local farmers, who suddenly found that their land was near the centre of a large city, started renting out their spare rooms for extra income. Traditional village houses were of poor quality, and the demand for cheap housing from the incoming migrants, combined with Government and developers' compensation for the loss of agricultural land, provided the farmers with an excellent opportunity to rebuild. Some of the additional rooms have become modern multi-storey buildings with a variety of units available for rent, some of which can comfortably accommodate married migrants with children. What is interesting about the model is that it exemplifies a purely "self-help", market-driven initiative, and represents a unique partnership between local rural residents and migrants with no Government support. The model is characterized by flexibility in meeting the needs of migrants and affordability for those with low incomes (Wang, Wang and Wu, 2010).

a http://www.cohre.org/index.php

## Men in families and as fathers

This chapter has examined numerous interconnections between migration and gender and families. For example, there tend to be differences in how men and women use remittance funds, and these differences are influenced by notions about what constitutes proper behaviour for women versus proper behaviour for men. The differences are also influenced by gender-related differences in labour demand and in labour conditions. A finding common to many different countries, however, is that although roles in families may shift depending on whether it is the mother or the father who goes out to work, fundamental gender norms may in fact be remarkably stable. When men go abroad to work they continue to fulfil their traditional breadwinner roles, and, when women go abroad to work, it is very often a female who steps in to take care of her tasks at home. The shift in roles when women can find work abroad and men cannot can also lead to tension, conflict and abuse within families, especially in traditional and patriarchal societies, where female labour migration had not been customary, and perhaps when the funds provided by the female family member who is able to find employment abroad are essential for a household's very survival. In such instances a man's loss of ability to provide for his family may be a source of intense shame.

Another key theme running through the chapter has been that of the importance of conditions in destination communities for influencing changes within migrant families. A man's ability to live and work in decent conditions, and attitudes towards

---

Box IV.9
**Programmes in support of migrant families**

The importance of support for families in the context of migration has been stressed in numerous studies and reviews. Families often receive substantial support from the extended family while one or more of their members works abroad, but those members, in turn, may also need support.

One programme designed to support the families of overseas workers was aimed at fostering resilience of children in Mexican communities with high levels of emigration and of poverty, as well as low levels of education. The programme offered support to girls, boys, nursery school teachers, mothers and/or caregivers in families likely to have a parent working abroad, focusing on helping to develop children's self-knowledge, independence and responsibility and their ability to communicate and establish relationships, to express feelings and affective needs, and to seek assistance. Results of the evaluation showed that in spite of the potential disadvantages with which they might have been faced initially young children could be helped to become conscious of and communicate their moods, ask for help appropriately, choose alternatives for solving problems, set up positive relationships with equals, and develop supportive and cooperative behaviours (Givaudan, Barriga and Gaal, 2009).

A few programmes for immigrant fathers have also emerged. They may have been developed by official entities like the Government of the sending or receiving country, or by Non-governmental organizations, foundations or churches, and may provide a wide range of services, including advocacy, information and counselling, help with reintegration, and workshops for children and their caregivers. Programmes developed specifically for immigrant fathers, such as one in Calgary, Canada, may include work support and help in acquiring language proficiency; help with interpreting new values and with interacting; support groups which provide men with a safe place for connecting with each other; and help with reconciling prior and new conceptions of fatherhood (Roer-Strier and others, 2005).

## Box IV.10
## Migration, HIV and AIDS* in Southern Africa

* Further discussion on migration and HIV/AIDS can be found *inter alia* in Belsey (2005): Migration: economic necessity and family vulnerability.

The potential relation between population mobility and HIV has been the object of debate ever since the beginning of the AIDS epidemic. On one side—and as with fears of, and stereotypes about, infectious diseases throughout the ages—migrants have been accused of bringing HIV into countries. On the other hand, numerous studies have shown that some groups of migrants are more vulnerable to HIV infection than their non-migrant counterparts: there is growing recognition that migration may well give rise to behaviours and situations that facilitate HIV transmission.

Southern Africa is one of the world's most severely affected areas, with an estimated 11.3 million adults and children living with HIV in 2009, out of 33.3 million people worldwide. That same year, 31 per cent of the new HIV infections worldwide occurred in 10 countries in Southern Africa, as did 34 per cent of all AIDS-related deaths. Globally, about 40 per cent of all adult women with HIV live in Southern Africa.

Migration has long been a feature of daily life in Southern Africa. Current migration flows are dominated by labour migration towards South Africa, and by rural urban migration in all countries of the region. Migration is largely seasonal and temporary, with workers returning home to their families on a regular basis. A large number of studies have examined the relationships between such mobility and the rapid spread of HIV, as well as the HIV-related risks experienced both by the migrants themselves and by the families and communities affected by mobility.

Such studies have shown that there are several common determinants of migrants' higher vulnerability and risk, including lack of access to public services (e.g. HIV/AIDS education and health services including STD treatment) due to legal and communication barriers, separation from families and regular partners, alienation and loneliness, and also the exploitation that reduces an individual's possibilities for making healthy choices.

As for gender aspects, male migrants, are often faced with dangerous working conditions and estranging environments, to which they may responds with exaggerated masculinity, a macho attitude that denies danger and even encourages risk behaviours. Gender norm prizing multiple sexual partners also increase the likelihood of HIV infection. For many years it was assumed that male workers who acquired HIV while they worked away from home in mines, in transport industries and in cities for example, would be responsible for carrying the virus back to their partners left behind in largely underdeveloped and impoverished rural areas. Evidence growing over the past decade is showing that the picture is much more complex than has been assumed, however. For example women whose partners are working away from home for long periods may be left without support, and with little recourse but to trade sex to survive. They may acquire HIV during such 'survival sex', or simply from relations established in the absence of a missing partner. As for women who migrate, many work in informal and seasonal employment that leaves them vulnerable to exploitation and to abuses that put them at risk, including the need to engage in sex for support and/or for security.

Partly based on the evidence generated by a large of studies focusing on population mobility and HIV in Southern Africa, a number of interventions have been carried out over the past 10 to 20 years to provide safe sex education and condoms to migrants, and to facilitate their access to STI and HIV care and treatment. A number of important regional initiatives have attempted to address the underlying economic, political, social and cultural factors that contribute to migrants' vulnerability, including poverty, poor social status of women, and inequalities linked to the migrant labour system itself.

More recently, and as former migrant workers infected while working abroad start to return home for care at the end of their lives, studies are beginning to explore the potentially heavy burden migration and HIV will be placing on families, in Southern Africa as in other areas of the world.

**Sources:** Brummer (2002) and Haour-Knipe (2009).

migrants, affect his self-image and influence his ability to carry out his fathering roles. Two different approaches to dealing with the effect of migration on individual men and on families were discussed, each of which has been the focus of a rather substantial literature. One approach entails analyzing the stress, loss, isolation, marginalization and domestic problems to which migration can give rise. The other entails focusing on the increased economic, social, individual and familial well-being to which it can also give rise. The first approach is necessary in order to deconstruct problems so as to be able to address them, while the second can provide indications of how to help make migration a positive experience for all concerned. A number of specific programmes have been developed to support migrant men and families, one example of which was discussed in box IV.5. Two others are discussed in box IV.9.

## Concluding remarks

This chapter has looked at numerous issues related to men, families and migration, and has outlined many approaches to dealing with the issues raised. At the same time, the lacks and needs in this domain are numerous; for one thing, there is a need for reviews of several major issues that it was not possible to cover here, including evaluations of the long-term effects of the major family-related migration policies, such as family reunification and social protection, and of policies for providing access to education for children of migrants, or to health care and health promotion. Several major conceptual themes should also be reviewed, such as that of how masculinity may be affected by migration; the theme of the repercussions of migration for families, especially for men and children; and the neglected theme of return migration and its effects on the men, women and families involved. There is a great need for good practice studies: while family-related changes due to migration are perhaps inevitable, there is need for studies with a resiliency approach, which examine the factors and perhaps the programmes that enable such changes to give rise to growth, learning and increased well-being, rather than to inflict harm within migrant families.

At the same time, the chapter has raised a number of very troubling unanswered questions:

How do men react, especially in traditional and/or patriarchal societies, when women can find jobs abroad more easily than men? In particular, how do such labour-market shifts affect the motivation and self-image of male workers? And how can men, women, and families best be protected in such circumstances?

How do destructive spirals arise within families, as, for example, in cases where men are not trusted with remittance funds or with the care of their own children, and become increasingly marginalized within their own households? How might such destructive spirals be averted or reversed?

How do countries' security concerns, and the links between such concerns and migration, affect migrant families in general and migrant men in particular? What are the medium- and long-term effects of the marginalization and relegation of migrant men and their families into insecure neighbourhoods and insecure employment?

A key focus of this chapter has been the observation that, after decades of being the model of reference for migration, men have increasingly been left behind, not only as labour migrants, but also in research and policy dialogue. It is now time for the pendulum to swing back in the other direction, so as to take into account women *and* men in relation to migration. Progress towards resolving some of the very troubling questions and extremely complex policy issues raised here can begin only once the significance of men is once again recognized.

# References

Abrego, L. (2009). Economic well-being in Salvadoran transnational families: how gender affects remittance practices. *Journal of Marriage and Family*, vol. 71, No. 4 (November), pp. 1070-1085.

Adepoju, A. (1997). *Family, Population and Development in Africa*. London: Zed Books.

Asis, M. (2003). International migration and families in Asia. In *Migration in the Asia Pacific: Population, Settlement and Citizenship Issues*, R.R. Iredale, S. Castles, and C. Hawksley, eds., Cheltenham, United Kingdom: Edward Elgar.

Behnke, A., B. Taylor, and J.R. Parra-Cardona (2008). «I hardly understand English, but ...»: Mexican origin fathers describe their commitment as fathers despite the challenges of immigration. *Journal of Comparative Family Studies*, vol. 39, No. 2 (spring), p.187.

Belsey, M.A. (2005). *AIDS and the Family: Policy Options for a Crisis in Family Capital*. United Nations publication, Sales No. E.06.IV.1.

Benach, J., and others (2010). Immigration, employment relations, and health: developing a research agenda. *American Journal of Industrial Medicine*, vol. 53, No. 4 (April), pp.338-343.

Brindis, C., and others (1995). The associations between immigrant status and risk-behavior patterns in Latino adolescents. *Health*, vol. 17, No. 2 (August), pp. 99-105.

Brummer, D. (2002). Labour migration and HIV/AIDS in Southern Africa. International Organisation for Migration: Regional Office for Southern Africa.

Bryant, J. (2005). Children of international migrants in Indonesia, Thailand, and the Philippines: a review of evidence and policies. UNICEF Innocenti Working Papers, No. 2005-05. Florence, Italy: UNICEF Innocenti Research Centre

CARAM Asia (2004). The forgotten spaces: mobility and HIV vulnerability in the Asia Pacific. Kuala Lumpur: Coordination of Action Research on AIDS and Mobility.

Carling, J. (2005). Gender dimensions of international migration. Global Migration perspectives, No. 35 (May). Geneva: Global Commission on International Migration.

_____ (2008). The determinants of migrant remittances. *Oxford Review of Economic Policy*, vol. 24, No. 3, pp.582-599.

Cassarino, J.P. (2004). Theorising return migration: the conceptual approach to return migrants revisited. *International Journal on Multicultural Societies*, vol. 6, No. 2, pp.253-279.

Castles, S. (1999). International migration and the global agenda: reflections on the 1998 UN Technical Symposium. International Migration, vol. 37, No. 1, pp.5-19.

Center for Global Development (2009). *Migrants Count: Five Steps Toward Better Migration Data–Report of the Commission on International Migration Data for Development Research and Policy*. Washington D.C.: Center for Global Development.

Chamberlain, M. (1998). Family and identity: Barbadian migrants to Britain. In *Caribbean Migration: Globalised Identities*, M. Chamberlain, ed., (pp. 148-161). London Routledge.

Charbit, Y. and C. Bertrand (1985). *Enfants, familles, migrations dans le bassin mediterraneen*. Cahier No. 110. Paris: Presses universitaires de France.

Charsley, K. (2005). Unhappy husbands: masculinity and migration in transnational Pakistani marriages. *Journal of the Royal Anthropological Institute*, vol. 11, No. 1 (March) pp.85-105.

Collinson, M.A., and others (2006). Highly prevalent circular migration: households, mobility and economic status in rural South Africa. In *Africa on the Move: African Migration and Urbanization in Comparative Perspective*, M. Tienda and others, pp. 194-216. Johannesburg, South Africa: Wits University Press.

Creese, G., I. Dyck, and A.T. McLaren (2008). The «flexible» immigrant? human capital discourse, the family household and labour market strategies. *Journal of International Migration and Integration,* vol. 9, No. 3, pp. 269-288.

Crush, J., and others (2010). Migration, remittances and gender: responsive local development; the case of Lesotho. Santo Domingo. United Nations International Research and Training Institute for the Advancement of Women (INSTRAW), and United Nations Development Programme (UNDP).

Davidson, J. and C. Farrow (2007). *Child Migration and the Construction of Vulnerability.* Stockholm: Save the Children Sweden.

de Haas, H. (2010). Migration and development: a theoretical perspective. *International Migration Review,* vol. 44, No. 1, (spring), pp. 227-264.

Docquier, F., B.AL. Lowell and A. Marfouk (2007). A gendered assessment of the brain drain. Bonn: IZA Discussion Paper, No. 3235. Institute for the Study of Labor (IZA).

Dreby, J. (2006). Honor and virtue: Mexican parenting in the transnational context. *Gender and Society,* vol. 20, No. 1 (February), pp. 32-59.

Dumont, J.C., J.P. Martin and G. Spielvogel (2007). Women on the move: the neglected gender dimension of the brain drain. IZA Discussion Paper, No. 2920.

Ehrenreich, B. and A.R. Hochschild (2003). *Global Woman: Nannies, Maids and Sex Workers in the New Economy.* London: Granta.

Findley, S. (1997). Migration and family interactions in Africa. In *Family, Population and Development in Africa,* A. Adepoju, ed., pp. 109-138. London: Zed Books.

Foner, N. (1997). The immigrant family: cultural legacies and cultural changes. International Migraton Review, vol. 31, No. 4 (special issue), pp.961-974.

Garcia, M. and D. Paiewonsky (2006). Gender, Remittances and Development: *The Case of Women Migrants from Vincente Noble, Dominican Republic.* Santo Domingo: United Nations International Research and Training Institute for the Advancement of Women (INSTRAW).

Gfroerer, J.C. and L.L. Tan (2003). Substance use among foreign-born youths in the United States: does the length of residence matter? *American Journal of Public Health,* vol. 93, No. 11 (November), pp. 1892-1895.

Ghosh, B. (2000). *Return Migration: Journey of Hope or Despair?* Geneva: International Organization for Migration.

Givaudan, M., Barriga, M., and F. Gaál (2009). Strengthening resilience in communities with a high migration rate: I want to, I can... learn and have fun at nursery school. *Early Childhood Matters,* pp. 47-51.

Glick, J. (2010). Connecting complex processes: a decade of research on immigrant families. *Journal of Marriage and Family,* vol. 72, No. 3 (June), pp. 498-515.

Global Commission on International Migration (2005). *Migration in an interconnected world: New directions for action: report of the Global Commission on International Migration.* Geneva.

Goulbourne, H. (2010). *Transnational Families: Ethnicities, Identities and Social Capital.* London: Routledge.

Gunatilleke, G. (1991). *Migration to the Arab World: Experience of Returning Migrants.* Tokyo: United Nations University.

Gushulak, B.D. and others (2010). Migration and health in Canada: health in the global village. *CMAJ,* pp. 1-7.

Gwaunza, E. (1998). The impact of labour migration on family organization in Zimbabwe. In L.M. Sachikonye, ed., pp. 49-55. *Labour markets and migration policy in Southern Africa*, Mount Pleasant, Harare: SAPPHO.

Haour-Knipe, M. (2001). *Moving Families: Expatriation, Stress and Coping*. London: Routledge.

_____ (2009) Families, children, migration and AIDS. *AIDS Care*, vol. 21, No. 1, pp. 43-48.

Hernandez, D.J. and others (1998). *From Generation to Generation: the Health and Well-being of Children in Immigrant Families*. Washington, D.C.: National Academy Press.

Herring, A. A. and others (2010). Differential mortality patterns between Nicaraguan immigrants and native-born residents of Costa Rica. Journal of Immigrant Minority. Health, vol. 12, No. 1 (February), pp. 33-42.

Hew, C. S. (2003). *Women Workers, Migration and Family in Sarawak*. London: RoutledgeCurzon.

Hirsch, J. (2002). Que, pues, con el pinche NAFTA? Gender, power and migration between western Mexico and Atlanta. *Urban Anthropology*, vol. 31, Nos. 3-4, pp. 351-387.

Holmes, S. M. (2007). Oaxacans Like to Work Bent Over: the naturalization of social suffering among berry farm workers. *International Migration*, vol. 45, No. 3 (August) pp. 39-68.

Holst, E., Schäfer, A. and M. Schrooten (2008). Gender, Migration, Remittances: Evidence from Germany. Discussion Papers of DIW Berlin, No. 200. Berlin: German Institute for Economic Research.

Hugo, G. (1994). Migration and the family. UN Occasional paper series for the International Year of the Family. Vienna: United Nations.

_____ (1998). Family dimensions of Asia-Pacific migration: theoretical and empirical issues. In P. Brownlee and C. Mitchells (eds.), «Migration research in the Asia Pacific: theoretical and empirical issues» pp. 41-62. Asia Pacific Migration Research network Working Papers, No. 3, Wollongong, Australia: Asia Pacific Migration Research Network.

Hunter, M. (2007). The changing political economy of sex in South Africa: the significance of unemployment and inequalities to the scale of the AIDS pandemic. Social Sciences and Medicine, vol. 64, No. 3 (February), pp. 689-700.

International Steering Committee for the Campaign for Ratification of the Migrants Rights Convention (2009). Guide on ratification of the International Convention on the Protection of the Rights of All Migrant Workers and Members of Their Families (ICRMW). Geneva.

Internal Displacement Monitoring Centre, Norwegian Refugee Council (2009). *Internal Displacement. Global Overview of Trends and Developments in 2008*. Geneva.

International Organization for Migration (2008). *World Migration 2008: Managing Labour Mobility in the Evolving Global Economy*. Geneva. Sales No. E.07.III.S.8. United Nations publication.

Jolly, S. and H. Reeves (2005). *Gender and Migration: Overview Report* Brighton, United Kingdom: Institute of Development Studies.

Jones, H. and L. Pardthaisong (2000). Demographic interactions and developmental implications in the era of AIDS: findings from northern Thailand. *Applied Geography 20 (2000)*, vol. 20, No. 3 (July) pp. 255-275.

Knodel, J. and C. Saengtienchai (2007). Rural parents with urban children: social and economic implications of migration for the rural elderly in Thailand. *Population, Space and Place*, vol.13, No. 3 (May/June), pp. 193-210.

Kofman, E. (2004). Family-related migration: a critical review of European studies. *Journal of Ethnic and Migration Studies*, vol. 30, No. 2, pp. 243-262.

_____ and V. Meeton (2008). Family migration. In *World Migration 2008: Managing Labour Mobility in the Evolving Global Economy*. Geneva. UN publication, Sales No. E.07.III.S.8.

Labib, A. (1997). Les familles restées en Tunisie. In *Migration internationale et changements sociaux dans le Maghreb: actes du colloque international de Hammamet, Tunisie (21–25 Juin 1993)*, A. Bencherita, ed., pp. 101-130. Tunis: Université de Tunis I.

Lean, L. and P. Hoong (1983). migrant workers in Asean: a review of issues and implications for government policies. *International Migration*, vol. 21, No. 2 (April), pp. 277-287.

Levitt, P. and N. Jaworsky (2007). Transnational migration studies: past developments and future trends. *Annual Review of Sociology*, vol. 33, No. 1, pp. 129-156.

Long, L. and E. Oxford (2004). *Coming Home? Refugees, Migrants, and Those Who Stayed Behind*. Philadelphia, Pennsylvania: University of Pennsylvania Press.

Massey, D. (2006). Patterns and processes of international migration in the twenty-first century: lessons for South Africa. In *Africa on the Move: African Migration and Urbanization in Comparative Perspective*, M. Tienda and others, eds., pp. 38-70. Johannesburg, South Africa: Wits University Press.

McKay, L., S. Macintyre and A. Ellaway (2003). *Migration and Health: a Review of the International Literature* (MRC Social and Public Health Sciences Unit Occasional Paper, No. 12). Glasgow, UK: MRC, Medical Research Council Social and Public Health Sciences Unit, University of Glasgow.

Mélika, H. Z. (1997). Les épouses des travailleurs migrants demeurées au pays: chefs de ménage ou substituts des absents. In *Migration internationale et changements sociaux dans le Maghreb actes du colloque international de Hammamet, Tunisie (21–25 Juin 1993)*, A. Bencherifa, ed., pp. 159-179). Tunis: Université de Tunis I.

Menjívar, C. and V. Agadjanian (2007). Men's migration and women's lives: views from rural Armenia and Guatemala. *Social Science Quarterly*, vol. 88, No. 5, pp. 1243-1262.

Monsutti, A. (2007). Migration as a rite of passage: young Afghans building masculinity and adulthood in Iran. *Iranian Studies*, vol. 40, No. 2 (April), pp. 167-185.

Nauck, B. and B. Settles (2001). Immigrant and ethnic minority families: an introduction. *Journal of Comparative Family Studies*, vol. 32, pp. 461-466.

Organization for Economic Cooperation and Development (2010). *International Migration Outlook: SOPEMI, 2010* Paris. Summary available from http://www.oecd.org.

Ondimu, K. (2010). Labour migration and risky sexual behaviour: tea plantation workers in Kericho District, Kenya. In *Mobility, Sexuality and AIDS*, F. Thomas, M. Haour-Knipe and P. Aggleton, eds., pp. 154-167). London and New York: Routledge.

Orellana, M.F., Thorne and others (2001). Transnational childhoods: the participation of children in processes of family migration. *Social Problems*, vol. 48, No. 4, pp. 572-591.

Orozco, M., B. Lowell and J. Schneider (2006). Gender-specific determinants of remittances: differences in structure and motivation. Washington, D.C.: Report to the World Bank Group, Gender and Development Group.

Parrado, E., C. Flippen, and L. Uribe (2010). Concentrated disadvantages: neighbourhood context as a structural risk for Latino immigrants in the USA. In *Mobility, Sexuality and AIDS*, F. Thomas, M. Haour-Knipe and P. Aggleton, eds. London and New York: Routledge.

Parrenas, R.S. (2003). The care crisis in the Philippines: children and transnational families in the new global economy. In *Global Woman: Nannies, Maids, and Sex Workers in the New Economy*, B.Ehrenreich and A.R. Hochschild, eds., pp. 39-54. New York: Metropolitan Books.

Patterson, J.M. (2002). Understanding family resilience. Journal of Clinical Psychology, vol. 58, No. 3 (March), pp. 233-246.

Portes, A., W. Haller, and P. Fernandez-Kelly (2005). Segmented assimilation on the ground: the new second generation in early adulthood. *Ethnic and Racial Studies*, vol. 28, No. 6 (November), pp. 1000-1040.

Portes, A. and R. Rumbaut (2005). Introduction: the second generation and the children of immigrants longitudinal study. *Ethnic and Racial Studies*, vol. 28, No. 6 (November), pp. 983-999.

Posel, D. (2006). Moving on: patterns of labour migration in post-apartheid South Africa. In *Africa on the Move: African Migration and Urbanization in Comparative Perspective*, M. Tienda and others, eds., pp. 217-231. Johannesburg, South Africa: Wits University Press.

Rajan, S. I. (2007). New trends of labour emigration from India to Gulf Countries and its impact on the Kerala economy. In *«International labour migration from South Asia»*, Hisaya Oda, ed. Tokyo: Institute of Developing Economies, Japan External Trade Organization.

Ramphele, M. (1993). *A bed called home: Life in the Migrant Labour Hostels of Cape Town*. Cape Town: David Philip, Publishers.

Ratha, D., S. Mohapatra and A. Silwal (2010). Outlook for remittance flows 2010-11. Migration and Development brief, No. 12. Washington D.C.: Migration and Remittances Team, Development Prospects Group, World Bank.

Razum, O. and others (1998). Low overall mortality of Turkish residents in Germany persists and extends into a second generation: merely a healthy migrant effect? Tropical Medicine and International Health, vol. 3, No. 4 (April), pp. 297-303.

Redfoot, D. L. and A.N. Houser (2005). *«We shall travel on»: quality of care, economic development, and the international migration of long-term care workers*. No. 2005-14 (October). Washington, D.C.: Public Policy Institute, AARP.

Reed, H., C. Andrzejewski, and M. White (2010). Men's and women's migration in coastal Ghana: an event history analysis. *Demographic Research,* vol. 22, No. 25 (April), pp. 771-812.

Rende Taylor, L. (2005). Patterns of child fosterage in rural northern Thailand. Journal of Social Science, vol. 37, No. 3, pp. 333-350.

Roer-Strier, D. and others (2005). Fatherhood and immigration: challenging the deficit theory. *Child and Family Social Work,* vol. 10, No. 4 (November), pp. 315-329.

Salt, J. (2001). The business of international migration. In *International Migration in the 21st Century: Essays in Honour of Reginald Appleyard*, M.A.B. Siddique ed., pp. 86-108. Perth, Australia: Edward Elgar.

Scalabrini Migration Center (2003). *Hearts Apart: Migration in the Eyes of Filipino Children*. Manila: Scalabrini Migration Center.

Siddiqui, T., R. Rashid, and B. Zeitlyn (2008). Information campaigns on safe migration and pre-departure training. Brighton, U.K.: Sussex Centre for Migration Research, University of Sussex.

Singh G.K. and M. Siahpush (2001). All-cause and cause-specific mortality of immigrants and native born in the United States. American Journal of Public Health, vol. 91, No. 3, pp. 392-399.

Sorensen, N. N. and L. Guarnizo (2007). Transnational family life across the Atlantic: the experience of Colombian and Dominican migrants in Europe. In *Living Across Worlds: Diaspora, Development and Transnational Engagement*, N. N. Sorensen, ed. pp. 151-176. Geneva: International Organization for Migration.

Stark, O. and J. E. Taylor (1989). Relative deprivation and international migration. *Demography,* pp. 1-14.

Staver, A. (2008). Family reunification: a right for forced migrants? (Refugee Studies Centre Working paper Series, No. 51. Oxford: Refugee Studies Centre, Oxford Department of International Development–University of Oxford.

Strier, R. and D. Roer-Strier (2010). Fatherhood in the context of immigration. In *The Role of the Father in Child Development*, M. Lamb, ed., pp. 435-458. Hoboken, New Jersey: John Wiley and Sons.

Suarez-Orozco, C., I. L. Todorova and J. Louie (2002). Making up for lost time: the experience of separation and reunification among immigrant families. *Family Process*, vol. 41, No. 4 (winter), pp. 625-643.

Thomas-Hope, E. (1999). Return migration to Jamaica and its development potential. International Migration, vol. 37, No. 1, pp. 183-207.

Tiemoko, R. (2003). Migration, return and socio-economic change in West Africa: the role of family (Sussex Migration Working Paper No. 15). Brighton, U.K.: Sussex Centre for Migration Research, School of Global Studies, University of Sussex.

Tienda, M. and others, eds. (2008). *Africa on the Move: African Migration and Urbanization in Comparative Perspective.* Johannesburg, South Africa: Wits University Press.

Treas, J. and S. Mazumdar (2004). Kinkeeping and caregiving: contributions of older people in immigrant families. *Journal of Comparative Family Studies,* vol. 35, No. 1 (January)

United Nations (2005). *2004 World Survey on the Role of Women in Development: Women and International Migration.* Sales No. E.04.IV.4.

United Nations, Commission on Human Rights (2002a). Report of the Special Rapporteur on specific groups and individuals: migrant workers, 15 February. E/CN.4/2002/94.

United Nations, Commission on Human Rights (2002b). Report of the Special Rapporteur on specific groups and individuals: migrant workers: addendum: mission to the Philippines. 1 November. E/CN.4/2003/85/Add.4.

United Nations, Department of Economic and Social Affairs, Population Division (2010). Bonn: Institute for the Study of Labor. Database on women among migrant 'stocks' world wide.

United Nations Development Programme (2009). Human Development Report 2009. *Overcoming Barriers: Human Mobility and Development.* Basingstoke, United Kingdom: Palgrave Macmillan.

United Nations High Commissioner for Refugees (2009). 2008 Global trends: refugees, asylum-seekers, returnees, internally displaced and stateless persons. Geneva.

United Nations Population Fund (2006). *State of world population 2006: A Passage to Hope, Women and International Migration.* New York.

_____ (2007). *Moving Young: State of World Population 2006 Youth Supplement.* New York.

United Nations International Research and Training Institute for the Advancement of Women (INSTRAW) and United Nations Development Programme (2010). Migration, remittances and gender-responsive local development. case studies: Albania, the Dominican Republic, Lesotho, Morocco, the Philippines and Senegal. Santo Domingo. Available from http://www.un-instraw.org/.

Van Parys, R. and N. Verbruggen (2004). Report on the Housing Situation of Undocumented Migrants in Six European Countries: Austria, Belgium, Germany, Italy, the Netherlands and Spain. Brussels: Platform for International Cooperation on Undocumented Migrants (PICUM).

Walsh, F. (2006). *Strengthening Family Resilience,* 2nd ed. New York: Guilford Press.

Wang, Y., Y. Wang and J. Wu (2010). Housing migrant workers in rapidly urbanizing regions: a study of the Chinese model in Shenzhen. *Housing Studies,* vol. 25, No. 1, pp. 83-100.

Wardlow, H. (2010). Labour migration and HIV risk in Papua New Guinea. In *Mobility, Sexuality and AIDS,* F. Thomas, M. Haour-Knipe and P. Aggleton, eds. pp. 176-186. London and New York: Routledge.

Whitehouse, B. (2009). Transnational childrearing and the preservation of transnational identity in Brazzaville, Congo. *Global Networks*: A Journal of Transnational Affairs, vol. 9, No. 1 (January), pp. 82-99.

World Bank (2010). Philippines quarterly update. Manila: World Bank group in the Philippines.

Zourkaléini, Y., and V. Piché (2007). Economic integration in a West-African urban labour market: does migration matter? the case of Ouagadougou, Burkina Faso. *Demographic Research,* vol. 17, pp. 497-540.

V

# Men, families and HIV and AIDS

Chris Desmond and Victoria Hosegood

## The authors

**Chris Desmond** is a research associate at the FXB Centre for Health and Human Rights at the Harvard School of Public Health. His research has focused on issues relating to HIV and children, including those related to the costs of care, the appropriate targeting of responses and policy development. Past work has included examining the possibilities for assessing country responses to HIV/AIDS, including investigating appropriate indicators of a successful response to children. Mr. Desmond was a contributor to the Joint Learning Initiative on Children and HIV/AIDS. Currently, he manages the "cost of inaction" research project at the Centre. The project examines alternative approaches to evaluating the response to children affected by HIV/AIDS. Prior to moving to FXB, he was a research specialist at the Human Sciences Research Council in South Africa and a research fellow at the Health Economics and HIV/AIDS Research Division at the University of KwaZulu-Natal.

**Victoria Hosegood** is a Reader in Demography with the Faculty of Social and Human Sciences, University of Southampton. Her research interests lie in the area of demography and health of families in sub-Saharan Africa, and she is particularly interested in the impact of HIV and treatment and the collection and analysis of longitudinal demographic and health data to inform family health interventions. She is the principal investigator of a Wellcome Trust-funded study of Fatherhood and Men's Health. Much of her South African research has involved collaborations with the Africa Centre for Health and Population Studies, University of KwaZulu-Natal, and the Human Sciences Research Council.

# Introduction

The consequences of illness and death associated with HIV and AIDS extend far beyond infected individuals. HIV is a family disease, and understanding how families are affected and how they respond to infection, ill health and mortality is crucial to efforts to strengthen family support. The present chapter highlights the role of men in influencing the risk and impact of HIV and AIDS within families, the support provided to adults and children affected by HIV and AIDS, and family resilience in such situations. It is argued in the chapter that relevant research and programmes have been hindered by assumptions about men and HIV, men and their involvement in families, and the messaging around HIV and AIDS that tends to apportion blame and innocence to specific types of people within families.

The assumptions on which policies are based need to be questioned, not only in terms of their validity, but also in terms of their usefulness. It is generally assumed that men play a limited role in affected families, particularly in relation to the physical care of those who are ill and in taking responsibility for the care of children. These assumptions relate to the widely held view that men, particularly in more traditional societies, have very limited involvement in care activities within families. In some areas, such as South Africa, there are strong negative perceptions of men in families, with absence, abandonment, violence and neglect emphasized within the discourse. Furthermore, in the context of providing support for families affected by HIV and AIDS, it is very common for commentators to refer to women and children as "innocent victims" of the HIV epidemic—an epidemic for which men are to blame. Attention is often focused on men with multiple sexual partners, men's reluctance to use condoms, the high HIV prevalence among men who have sex with men, and men's risk-taking behaviours such as drug use and alcohol consumption.

If families are to be more effectively supported in their efforts to deal with the consequences of HIV and AIDS, the assumptions on which family-strengthening policies are based, need to be questioned. A failure to do so may well lead to missed opportunities to involve men in the support of families—involvement that could well benefit men and other family members.

In this chapter we argue that, while negative images of men have been used to raise awareness and financial support for programmes and services targeting women and children affected by HIV and AIDS, basing public-health and welfare policies on such negative assumptions leads to a number of problems. Suffering that is particular to men may be overlooked, with undesirable outcomes that may include their underutilization of antiretroviral treatment (ART) and other health services. Moreover, a potentially powerful resource for families may be missed. Assuming men do not want to be involved in family services, or are not able to take on supportive roles within the family, may translate into missed opportunities. It is also suggested in the chapter that involving men not only helps others but also represents a way to strengthen the health and well-being of the men themselves.

The problems that arise from casting men in a wholly negative light do not mean that we should simply rush to offer a more positive image of men more positively.

Understanding how sexism, unequal power relations and other forms of discrimination shape the course of the HIV epidemic is essential. Identifying ways to respond to these injustices should be a priority. Indeed, addressing such inequalities may be one of the best ways to stop the continued spread of HIV. What is needed, however, to avoid the problems of casting men in a negative light is to decrease the importance of blame and rigid assumptions in policy design.

The aim of this chapter is to highlight multiple aspects of men and families in the context of HIV and AIDS, and consider how the relationships and roles that men have within their families can be incorporated into the design and implementation of family policies and programmes. The first part of the chapter includes a review of what is known about men and families within this context, with the authors demonstrating that the limited extent to which men have been considered in studies and commentaries is wholly unrepresentative of men's presence within families and their experience of HIV as members of families and as HIV-infected individuals. Consideration is then given to ways in which family policies reflect society's understanding of how families respond to and are affected by HIV and AIDS, and to ways in which such policies might be strengthened.

## What is meant by "family"?

With its global impact and disproportionately high incidence in some marginalized groups and communities, HIV, more than any other disease, has highlighted the diversity of contemporary family forms and the varied ways in which families respond to infection, ill health and death. Families are not composed of individuals related solely through marriage or biology. Twenty years ago, seeking to identify who counted as family in the context of AIDS, Carol Levine (1990) provided the following working definition:

Family members are individuals who by birth, adoption, marriage or declared commitment share deep, personal connections and are mutually entitled to receive and obligated to provide support of various kinds to the extent possible, especially in times of need.

This definition continues to be a useful one. The term "family" encompasses a variety of traditional and non-traditional groupings, including heterosexual and homosexual partnerships, biological and social parents and children, polygamous and polygynous relationships, close friends, and other relatives. Also, families are made up not only of those people with whom we are in daily contact. Support may come from relatives living far away who send financial assistance, or entail a new arrangement: for example, adult children who return to live with their parents upon becoming ill, or relatives who foster children whose parents are ill or have died.

How do men fit into this definition of the family? They may be part of the central family unit as partners (of women or men), biological fathers or biological children. They may also maintain family relationships as uncles, grandfathers, stepfathers and close friends. Men's family relationships can vary to the extent to which they are recognized by others in the community and by the State. In some societies, men's relationships are highly privileged; may all biological children are considered the property of the father, regardless of the marital status of the children's parents. In others, neither social nor legal recognition is accorded to the biological fathers of any children born to unmarried couples. For some men, the lack of recognition may be within the context of the wider family—for example, where unmarried young men are not acknowledged by a partner's family due to conflict. In other situations, the status of men in less traditional family relationships is not sanctioned at the level of the State, as in countries where homosexuality is illegal.

## HIV as a "family disease"

The incidence, prevalence and impact of HIV can be addressed from a number of different perspectives. When the focus is on infected individuals, discussions relating to men and HIV tend to highlight the burden of disease for men relative to women. Estimates published by the Joint United Nations Programme on HIV/AIDS (UNAIDS) suggest that roughly equal numbers of men and women are infected with HIV globally. However, there are large regional variations in the sex distribution of HIV infection (see table V.1). In sub-Saharan Africa, where HIV is most prevalent, more women than men live with HIV, and the same is true in the Middle East and North Africa. In the Caribbean, HIV infection is evenly distributed between men and women. In the rest of the world, it is more concentrated in men.

The significant regional variations in the sex distribution of HIV infection reflect the different types of HIV epidemics prevailing around the world. When a region's epidemic is driven primarily by heterosexual transmission, a higher proportion of women are infected than is the case when the epidemic is driven by transmission through homosexual sex and intravenous drug use. When HIV is concentrated among men, relatively fewer children are infected, since children are typically infected by their mothers.

While focusing on the individual is critical in HIV research and programme planning, this limited perspective fails to acknowledge the key importance of the family

Table V.1
**Women, men and children living with HIV**

| Region | Number of people living with HIV | | | | Percentage of total | | |
|---|---|---|---|---|---|---|---|
| | Women (15+) | Men (15+) | Children (0-14) | Total | Women (15+) | Men (15+) | Children (0-14) |
| **Global** | **15 500** | **15 300** | **2 000** | **32 800** | **47** | **47** | **6** |
| Sub-Saharan Africa | 12 000 | 8 300 | 1 800 | 22 100 | 54 | 38 | 8 |
| East Asia | 200 | 530 | 7.8 | 737.8 | 27 | 72 | 1 |
| Oceania | 22 | 51 | 1.1 | 74 | 30 | 69 | 1 |
| South and South-East Asia | 1 500 | 2 600 | 140 | 4 240 | 36 | 61 | 3 |
| Eastern Europe and Central Asia | 460 | 1 040 | 12 | 1 512 | 30 | 69 | 1 |
| Western and Central Europe | 200 | 530 | 1.3 | 731.3 | 27 | 72 | 1 |
| Middle East and North Africa | 190 | 160 | 26 | 376 | 50 | 43 | 7 |
| North America | 250 | 950 | 4.4 | 1 204 | 20 | 79 | 1 |
| Caribbean | 110 | 110 | 11 | 231 | 48 | 48 | 4 |
| Latin America | 550 | 1 150 | 44 | 1 744 | 32 | 66 | 2 |

Source: Joint United Nations Programme on HIV/AIDS (UNAIDS) and World Health Organization, 2008 Report on the Global AIDS Epidemic, Geneva, July 2008.

within the context of HIV and AIDS. Regardless of the cause, the illness and death of any family member can potentially have significant emotional, financial and practical consequences for the family as a whole. The consequences of HIV/AIDS for families are often particularly severe and as a result HIV has been described by some commentators as a "family disease", primarily because it often involves the clustering of infections within a family and the loss of an important income earner or caregiver, and because of the role the family can play in HIV prevention (Richter and others, 2009).

## The clustering of infection

The clustering of infection within a family can occur as a result of sexual or mother-to-child transmission. In Rwanda and Zambia, for example, relations between cohabiting partners are responsible for an estimated 60-90 per cent of new infections (Dunkle and others, 2008). Mother-to-child transmission also derives from a family relationship.

The sexual nature of transmission obviously leads to the clustering of HIV infections within the family in both heterosexual and homosexual contexts. When the individual is infected through intravenous drug use, the clustering may still occur, either as a result of partnering with other infected drug users, or through sexual transmission. Thus, it is not uncommon for families to have more than one HIV-infected member and to experience multiple episodes of illness and death (Belsey, 2005; Hosegood and others, 2007).

## Consequences for families

Providing care to a member who is suffering from HIV and AIDS places enormous pressure on a family's human and financial resources. Research on the age distribution of HIV incidence indicates that infected family members are likely to be prime-age adults (aged 15-45), and ill health within this economically productive group is often associated with a decrease in income. Individuals in this age bracket also play a major role in domestic activities such as providing physical care for children and other dependants. Essentially, financial resources and the capacity to provide care may decline at a time when they are most needed within the family.

The negative consequences of HIV and AIDS on the family may well be very different, depending on the circumstances of the family prior to the illness and what role the family member or members who became ill played prior to their illness. The loss of a primary earner can be particularly serious for families who are poor or close to the poverty line. The financial situation in such a household is affected not only by the loss of a major source of income, but also by the expenses incurred in dealing with a major illness and by the fact that the provision of physical care and support by family members prevents them from engaging in other productive activities. If a household is labour-constrained and the family is already finding it difficult to provide sufficient physical care to members, the illness or loss of a provider of such care is particularly serious. Essentially, the direct impact of the disease is magnified by the need to allocate financial and human resources to provide care for the infected member.

In many of the regions with generalized HIV epidemics, men play a leading role in income-generation. Male illness is therefore typically associated with the loss of a primary earner. While women often have an important income-generating role, they tend to also play a primary role in the provision of physical care within the home. The sex of the person(s) infected may therefore have different implications for an affected family. Another consideration is status within the family: if more resources are directed towards the care of men when they are ill, the impact on the family will be greater than if it is a woman in the family who falls ill.

Numerous studies undertaken in various parts of the world have examined the negative impact of HIV-related illness on family finances. The focus has typically been on consequences at the level of the household—the most common unit for data collection. While concerns have been raised about the methodological difficulties of measuring the extent of impact (Beegle and De Weerdt, 2008), it is clear that HIV/AIDS has a detrimental impact on the household financial situation. Households in South Africa have been shown to decrease expenditure as a result of being affected (Bachmann and Booysen, 2004). Reduced earning potential as a result of illness and the time and money spent on providing care have been identified as the major causes of financial strain in such contexts. In Cambodia, high expenditures on medical care have been linked to lower expenditures on other household members and the sale of assets (Alkenbrack Batteh and others, 2008). Similar consequences have been observed in other African and Asian countries.

Efforts have been made not only to measure the financial impact of illness and death resulting from AIDS but also to compare this impact with that linked to illness and death from other causes. Research results from Ethiopia, for example, indicate that illness and death associated with AIDS have a greater economic impact on households than do illness and deaths from other causes (Tekola and others, 2008). While this type of information is useful, it is more important to understand what determines the severity of the financial impact, which factors influence the short- and long-term consequences of changes in financial status, and the implications of these changes for family well-being.

One major factor affecting family well-being is the availability of financial and human resources prior to the occurrence of HIV infection within the household (Desmond, 2009). For families that have the financial resources, needed to deal with the loss of income and increased costs associated HIV and AIDS, the impact of the disease on other aspects of their well-being may not be as serious. For example, they may not have to sacrifice their children's education to pay medical costs; and while expenditure on food may decrease, it may still be sufficient to prevent malnutrition. However, when families face a multitude of stressors, including poverty and food insecurity, the impact of HIV and AIDS can be especially damaging (Drimie and Casale, 2009). In such situations, the financial costs of illness and death may not only affect families in the short term may also put them on a downward trajectory, particularly if productive assets are sold during the crisis (Donahue, 2005; Heymann and Kidman, 2009). When families do not have the resources to respond to HIV and AIDS, the health and education of children, the nutritional status of all household members, and many other aspects of well-being may be seriously affected (Desmond, 2009).

The consequences of both illness and death have been examined in relevant financial-impact studies. Each is associated with lost income if infected adults or their caregivers were previously employed. Death, however, relieves the pressure of recurrent costs of care and allows caregivers to direct their attention to other tasks. However, the death of a family member can have serious financial implications, starting with high funeral costs which can be difficult to meet. Long-term economic prospects for a family may be greatly reduced if the family has to exhaust savings or sell productive assets to meet the costs of the funeral (Donahue, 2005).

In some parts of the world, the negative consequences of a family member's death are exacerbated by difficulties relating to inheritance, particularly when a male head of household dies. When a man's life ends, the disposition of his land, house and other assets may be challenged. This occurs all over the world, but Rose (2006) provides specific examples of its occurrence in eastern and southern Africa. The relatives of the deceased may argue that customary law allows them to seize his property, possibly leaving his partner and children without a home or the means to live. Counter-arguments have been made that such seizures are not sanctioned by customary law and that, where they are, the inheritors often have a duty (at times ignored) to care for the dead man's family (ibid.).

While quantitative studies have typically focused on the household, family networks of support, particularly in the highly-affected Southern African region, stretch far wider (Mathambo and Gibbs, 2009). Households may experience negative consequences due to the death or ill health of non-resident household members and extended family (Hosegood and others, 2007). Families often send the individual with the highest income-earning potential away to work, and the loss of that person can have very serious implications for family finances (Haour-Knipe, 2009). The financial impact of illness and death may be even greater if the migrant returns home to die, as not only will the migrants' income be lost, but the costs of care (human and financial) will increase. The issues of migration and employment are particularly important when considering the role of men in families affected by HIV and AIDS. While a growing number of women now migrate for work, it is more frequently men who are absent. The discourse on labour migration among men tends to focus on their absence and not on their financial contribution, which draws attention away from the impact the loss of such support can have on families.

Much of the evidence relating to the household- and family-level impact of HIV and AIDS comes from Africa and Asia. It is in these regions that families are most likely to face the prospect of dealing with the direct consequences of the disease as well as poverty and other stresses, while receiving very little support from the State or non-governmental organizations. The impact on families in such contexts can be extremely serious. A number of commentators have expressed concern that family systems in high-prevalence areas are breaking under the strain. In spite of these circumstances, households continue to be the main source of care and support for HIV-affected individuals, even in the most highly affected regions (Hosegood, 2009).

As mentioned previously, HIV is considered a family disease not only because infections tend to cluster within households and affect the family as a whole, but also because the family plays a role in determining individuals' risk of infection.

## The role of the family in HIV prevention

A family can influence the risk of HIV infection among its members in many different ways. The most direct influence is exerted through the family's efforts to reduce the chances of sexual transmission between its members and to prevent vertical transmission from mother to child.

The important role played by the family in child development may also influence the risk of HIV infection. A study carried out in the United States of America found, for example, that homosexual men who perceived a lack of family support were more likely to engage in risky behaviours (Kimberly and Serovich, 1999). Factors such as family structure and socio-economic status and their link to children's risky sexual behaviour (Miller and others, 2002), drug use (Denton and Kampfe, 1994), and other risk behaviours (Blum and others, 2000) have been well studied.

There are also interrelationships between the role of families in prevention and the impact of HIV on the family. There is some evidence from studies conducted in sub-Saharan Africa suggesting that children orphaned as a result of AIDS may be especially vulnerable to HIV infection (Cluver and Operario, 2008). The findings are stronger for girl orphans than for boy orphans and are typically associated with early sexual debut and other risk behaviours (Richter and others, 2009). Efforts to strengthen the capacity of families to deal with the impact of HIV and efforts to help families prevent HIV infection may well involve the same families.

The family environment plays an important role in determining the risks and consequences of HIV and AIDS. Therefore, it is important to examine the way in which family policy influences the situation of affected families. This requires an understanding of how families operate—and particularly the role men play in families—in the context of HIV and AIDS. It is not simply that men are the earners and women take care of the home; such a simplistic view can lead to inappropriate policy recommendations. It is necessary, therefore, to carefully examine both what we know and what we don't know about what role men play in families affected by HIV and AIDS.

## Involvement of men in families affected by HIV and AIDS

Research on HIV and the family can be divided into two broad groups of studies: those that examine the impact of HIV and AIDS on families and those that examine ways in which families have responded to the experience of HIV and AIDS. The distinction between "impact" and "response" may at first appear somewhat artificial. Part of the difference in emphasis derives from the type of data used (qualitative or quantitative) and from disciplinary perspectives (economics/demography or psychology/sociology). It also reflects the way in which the focus of research on HIV and the family has changed as effective HIV treatments have become available and accessible in high-income countries and, more recently, around the world. Bor and Elford (1994) edited one of the first books to address HIV and families. Several of the book's chapters focused on HIV- and AIDS-affected families in Africa and Asia, but the emphasis tended to be on the impact of the disease, as the contexts described were not ones in which the prevention of mother-to-child transmission (PMTCT) or antiretroviral treatment (ART) were widely available within the public-health sector. More generally, the earlier studies concentrated on the effects of adult illness and death on families (focusing, for example, on the changing composition and dissolution of households, economic vulnerability, and orphanhood and widowhood), while research conducted more recently is increasingly exploring the experiences of HIV-infected individuals and their families (focusing, for instance, on health and well-being, employment and family relationships).

To answer the question, What role do men play in HIV and AIDS-affected families? requires a more general understanding of their involvement in the contemporary lives of families and children across different regions. Only then can other, related questions be asked: Does the involvement of men in families change in response to the short- and long-term effects of HIV? If so, how? Is their level of involvement increased (for example, through the provision of more financial support or the assumption of personal care for children or sick adults) or decreased (perhaps because of growing union instability)? Some of these questions are addressed elsewhere in the present publication. Two chapters provide an overview of men's involvement in families: chapter I examines the issues of men in the lives of women and children, and chapter II examines several aspects of fatherhood. As noted in these chapters, and in a number of commentaries, research on men's involvement in Western families has advanced considerably in the last two decades, while progress has been less pronounced in Africa and Asia. Major research constraints derive from theoretical and conceptual limitations in relation to fatherhood and father involvement in these contexts (which have been well described) and the fact that data on men's roles in families generally are limited and data relating specifically to families affected by HIV and AIDS are extremely rare (Hosegood and Madhavan, 2010; Sherr, 2010).

Most families throughout the world include men. However, in families arrangements in which men live, and the roles that they play, are diverse and complex. For men in affected families, the experience of HIV infection, AIDS and HIV treatment of family members and/or of themselves has many possible consequences for how men live and what roles they are called upon, are able or choose to play. Given that the dominant routes of HIV transmission are sexual and vertical, in severely affected groups or communities, several members of the family may be infected. Men living in affected families may experience many family changes resulting in new or multiple roles. HIV-infected men can be healthy or ill, may be receiving treatment, or may have lost partners or children to AIDS. Uninfected men may be at risk of contracting HIV from one or more infected sexual partners that may or may not be considered family members. Men, whether infected or uninfected, may have social, emotional and economic relationships with other HIV-infected members of their immediate or extended family. As all of this suggests, the simple dichotomy between infected and non-infected is problematic in relation to HIV, particularly when considering family responses over time.

Very few published studies have specifically documented men's involvement in HIV-affected families. The most detailed information about the men's roles in such families are available from studies that have examined the experience of HIV-infected homosexual men, their male partners and male friends in relation to physical, emotional and material care and support. Although many different roles have been documented for men in families, the understanding of men's roles in affected families in Africa and Asia is narrowly circumscribed in HIV and family studies, which focus almost exclusively on roles of economic provider. This is in marked contrast to the large number of studies describing the multiple roles that female family members and children play in affected households. Some authors do not specify whether they are referring to males or females when they describe family members or caregivers, though, in most cases, the general tenor of the study suggests that the terms are used in reference to women within families.

Provided below is an examination of how the experience of HIV and AIDS in families influences the roles men play in those families. Both commonly performed and new or modified roles are considered. Also explored are some of the specific ways in which families respond to ill health and the death of HIV-infected men.

## Men's roles as partners

The gendered context of cultures and societies means that the roles of men who are partners of HIV-infected women may differ from those of women who are partners of HIV-infected men. Many studies report that among heterosexual married couples, particularly in Africa and Asia, wives are more likely than husbands to be the primary carer for an infected spouse. This assumption bears further scrutiny, however, as the term "carer" or "caregiver" encompasses a broad range of meanings, with apparent disparities largely influenced by gender norms. Most studies do not define or specify the roles associated with primary caregiving; but in the context of severe illness, there seems to be a tendency to associate the provision of care with intimate activities such as washing and feeding. The influence of cultural gender norms, particularly in more traditional societies, will lead to the predominance of women in these types of care activities. Societal norms notwithstanding, there are some males who assume primary, or at least substantial, responsibility for various aspects of care and support for their female partners, whether by attending to daily needs or by ensuring that health-care needs, such as transport, medicines and health care, itself are met. However, because of prevailing social attitudes, men who perform such intimate care roles for their female partners, or indeed for other HIV-infected members of the family, may be reluctant to report this to researchers (Montgomery and others, 2005). Given that economic, social and legal conditions tend to be more favourable for men than for women in many societies, heterosexual male partners of HIV-infected women may generally be in a better position than female partners of HIV-infected men to meet many of the care needs, which can include covering food and living expenses, providing transport, and accessing health and social services, grants and employment benefits.

Gender norms also influence the psychosocial experiences of HIV-infected men, and these have implications for the roles they play in families and for the responses of their partners. Studies have reported gender differentials with regard to stigma, disclosure, depression, health-seeking behaviours, and health-care access and provision. For example, the pattern and timing of disclosure following diagnosis differ between women and men, with the latter more likely to inform their partners of their HIV-positive status (Skogmar and others, 2006). The family environment also influences the experiences and roles of men and women and their partners with regard to HIV infection and treatment. In a recent study, Fitzgerald, Collumbien and Hosegood (2010) examined the experiences of men and women participating in an ART programme in a rural area of KwaZulu-Natal, South Africa, highlighting a number of family-related factors that characterize the experience of men undergoing treatment.

Gender-based differences in the challenges faced by men and women following the death of a partner from AIDS have not been conclusively identified or defined. A study by Sikkema and others (2000) examined the coping strategies and emotional well-being of 199 HIV-infected men and women who were participating in AIDS services in Milwaukee, Wisconsin, and had experienced AIDS-related bereavement. High levels and serious experiences of bereavement were reported but did not appear to differ on the basis of gender or age. It should be noted, however, that the study did not explicitly examine parenting roles or differentials in coping strategies between parents caring for young children and other participants.

## Men and their absence in the literature on the care of children in families affected by HIV and AIDS

Prior to exploring some of the ways men can be involved in the care of children, it might be beneficial to consider the extent to which the absence of men from the literature on HIV and families reflects the reality in affected families. There are several reasons for the "absence" of men from accounts of families and HIV with respect to the care of young children. One reason is that researchers seeking to understand and describe men's involvement in families, particularly in their role as fathers, face a number of difficulties in measuring and documenting such involvement. One of the key issues is how to avoid the narrow conceptualization and evaluation of men's roles within the framework of a "maternal template" of parenting roles and activities. When considered in such a context, men are likely to be viewed as deficient in that they are less involved in specific activities typically performed by women, including the physical care and feeding of young children. Notwithstanding the lack of studies with direct reference to HIV and AIDS, a growing body of scholarship has documented the diverse roles that men, in particular biological fathers, perform in relation to children and families in different social and cultural contexts (Day and Lamb, eds., 2004; Townsend, 2002). There is increasing recognition that the involvement of men, especially fathers, directly and indirectly influences a wide range of outcomes for children in areas such as development, adjustment and education (Tamis-LeMonda and Cabrera, eds., 2002).

Another factor contributing to the relative absence of men in literature on HIV and families is the emphasis placed on the size and importance of the contributions made by women in the care of children in affected households. It is often asserted in policy statements and publications that women play the most important role in affected families—a view reinforced by the general belief that women provide essential care and support on a consistent basis and tend to take on "more" roles and responsibilities than men do within the family (Joseph and Bhatti, 2004). These portrayals of women by researchers and policymakers as the bulwark for affected families can combine with strong social norms related to childcare to create a situation in which studies are unlikely to seek to document men's involvement in the care of children.

The exclusion of men from the dialogue centred around care and support is also the product of perceptions linked to common descriptors; for example, women are often referred to as "innocent" or as "victims" of a problem created by men's aberrant sexual behaviour. Men tend to be seen as part of the problem or risk rather than part of the response. Slogans such as "HIV wears a woman's face" promulgated by well-known public figures such as former UNAIDS Special Envoy Stephen Lewis have been widely disseminated through the media. Most of the attention given to men in the context of HIV and AIDS has focused on changing their behaviour with respect to sex, condom use, testing, or treatment adherence; very little has been done to promote or support caregiving behaviour among men in families.

In a 2005 study, Montgomery and others examined the extent to which men's involvement was described in transcripts from a two-and-a-half-year ethnographic study of households affected by HIV and AIDS in rural KwaZulu-Natal, South Africa. Re-examining the interview transcripts, researchers identified the fact that men had been observed participating in caretaking, feeding, cooking and washing, making themselves available to children through continuous physical presence or visits, and taking responsibility for children by, for example, providing financial support and facilitating access to health care and schooling. However, these types of involvement by men were rarely directly reported in response to questions about the care of children. The authors identified several possible reasons for this. Women were much more likely than men to be interviewed, and female respondents, when asked about men's involvement, tended to focus on issues of financial support. Furthermore, female interviewers aware of Zulu cultural gender norms assumed that women would be the active caregivers for young children and seldom asked men about their involvement. Those men who were engaged in the direct personal care and support of young children tended to be the victims of extreme circumstances and to live in relative isolation—compelled to reside alone with their children following the death of a female partner, for example. Such men appeared to have been deterred from openly reporting their involvement in what were perceived, in that rural context, to be female roles.

A third feature of the research and policy environment has been the dominance of particular types of families in HIV impact studies, particularly in Africa. Intentionally or unintentionally, researchers conducting HIV/AIDS studies have tended to concentrate on families in which men are less central, including female- or child-headed households. Denis and Ntsimane (2006), considering the reasons why fathers were not featured in stories of 33 families affected by HIV/AIDS in KwaZulu-Natal, observed that in all of the accounts, the families were identified as female-headed. No fathers were interviewed, and grandfathers were interviewed only where the children's mothers or grandmothers were deceased or unavailable. Furthermore, although 38 per cent of the fathers in these families were dead, information was tabulated on their failure to contribute to the support of their children.

Research and policy attention relating to men's involvement in affected households has focused on two broad themes: the parenting experiences of HIV-infected fathers and the consequences for children of paternal deaths. The emphasis on paternal orphaning rather than on men's involvement with affected children was particularly dominant in research on Africa prior to public access to HIV treatment. The present authors identified no literature describing the roles of men in caring for children in affected households more generally, leaving open such questions as, what role do men other than biological fathers (including stepfathers, older brothers, and grandfathers) play in the care of children in affected households? Do role strain and stress affect the parenting roles of non-infected adults in affected families?

In spite of the research limitations, a picture is beginning to emerge—from studies open to acknowledging possibilities extending beyond preconceived notions—of the various roles men can and do play in relation to children. Particularly important is the role of men as fathers in the context of HIV and AIDS. Provided directly below is an examination of some of the critical issues relating to men as potential fathers, men as fathers of young children, men as fathers of adult children, the benefits of fatherhood, and homosexual men as fathers.

## Men as potential fathers in the context of HIV and AIDS

One area that is becoming increasingly important is HIV-infected fathers and the care of children. The advent of available and effective HIV treatment has resulted in gains in life expectancy and improvements in the quality of life for HIV-infected people. A growing number of young HIV-infected individuals will seek to balance complex concerns relating to health, the future and social attitudes with the desires and expectations they, their partners, and the wider family have with regard to childbearing and family building (Cooper and others, 2007). Advances in medical techniques and understanding have reduced the risk of HIV transmission between inseminated and inseminating partners and between mothers and children. The consequence is likely to be an increase internationally in the proportion of HIV-infected people who have children after diagnosis. In this context, the importance of understanding and supporting the fertility choices of young HIV-infected people and their partners is being increasingly recognized in all affected groups and populations and within the health-care sector (Delvaux and Nostlinger, 2007; Myer and others, 2010; Myer, Morroni and Rebe, 2007; Paiva and others, 2007; van Leeuwen and others, 2007). While ART and fertility treatments have reduced the risk of HIV transmission from infected men to their partners, the desire of these men for, and the possibility of, fatherhood may be challenged by their own attitudes and by perceived social attitudes towards fathering by HIV-infected men. Sherr and Barry (2004) interviewed 32 HIV-infected heterosexual men attending an HIV clinic in London. Thirty-eight per cent of the men had become fathers prior to HIV diagnosis. Although 81 per cent of those interviewed expressed very positive views about the importance of fatherhood, nearly half believed they would experience discrimination if they became fathers in the future. A similar study featuring 84 gay fathers showed that issues of current or future fathering were discussed only rarely with clinic staff (Sherr and Talia, 2003). Sherr and Barry (2004) noted that the needs of the heterosexual HIV-infected men who were already fathers might require attention by health and social services, though they did not specify the types of support required. In Africa and Asia, the relatively recent roll-out of effective treatment options means that for men receiving antiretroviral drugs and therapy, research and programmes focusing on their parenting and fathering roles have been limited.

Obviously, many men are already fathers by the time they are diagnosed. The involvement of a father will depend on many factors, including the children's ages and needs, the characteristics and circumstances of the father, residential arrangements, the father's relationship with the mother, and the wider family and social contexts (including conflict and custody issues). It is essential that these factors be understood if policies are to support male involvement with children.

## Men as fathers in the context of HIV and AIDS

Fatherhood is a key part of the male adult identity throughout the world (Hobson, 2002). The meaning and types of father involvement have been the subject of considerable scholarship during the past two decades (Lamb, 2000; Tamis-LeMonda and Cabrera, eds., 2002). The bulk of the research has focused on fathers and families in the United States and other Western societies, though there have been efforts to engage in similar scholarship in Africa, Asia and Latin America (Barker and Verani, 2008; Morrell, 2006). The most widely utilized framework for studying father involvement was proposed by Lamb, Pleck, Charnov and Levine in 1985 (Lamb and others, 1987). Within this framework, father involvement is conceptualized as including three components: (a) paternal engagement (direct personal interaction with the child in the form of caretaking, play, teaching or leisure activity); (b) accessibility or availability to the child (positioning that allows the child to engage with the father if desired or necessary); and (c) responsibility for the care of the child (making plans and arrangements for care as distinct from the performance of care activities).

Qualitative and quantitative research has encompassed a detailed examination of father involvement with young children in a range of different family circumstances, types and social contexts, focusing on low-income and immigrant families, non-residential fathers, gay fathers, and other traditional and non-traditional arrangements. However, the same detailed data are not available for father involvement in families affected by HIV and AIDS (Hosegood and Madhavan, 2010; Sherr and Barry, 2004; Sherr and Talia, 2003).

A frequently cited Canadian study examined the parenting challenges of HIV-infected parents, including 28 fathers (Antle and others, 2001). The research identified key themes for affected families influenced by the context of sorrow, joy, guilt, stress and disclosure in which HIV-infected parents were raising their children. These themes included family life as "precious time", ill health and resource constraints affecting parenting, preparing children for bereavement, and future planning. Fathers were quoted as expressing concern about their ability to cope with family responsibilities and fathering in the future should their female partners die. HIV-infected mothers also appeared to be extremely anxious about the future and whether the child's father, their male partners, or other men would assume parenting responsibilities and guardianship. However, the study did not explicitly describe the roles that HIV-infected fathers played in the lives of their children, nor did it examine how HIV/AIDS altered the types, level and quality of involvement by fathers in families generally, and specifically in the care of children.

Knowledge of father involvement and the consequences for children in affected families is particularly constrained in sub-Saharan Africa, where family studies and household surveys provide very little detailed data on fathers (Hosegood and Madhavan, 2010;). Few researchers have collected longitudinal family data or examined the nature of fathers' involvement with respect to crucial dimensions of the father-child relationship (including the amount of time spent together, the quality of interaction, and levels and types of communication); nor have studies investigated the impact of this relationship over a longer time period, including that extending beyond father-child involvement. Studies of fathers and affected children in Africa have largely examined the association between fathers' co-residence and the outcomes associated with HIV incidence in adolescents, particularly in the areas of school enrolment, early sexual debut, marriage and pregnancy (Birdthistle and others, 2008; Case, Paxson and Ableidinger, 2004; McGrath and others, 2008; Timaeus and Boler, 2007). These and other child outcomes are also considered in a recent paper by Sherr (2010) on fathers and

HIV/AIDS, which reviews the evidence from 17 international studies whose aims were to describe the effects of a father's death from AIDS on a range of outcomes relating to sexual behaviour, education, child mortality and mobility, living in institutions, nutritional status, and kinship care. While the findings are somewhat mixed, particularly with respect to the timing of paternal orphaning and the sex of the offspring, the evidence overall suggests a protective effect of the presence of fathers in child outcomes.

For a number of reasons, many children affected by HIV and AIDS do not live in the same households as their fathers. Residential separation of biological fathers and children is common throughout the world, reflecting contemporary social patterns rather than the impact of HIV. Increasing rates of extramarital fertility, divorce and separation in high- and middle-income societies mean that many children grow up living in households separate from their biological fathers, and a significant number live with men other than their biological fathers who may or may not be involved in their parenting. HIV/AIDS may be a factor in that it tends to increase the risk of relationship instability. Studies have shown that for discordant couples, relationship dissolution is particularly prevalent (VanDevanter and others, 1999). Stressors on couples where HIV-infected partners have other medical conditions (such as haemophilia) or are drug users may also influence the duration of relationships (Tangmunkongvorakul and others, 1999). In the severely affected Southern Africa region, labour migration and low rates of marriage mean that the majority of fathers will be not be co-resident with their children for some or all of their childhood (Hosegood and others, 2008; Posel and Devey, 2006).

While non-resident fathers are typically less available to participate in the physical care of children, residential separation does not necessarily indicate a lack of involvement in other dimensions of care and support. The quality, levels and types of roles that fathers play in relation to their children are influenced by multiple factors, including the reasons for father-child separation, the quality of the father-mother relationship, and the amount of time spent with the child or children (Lamb, 2002). Madhavan and Townsend (2007) and Madhavan, Townsend and Garey (2008) found that financial contributions by resident and non-resident fathers in rural South Africa were similar. Unfortunately, many of the sources of data used in empirical studies of HIV-affected families in Africa do not provide a clear distinction between the types of circumstances in which fathers do not reside with their children. In a recent review article, Hosegood and Madhavan (2010) examine the availability of data on men's involvement in families in sub-Saharan Africa for informing family-centred programmes for children affected by HIV and AIDS. The authors note that while the survival status of parents is often recorded, very little information is available about the characteristics or involvement of non-resident fathers whose children have experienced the death of their mothers or who live in households otherwise affected by HIV and AIDS. In situations where labour migration is common, non-resident fathers may be more able than resident fathers to meet social obligations and play the family roles expected of them, particularly with regard to their children.

Illness and death of mothers may affect the level and type of involvement fathers have in the care of their children. The high rate of maternal orphanhood in countries with generalized HIV epidemics means that many surviving fathers are caring for children under extremely difficult circumstances. These fathers often lose the benefits of sharing care with a second parent, experience the poor emotional well-being associated with bereavement, and suffer a decline in their financial status owing to the mother's illness and death; some, moreover, may recently have become aware of their own HIV-positive status. The psychological challenges for men of coping with the ill-health and death of their partners can be severe, particularly when they themselves are infected with HIV. Grief and distress associated with AIDS-related loss have been shown to increase the risk of depression and reliance on maladaptive coping mechanisms (Sikkema and others, 2000). Most studies examining the effects of bereavement on male partners have focused on post-bereavement consequences relating to their mental and physical health and substance abuse. For those grieving partners who are also fathers, the psychological burdens of coping with profound loss can affect the level and quality of paternal involvement.

Comparative studies of household survey data from different African regions suggest wide variations in the patterns of fathers' co-residence with their children following maternal death. In a study comparing longitudinal demographic data from three African populations, Hosegood and others (2007) found that the proportion of maternal orphans living with their fathers in rural Malawi (68 per cent) was almost twice that in rural South Africa (38 per cent). The co-residence of fathers and maternal orphans is strongly reflective of the different residential arrangements of children and parents common in these populations. A much lower proportion of non-orphaned children co-reside with parents in South Africa than in other countries in the region (Hill, Hosegood and Newell, 2008; Monasch and Boerma, 2004). While data on household composition are readily available, the influence of maternal death on fathers' role in the care of children in relation to more than just the simple fact of co-residence is very poorly described in Africa and Asia.

In the context of HIV and AIDS it is necessary to focus not only on the role of fathers in affected families, but also on families more generally. As noted previously, HIV is a family disease in part because the family has a role in determining the risk of infection of its members. Fathers play an important role in providing information and in shaping their children's attitudes and behaviours. A number of researchers interested in identifying family predictors of HIV risk behaviours in adolescents have conducted studies examining the convergence/divergence in parent-child knowledge, attitudes and behaviours related to HIV risk, prevention, stigma and treatment. In this context, as in others, the findings generally indicate that children learn from observing and interacting with their parents and other family members. A study investigating the extent to which fathers influence high-risk sexual behaviour among African-American male adolescents found that greater communication between fathers and sons about HIV and sexual behaviour and fathers' belief in their sons' ability to practice abstinence or safe sex were associated with lower rates of high-risk sexual behaviour among sons (Glenn, Demi and Kimble, 2008).

## Fatherhood and adult children

The focus has thus far been on the roles of men as fathers of young children. The relationship men have with their offspring can be lifelong, however, and many fathers continue to be an important source of emotional and material support for their adult children and their families. The discourse on parents and adult children in relation to HIV and AIDS has largely centred around parental responses to HIV disclosure by grown children and parental involvement in the care and support of HIV-infected adult children and affected grandchildren. Many mothers have a strong relationship with their adult children and are actively involved in their lives; indeed, the importance of the maternal role beyond childhood and adolescence is widely acknowledged and has been the focus of considerable attention in research and programmes. Much less is known about the support provided by fathers and grandfathers. It is therefore difficult to assess whether men play a less important role than mothers do in caring for their adult children and grandchildren, or whether their contributions have been significant but largely unrecognized and overlooked. Certainly the lack of interest in exploring older fathers' roles is at odds with the importance attached to older men in the functioning of families in more traditional societies and the growing evidence of increased involvement among older parents in the lives of adult children in Europe and the United States (Clarke, Cooksey and Verropoulou, 1998).

In Africa, social and cultural norms reflect a strong emphasis on the relationship between adult men and their fathers—a relationship characterized by continued acknowledgement of the authority of male elders, respect for parents, and well-defined paternal and filial duties and obligations (Mkhize, 2006; Morrell, 2006; Townsend, 2002). In a study of stigma and support in an ARV programme in rural South Africa, the quality of the relationship between HIV-infected men and their fathers was a strong theme in the men's descriptions of their treatment experience (Fitzgerald, Collumbian and Hosegood, 2010). In some cases, the fathers were deceased or no longer in regular contact with their sons; however, where relationships were maintained, fathers played positive and negative roles in the lives of their adult children. Some older fathers offered material and practical support, which might include providing a son and his immediate dependants with financial assistance, housing and transport. In certain situations, particularly where the men's fathers were heavy alcohol users, this physical support was not provided within an emotionally supportive context. In other cases, fathers maintained contact but extended no support. The men were highly conscious of and sensitive to their fathers' opinions of them; several reported experiencing distress when their fathers openly criticized their past behaviour and their reduced ability to provide for their families. The sons bore their own and their fathers' disappointment that expectations were not being met and felt responsible for the shared sense of frustration over the reversal of care and support roles. Interviews with HIV-infected women from the same programme did not reflect the same sense of anxiety about the responses of fathers, likely owing to differences in the nature of father-son and father-daughter relationships in this population. Many women actually reported having received positive emotional and physical support from their fathers. In ARV programmes in resource-constrained areas, support for fathers of adult HIV-positive children has not been a major focus; where available, counselling support for carers and bereaved family members have generally targeted partners and children rather than parents.

In relationships between children and their fathers, care is most often thought of as being provided by the latter. However, care roles can be reversed in families that include HIV-infected fathers in poor health, with children providing physical, emotional and even financial support (Skovdal and others, 2009). This reversal is often noted in the literature, but it is rarely straightforward or absolute. Caregiving is frequently bidirectional; HIV-infected men may continue to provide certain aspects of care, remaining available for their children and ensuring that they have access to food and schooling, even when the fathers themselves require assistance from their children with regard to daily activities, including maintaining personal hygiene and cooking.

## The benefits of fatherhood in the context of HIV and AIDS

Fatherhood can have an impact on men's health. Men involved in affected families as fathers are likely to experience considerable stress as they struggle to fulfil paternal roles while also responding to the challenges of HIV/AIDS. The difficulties in dealing with the dual burdens of parenting and coping with serious illness are widely acknowledged and produce support for women but have largely gone unrecognized for men. Much is written about the impact fathers have on maternal and child health, but the impact of fatherhood on the physical and mental health of men is understudied and largely unknown (Garfield, Clark-Kauffman and Davis, 2006). This gap is cause for concern, as there is evidence to suggest that bidirectional associations exist between fathers and children and between fathers and mothers in terms of health.

Being a father can have a positive impact on a man. Men frequently report that fathering is "good for them", and the evidence generally supports this assertion (Levine and Pitt, 1995; Richter, 2006). Physical and emotional benefits can include increased levels of fitness, happiness, contentment and self-esteem (Henwood and Procter, 2003; Umberson, 1989). Fatherhood may improve men's health in that it tends to be linked to reductions in risk-taking behaviour (such as smoking and alcohol consumption) and to the adoption of certain positive behaviours (including a healthier diet and exercise) (Umberson, 1987; 1989).

Fatherhood is linked to a number of negative possibilities as well. Many men experience anxiety when faced with the assumption of new responsibilities (McLanahan and Adams, 1987; 1989). Paternal depression before and after the birth of a child has begun to receive wider attention as evidence has emerged from prospective studies carried out over the past several years (Ramchandani and others, 2005). Having children can also lead to changes in a couple's relationship. Conflicts within relationships, particularly those resulting in divorce or separation and the separation of fathers from their children, are known to have a significant adverse impact on men's health (Booth and Amato, 1991; Gove, 1973). Illness and mortality among children can increase parental stress, contribute to divorce, and lead to unemployment, which can also negatively affect parental health (Reichman, Corman and Noonan, 2004).

## HIV-infected men who have sex with men and their roles as fathers

Many men who have sex with men (MSM) play a fathering role, regardless of their biological relationship with their children. In the *2000 United States Census,* one third of female same-sex-couple households and more than one fifth of male same-sex-couple households reported at least one child under age 18 living in the home (American Psychological Association, 2004).

The extensiveness of social science research on the long-term experiences of HIV-infected men who have sex with men means that information is available (if somewhat limited) on fatherhood and fathering among gay and bisexual males. MSM may become biological or social fathers through their involvement in heterosexual relationships, artificial insemination or sperm donation, adoption or fostering, or various other means—including parenting arrangements with women (Sherr, 2010). While fatherhood and fathering are similar in many respects for heterosexual and gay men, the latter face unique challenges linked to heterosexism, homophobia and other negative attitudes towards non-normative family forms (Tasker, 2005). For a number of reasons—embarrassment, discomfort, underlying attitudes or even a lack of awareness—the issue of fatherhood and fathering is often not raised by health professionals, or indeed by the men themselves, in the provision of health services for gay HIV-infected men.

Not much is known about the role HIV-infected gay men play as fathers because HIV/AIDS research relating to MSM tends to include little or no information about family relationships or involvement with partners or children; the same is true for research on male injecting drug users (IDUs). Instead, attention is generally focused on family responses and support for HIV-infected MSM and IDUs. The discrimination experienced by HIV-infected men in these groups is well documented, with the stigma attached to HIV layered upon a pre-existing bias against homosexuals and drug users (Solomon and others, 2010). The social marginalization of MSM and IDUs is mirrored in the scarcity of literature relating to the family environment in general—and specifically to the roles these men play as partners and fathers—in HIV- and AIDS-affected families (Makusha and Richter, 2010). Although the role played by MSM in providing social support for HIV-infected MSM is well documented, very few studies explore the role of MSM and male IDUs in extending support to immediate family members affected by HIV/AIDS (Fisher and others, 1993).

## Men in high-risk groups as members of affected families

### Men who have sex with men as members of affected families

Large numbers of MSM live with their families of origin or are part of another type of family unit or network. In one study of 502 MSM recruited from community and clinic sources in London, only 36 per cent indicated that they lived alone (Hart and others, 1994); approximately 60 per cent resided with a male or female partner or with parents. Domestic family arrangements vary widely, ranging from men living with male partners in openly gay relationships to men living with their wives or female partners while openly or secretly maintaining homosexual relationships outside the home. The diversity of the families in which MSM live derives in part from the risks and social pressures linked to the acceptance and legality of homosexuality but is also a reflection of more general variations in family forms and functioning in different regions and communities.

Extensive research has been carried out on the critical role MSM play in the care and support of HIV-infected MSM (Munro and Edwards, 2009). In a 1994 study by Hart and others, 17 per cent of the men interviewed had had a close friend, partner or former partner who had died of AIDS, and three quarters of these men had provided some form of care for them. In a study conducted in 1988-1989, 125 informal carers for HIV-infected gay men attending genito-urinary medicine and immunology clinics in London were interviewed about their care experiences (McCann and Wadsworth, 1992). Among the carers, 42 per cent were partners and 45 per cent were close friends; the majority (77 per cent) were male. It should be noted that many MSM involved in caregiving are also infected with HIV, which adds to the physical, emotional and financial strain of providing informal care—particularly when the carers themselves require support.

For gay HIV-infected men, knowledge of and attitudes to both sexual orientation and HIV status are important in determining the responses of parents and the level and quality of emotional and material support they provide. Several studies conducted in the United States have explored these issues. An early national survey of parents and of adult gay and lesbian children who had recently disclosed their sexual orientation found similar attitudes towards AIDS among men and women (Robinson, Walters and Skeen, 1989). In a study of HIV-infected MSM, Fisher and others (1993) found that fathers were less likely than mothers to be aware of a son's sexual orientation. A more recent study of HIV-infected MSM found that mothers and siblings provided a significantly higher level of support than did fathers; their positive involvement was nonetheless important, given that families tended to be a key source of emotional and material support (Kadushin, 1999).

## Male injecting drug users as members of affected families

The nature of family relationships constitutes part of the risk environment that influences drug use, HIV infection risk, access to medical care, and the uptake of harm-reduction strategies (Rhodes, 2009). While this general fact is widely acknowledged, the status and involvement of men who abuse drugs as family members, and especially as fathers, are often overlooked in research and service delivery (McMahon and others, 2005). Many studies on drug use and other risk behaviours make little or no mention of men's family arrangements and involvement. It has been determined, however, that the original and immediate families of men using drugs can be negatively affected by the stigma attached to drug addiction, the economic disadvantages linked to poorer partnering, and other detrimental partnering patterns and behaviour. Studies comparing opioid-dependent fathers with other fathers have shown significant differences in economic resources to support family formation, the quality of parental bonding, patterns of procreation, and parenting behaviour (McMahon, Winkel and Rounsaville, 2008; McMahon and others, 2007). While relevant studies tend to highlight the threats posed to children, partners and other family members by drug use among men, there is growing recognition of the possibility that these men may be able to maintain positive family relationships and involvement under certain circumstances. Research progress in this area is limited, however, by the fact that very little is known about the role fatherhood plays in the lives of drug-using fathers, particularly with respect to psychological distress, drug-use behaviours, and treatment motivations (McMahon and others, 2005).

The continued expansion of the HIV epidemic among IDUs, especially in Eastern Europe, has given impetus to efforts to understand the social and physical contexts of injecting drug use. As with MSM, however, HIV and family research has primarily focused on understanding issues related to family support provided to HIV-infected

IDUs (see, for example, Risser and others, 2010); most studies have not explored the contribution of male IDUs to the care and support of parents, partners and others affected by HIV and AIDS within their family networks (Stowe and others, 1994). A small number of studies have investigated the father-child relationship within the context of HIV and AIDS and drug use among men. One recent study of 505 HIV-positive and HIV-negative drug-abusing fathers examined the effect of the fathers' drug addiction and HIV infection on adolescent children's psychological distress (Brook and others, 2008). The findings indicated that the children with HIV-infected drug-abusing fathers appeared to experience higher levels of psychological distress than did those with drug-abusing fathers who were HIV-negative.

Thus far, the main focus has been on the immediate family. However, the severity of the impact HIV has on family health and well-being often compels affected families to seek support from people outside this inner circle. These will most often be individuals related by kinship but they may also be friends or neighbours. To ensure that family policies make the best use of available resources, it is necessary to consider the role played by the extended family in the context of HIV and AIDS.

## HIV/AIDS and the extended family

For African and Asian families, kinship obligations are a prevailing feature and are central to family coping strategies. Men are often key figures in making decisions regarding financial and material support for kin, including the provision of money or food, permitting or encouraging other family members to offer assistance, or allowing affected relatives to become part of one's household. Fathers, brothers and uncles have a social obligation to extend support to needy relations both within and outside the immediate family. Men from the wider family may take specific steps to assist those who find it difficult to fulfil their responsibilities as fathers, husbands or heads of household in HIV-affected families. In situations in which brothers or sons become ill or die due to AIDS, male relatives will assume partial or full responsibility for raising their children and supporting their emotional, cognitive, educational and social development.

In severely affected communities in Africa, the sense of collective social responsibility for the family underlies a well-established tradition in which men other than biological fathers can play a fathering role. The phenomenon of extended family membership and support was well-established prior to the HIV epidemic (Mkhize, 2006). In some African cultures, the relationship with the maternal uncle is of particular social importance; he plays many important roles throughout a child's life, even negotiating for and contributing towards marriage (Townsend, 2002); not surprisingly, there are indications that children within such contexts tend to experience a high level of emotional closeness with maternal uncles. In other cultures, paternal grandfathers or uncles have the strongest social obligations towards children. "Social fathers"—individuals other than biological fathers who play fathering roles—constitute a well-established phenomenon in both Eastern and Western cultures.

This brief overview of the literature has highlighted how assumptions about men and their involvement with other family members have shaped the existing body of knowledge on the subject. The perception of men affects not only research, but also policy. The following section examines examples of the consequences of these perceptions on HIV and AIDS-related policies.

# The impact of perceptions on policy and practice

There is a wide range of community and State organizations that have emerged to support HIV- and AIDS-affected families. These vary by country in terms of their coverage, types of service provision, and target groups. The attitudes of these organizations towards the roles of men and women in families shape the ways in which they design and implement support activities and services. Where there are strong perceptions that men are not involved in the kind of care and support activities required by affected families, organizations are likely to engage only with women, thereby reinforcing perceptions about men's lack of involvement. For example, support groups for HIV-infected women typically include their children; however, men's groups are not set up to include their children.

In developing countries, family support organizations are primarily involved in activities relating to home-based assistance, the care of orphans and vulnerable children, and poverty alleviation, with most directing their efforts towards women and children. Certain groups may be actively targeted for specific purposes; in this regard, for example, organizations frequently focus on female economic empowerment through the development of craft, community garden, or micro-lending projects. On the other hand, this could be due to the fact that women form the largest group of volunteers; for example, the majority of volunteer caregivers for children and sick adults are women, especially in faith-based organizations.

Structuring services in such a way result in missed opportunities to help and strengthen families in crisis. Men may choose to become engaged with family support services if they are encouraged and given the chance to participate. Even when the opportunity is theoretically available to men, it is important to ensure that the attitudes of the staff involved in service delivery do not discourage men's involvement as service users or volunteers. If support staff do not acknowledge a man's role in caring for a child, or if the organization considers it odd that a man would volunteer to provide home-based care in his community, it is unlikely that he will take advantage of engagement opportunities.

Not involving men in family services can deprive others of benefit, but it can also leave the men themselves in a difficult situation, particularly if they are infected with HIV.

## Men's lack of access to HIV services

As access to ART has expanded, it has become apparent that the proportion of HIV-positive men in the total HIV-infected population is higher than the share of men in the total number of individuals receiving treatment. Analysis of data from a network of clinics providing highly active antiretroviral therapy (HAART) in 29 centres based in 13 countries in Africa, Asia and Latin America highlights this underrepresentation (see Braitstein and others, 2008). Of the 33,164 individuals included in the study, 60.3 per cent were female. In all but two centres, the proportion of women receiving treatment was similar to or higher than the UNAIDS estimate of the proportion of HIV infections among women in that area. Braitstein and others (2008) also conducted a systematic review of 21 published studies from Southern Africa and found that in all but 2, the ratio of women to men receiving treatment was greater than one.

One of the reasons frequently cited to explain the underrepresentation of men is that, in comparison with women, they tend to access treatment services when their disease is at a more advanced stage. Indeed, Braitstein and others (2008) found that men were more likely than women to have progressed to AIDS by the time they enrolled in treatment. The more advanced the disease when an individual begins treatment, the lower his or her chances of survival (Cornell and others, 2009). Enrolling at a more advanced stage of the disease means higher mortality rates among men, leaving treatment cohorts with a relatively high proportion of women. It is important to determine whether men are underrepresented among new clients and/or among those established on treatment. It is possible that men enrol in treatment in numbers corresponding to their representation in the HIV-positive population but are underrepresented in the treatment cohort because of the greater likelihood of their having died at an advanced stage of illness.

There is strong evidence supporting late enrolment and its negative impact on survival rates among men in treatment programmes. In the AMPATH ART programme in Kenya, men were seen to be at greater risk than women of being lost to follow-up because men tended to enter the programme at a more advanced stage of infection. Of the 8 per cent who never returned after their first visit, 65 per cent were men (Ocheieng-Ooko and others, 2010). A poorer survival rate may also explain, in part, why a study of four hospitals in northern Thailand found more women than men enrolled in treatment; the results (a male-female ratio of 1 to 1.4) were surprising given that more men than women in the region are infected with HIV (Le Coeur and others, 2009).

Underrepresentation in treatment cohorts is associated not only with high mortality rates, but also with underrepresentation at the time of enrolment. In one South African study, two thirds of the more than 2,000 newly recruited ART clients were women (Cornell and others, 2009). Similarly, in Burkina Faso, despite prevalence being similar between men and women, a recent study found more (by a factor of 2) women than men being enrolled in treatment (Bila and Egrot, 2009).

A number of factors may influence differential patterns of access to and enrolment in HIV treatment among men and women. It is often argued that men's health behaviours are shaped by the constructs of masculinity dominant in the community. The belief that men should be tough, and that using health services is a sign of weakness, is common in much of the world (Bila and Egrot, 2009; Braitstein and others, 2008; Jewkes and Morrell, 2010; Peacock and others, 2009; Remien and others, 2009). Another often mentioned reason is that men do not come into contact with health services as frequently as women do (Peacock and others, 2009; Braitstein and others, 2008). Women access the health system during pregnancy and when accessing services for their children. As a result, there are more opportunities to reach women with HIV testing programmes. This, in turn, leads to early identification of infection and enrolment in treatment programmes. For example, in the previously mentioned study in northern Thailand, women reported having been tested in connection with an event such as pregnancy or child death, while most of the men said they had been tested because they were not feeling well (Le Coeur and others, 2009). Another possible reason for delayed enrolment among men, identified in a study conducted in rural South Africa, is the perceived need to reduce alcohol consumption before initiating treatment. The male study respondents knew that alcohol use could interfere with treatment and felt they needed time to cut back; none of the women surveyed reported this as a concern (Fitzgerald, Collumbien and Hosegood, 2010).

The stigma associated with HIV and AIDS may affect men's access to and participation in testing and treatment in specific ways. In the Middle East, where ARV uptake is low among both sexes, research has highlighted stigma as a major constraint. In an examination by Remien and others (2009) of the problems faced by men in this context, the association of HIV and AIDS with MSM and the view that it is punishment from God is highlighted as particularly stigmatizing. The authors of a study in Burkina Faso (Bila and Egrot, 2009) indicated that men reported feeling shame when accessing HIV services; they noted that women also felt shame but overcame this obstacle in order to maintain good health for the sake of their children. Men in the study stressed that the sense of shame was linked to the stigma associated not only with HIV/AIDS itself but also with having to line up for services with women; some men would ask their wives to stand in line for them and call them when they reached the front. Similarly, in India it has been reported that men will travel away from their local communities to access treatment in order to avoid services typically associated with women (Sinha, Peters and Bollinger, 2009). Stigma may also derive from the portrayal of men as perpetrators and women as victims of the epidemic (Muula and others, 2007). This stigma may even shape policy. In Thailand, for example, treatment was first targeted at mothers, who were seen as victims of the epidemic, and not at men, who were seen as responsible for spreading the virus (Le Coeur and others, 2009).

Although men's underrepresentation in populations accessing treatment has been reported in a wide variety of settings, this finding is not universal. In the cross-country analysis conducted by Braitstein and others (2008), one of the two centres at which the proportion of men receiving treatment exceeded the proportion of HIV-positive men was in India. The Indian centre reported that only 20 per cent of their clients were women, while UNAIDS estimates indicate that women accounted for 38 per cent of the country's HIV-infected population at the time of the study. The authors suggest that such a finding may be due in part to the fact that clients at this site, unlike those at the other centres studied, were required to pay for treatment. Other studies have shown that HIV services offered in the India's private sector are more often accessed by men than by women (Joseph and others, 2010). Moreover, a review of studies on HIV testing in rural India suggests that women are often tested only after their husbands have tested positive (Sinha, Peters and Bollinger, 2009).

The attitudes of men to HIV, and health generally, contribute to different access and treatment experiences compared with women. However, the other major factor is men's lack of contact with health services. Men's lack of involvement in child and family health services is an important factor that exacerbates the challenges associated with health and help-seeking behaviours among men. It is easy to identify men's avoidance of health support as an extension of their attitudes. What is needed is to identify what changes are required in service delivery to promote greater participation among men.

## Policy implications

The problems and missed opportunities arising from the assumptions made about men's involvement in families have important implications for direct and indirect policies related to HIV and AIDS. Governments, civil society, United Nations organizations, and other interested parties must seek out ways to positively involve men. Within the realm of family services, Governments need to assess the effectiveness of current policies and implementation approaches, civil society must consider changing the way services are delivered, and United Nations organizations might re-examine policy advice. Action in these areas is unlikely unless the attitudes of men, women, service providers, policymakers, and researchers change in such a way as to recognize and promote positive roles of men in families.

### Involving men in family health services

Although family health services tend to concentrate primarily on child and reproductive health, the potential exists to reach all family members, including men. Family health services may be particularly well placed to promote preventative and screening services for men. In a cross-country analysis conducted by Braitstein and others (2008), men identified as HIV-positive through family clinics were less likely to have progressed to AIDS than those identified in other service settings. In the family clinics included in the study, 43 per cent of men enrolled for treatment had progressed to AIDS at the time they were enrolled, compared with 69 per cent in other types of clinics.

There are indications that including men in services aimed at preventing mother-to-child transmission (PMTCT) can contribute to the early identification and enrolment of HIV-positive men in treatment programmes. The participation of men may actually help increase the uptake of health services for both sexes. Concerns have been raised regarding women not testing because they fear blame and rejection by their partners (Gupta, 2004). Involving men by providing couples counselling and promoting mutual disclosure of HIV status can be an effective approach which can be offered alongside individual counselling and testing. Clearly, care must be taken to guarantee that appropriate counselling is offered to ensure that partner testing does not create problems. Interventions such as PMTCT-Plus established at the Mailman School of Public Health at Columbia University, New York City, have demonstrated that partners can and want to be involved in PMTCT services (Myer and others, 2005). Once involved, men can be part of the programme implementation by, for example, supporting the infant feeding choices made. Including men is such decisions needs to be approached carefully in order to manage conflict and to prevent existing inequalities from shaping the way feeding decisions are made (Tijou Traore and others, 2009).

Involving men in PMTCT interventions is one way to increase their contact with the health system. PMTCT programmes are implemented widely, have a specific HIV focus, and involve trained counsellors who can provide testing and refer adults for HIV treatment. Involving men in antenatal care, delivery, and child services may also increase men's engagement with the health system more generally. Measuring the effectiveness of these different types of services in promoting the health of men and their families is beyond the scope of this chapter. However, such assessments are undoubtedly needed. Furthermore, those involved in the delivery of health-care services can usefully question whether they contribute to the exclusion of men by approaching clients as individuals rather than as partners and members of a family. The emphasis here is on seeing the family as a whole, recognizing the importance for health of relationships that women and children have with men, and acknowledging men as part of families rather than as existing alongside them.

## Promoting positive change in men's attitudes towards family health

Promoting positive changes in men's attitudes towards their own health and that of their partners and children has been identified as an important factor in reducing the vulnerability of families to HIV and AIDS (Peacock and others, 2009). While men's behaviours are often the focus of health research and programmes concerning families' vulnerability, men's knowledge and attitudes towards health, risks, illness, healing and treatment also have an important influence on their own health-related behaviours. Men's attitudes towards HIV cannot be isolated from their broader understanding of health and well-being. While many men have positive attitudes towards protecting their own health and that of their families, others continue to place themselves and those close to them at risk of HIV infection, ill health and death.

It has been argued that in effecting changes in men's attitudes towards health there is a need to move beyond the instrumentalist approach, that is, seeing men only in terms

---

Box V.1
**Programme H: Brazil**

---

Programme H was developed in 1999 and was first implemented in low-income areas of Rio de Janeiro. The "H" stands for *homens*, which means "men" in Portuguese. The programme focuses on helping young heterosexual men living in deprived areas to examine and question traditional ideas of masculinity. Five major themes are addressed with the participants: sexuality and reproductive health, fatherhood and caregiving, moving from violence to peaceful coexistence, reasoning and emotions, and preventing and living with HIV and AIDS. The programme is activity-based and includes role playing, individual reflection and brainstorming. Sessions are conducted by adult men who can serve as role models for the younger participants. Implementation typically involves two-hour weekly sessions held over a six-month period.

In addition to working directly with young men, Programme H is engaged in social marketing campaigns. As the programme designers recognized early on, changing behaviour is difficult if attention is focused on individuals alone. Young men's attitudes and behaviour are influenced by many factors, and it is essential to create an environment conducive to positive change. Programme H uses posters, radio shows, dances and other media to promote its messages and to strengthen the perception that developing more positive attitudes towards gender relations is a worthy goal.

Evaluations suggest that Programme H has been successful in modifying attitudes and moderating risk-taking behaviour. Post-intervention participants express a relatively high level of support for more gender-equitable norms. Moreover, there are indications of higher rates of condom use and fewer reports of sexually transmitted infection symptoms among those who have been in the Programme.

**Source:** Barker and Verani (2008).

of how they can be involved in the protection of others (Peacock and others, 2009). In the 2001 Declaration of Commitment on HIV/AIDS,[1] no mention is made of the vulnerability of some men or of the need to address the lower rates of health-care access among men. Emphasis is placed on men's responsibilities towards others, with little said about the rights men have (ibid.). The Political Declaration on HIV/AIDS,[2] adopted without a vote by the General Assembly on 2 June 2006 at its High-level meeting on AIDS, is similarly framed (ibid.). Engaging with men solely in terms of how they can help others results in missed opportunities to respond to men's own concerns and health needs.

Behaviours such as violence, dominance, substance abuse, unprotected sexual intercourse and resistance to accessing health services pose risks to men's own health and that of their families. These behaviours are also associated with elevated risks of HIV infection and AIDS mortality (Peacock and Levack, 2004; Peacock and others, 2009). Several programmes have been developed with a view to engaging with men in order to reduce the risk of infection for themselves, their partners, and their families from HIV. Many of these interventions have been inspired by Program H and its success in Brazil (see box V.1) (Pulerwitz and Barker, 2008). The Yaari-Dosti is one such programme targeting young men in India (see box V.2).

Interventions to address male attitudes have also been included in programmes designed to involve both men and women. One example is the popular Stepping Stones intervention, first implemented in Uganda in 1995 and later exported to more than 40 countries (Jewkes and others, 2008). The aim of the programme is to prevent HIV infection by building more gender-equitable relationships. A cluster-randomized control trial was conducted comparing an adapted version of the Stepping Stones intervention with a control HIV prevention information intervention. The modified Stepping Stones intervention involved working with groups of young men and women separately and together. The participants ranged in age from 16 to 23 years. Outcomes related to sexual behaviour and the incidence of HIV and HSV-2 were assessed using baseline data and two rounds of follow-up at 12 and 24 months. The results suggested that the Stepping Stone intervention had no impact on HIV incidence but was associated with a reduction in HSV-2 incidence and violence against women (ibid.).

Male attitudes towards risk are shaped by a variety of factors. Some of these factors can be addressed by working directly with the individuals concerned. Other factors may

---

Box V.2
**The Yaari-Dosti programme: India**

The Yaari-Dosti programme in India targets young men in urban and rural settings, seeking to change gender attitudes and associated risk behaviours. Three major areas of focus within the programme are condom use, violence against partners, and communication with partners. In one evaluation, a baseline assessment suggested that only 10 per cent of participants could be considered to hold highly equitable gender attitudes. More than one third reported violence against a partner in the preceding three months. Poor attitudes towards gender equity were linked to risky behaviour at baseline. The intervention, involving workshops and education, led to a positive change in attitudes. Communication with partners increased, and reports of partner violence declined. The urban and rural men who participated in the intervention were, respectively, 1.9 and 2.8 times more likely than those in the control group to report using a condom.

**Source:**  Verma and others (2006).

be influenced by the social context. The pervasiveness of poverty, unemployment, crime and the general acceptability of violence may all play a role in shaping men's attitude towards risk. Peacock and Levack (2004) found that unemployment among men was linked to a higher probability of committing violence against women. Challenging prevailing gender norms may require action that involves the entire community, including local leaders and other community members. Interventions that seek to address the social context should be considered an essential part of HIV and AIDS mitigation efforts. The importance of structural prevention has long been recognized. Since male attitudes also have implications for treatment, care and support, there may be a need to think about structural interventions aimed at improving outcomes in these areas as well.

## Promoting attitude changes among service providers and policymakers

For family policies to be as effective as possible, attitudes and assumptions of a whole range of actors may need to be modified. Altering men's attitudes towards family members is crucial, but if service providers are not supportive of positive changes in men's roles and perspectives, there may be little impact. For example, if fathers who bring children to a clinic are always questioned as to why the child's mother has not brought them in and assumptions are made that he is not a primary caregiver for the child, fathers may become discouraged. Box V.3 highlights a programme in Chile that involves multiple stakeholders in exploring the role of men as fathers.

Family policies and programmes that are based on negative assumptions regarding the probability of male involvement are likely to play a role in supporting and fortifying such assumptions. Low expectations become self-reinforcing, and a negative cycle is established: policy and practice make no effort to involve men; thus men are not involved, which appears to validate the assumption that men do not want to be involved. Similarly, researchers who assume that men in a particular community do not fulfil certain roles and responsibilities within families will direct the focus of their

---

**Box V.3**
**Centro de Investigación y Desarrollo de la Educación: Chile**

Centro de Investigación y Desarrollo de la Educación (CIDE), a non-governmental organization in Chile, has developed and implemented a programme designed to address attitudes towards men as fathers. The intervention is built around group education sessions and involves both men and service providers in discussions about what role fathers should play. In order to encourage the engagement of participants, the curriculum incorporates activities that require them to reflect on their relationship with their own fathers. This reflection provides the starting point from which men and service providers can begin more general discussions on the role of fathers.

The programme was initially directed at men; however, with the involvement of non-governmental organizations staff and service providers, women tend to be in the majority. There are certain advantages associated with this outcome. Female service providers who have a very narrow view of fatherhood may discourage or prevent male involvement. Promoting reflection on, and discussion of, the role of fathers may encourage changes in thinking that would make it easier for men to be more involved.

**Source:** Barker and Verani (2008).

work towards families and away from men, with the consequence that their findings will confirm the "absence" of men in family life and may overlook positive deviance among particular groups of men or even large-scale behavioural and attitude changes by men and their communities. Taking a fresh look at assumptions about men can lead to greater recognition of the need to collect more informative data about men and affected families and to initiate discussions and creative intervention strategies that promote and support men's active involvement in safeguarding the health and well-being of their families.

Although the positive contributions men make within affected families should be documented and supported, it must also be acknowledged that there are deep-rooted problems—including gender inequalities, intimate-partner violence, and child sexual abuse—that reflect and reinforce men's perceptions of their role in the family. Programmes designed to support families need to continue to raise awareness about these issues and to take steps to address them. Compartmentalization should be avoided. Programmes and policies should seek to integrate efforts to promote men's support of affected families with HIV prevention and treatment efforts targeting men. Men and families live in complex risk environments and experience HIV and AIDS in many different ways (as parents, as partners, and as dependants or main income earners) at the same time and over time.

There is a need to recognize that marginalized groups of men (including IDUs, MSM and male sex workers) who are severely affected by HIV and AIDS are not isolated individuals but are members of families and the larger community. As fathers, children, partners, friends and relatives, they play various roles in shaping the lives of others. Programmes targeting support for marginalized groups can extend their reach, addressing family concerns, responsibilities, engagement and other key issues with all the men involved, whether they are clients or family members. The opportunities are there; policy-makers just need to be prepared to recognize them.

## Shifting decision-making power to those most affected

Many of the problems associated with responding to the needs of men and families affected by HIV/AIDS derive from the distance between those making and/or dictating policy and those most affected. HIV infection rates are highest in poor countries and in marginalized communities in wealthy countries; hence those most affected are rarely in a position to influence the response to the crisis. Poorer countries and their advocates may appeal to richer countries for resource and technical support, but such assistance is often tied to programme approaches dictated by the donors. Marginalized communities, even in wealthy countries, are among the least involved in policy decisions, although there are some important exceptions: While the homosexual community in the United States is marginalized in many ways, it has strongly influenced the response to the epidemic.

United Nations organizations, the United States President's Emergency Plan for Aid Relief (PEPFAR), the World Bank, the Global Fund to Fight Aids, Tuberculosis and Malaria, and many other entities involved in efforts to combat HIV/AIDS are committed to supporting affected families; however, they limit their direct involvement in shaping programmatic responses. Some organizations, including the Global Fund, direct their funding appeals to people with no direct experience of HIV and AIDS. Involving the members of affected communities in resource allocation decisions can help; but this is not enough, as tensions can still arise when the efforts to garner support and the efforts to design effective programmes are at cross-purposes. The advocacy necessary to secure donor support can lead to inappropriate or suboptimal policy design. One of the primary sources of this tension is the need to portray the recipients of support as deserving. For example, as the increases in HIV/AIDS funding demonstrate, raising money for HIV treatment appears to be far easier than raising money for HIV prevention. A reluctant donor may argue that becoming infected with HIV is an individual's fault, given the link with sexual and other risk behaviour, and that it is the responsibility of those engaged in such behaviour to change. It is more difficult to argue that individuals should die because they cannot afford life-saving medication. The depiction of the drug company as a villain makes efforts to drum up support for treatment even easier. Drug companies wanting to protect their profits at the expense of poor people's lives provide good material for powerful campaigns. While identifying the appropriate balance of investments in prevention and treatment is beyond the scope of this chapter, the point that effective advocacy may sometimes lead to inappropriate policy and programme design is very relevant.

Advocacy relating to men, families and HIV has arguably contributed to the development of suboptimal policies and programmes. It is not so much that the wrong steps have been taken, but that opportunities have been missed and stereotypes reinforced. A popular form of advocacy for national and international responses has entailed utilizing images of "innocent" women and "guilty, risk-taking" men and depictions of husbands "bringing" HIV infection home to their wives and of women bearing the burden of providing care and support for ill family members and children. One can make a case for including men in policy responses; but, typically, this seems to be done by outlining how the proposed beneficiaries are outside the norm: they are good men who want to help, unlike most men, who do not. At times it appears that in response to the success of campaigns designed to portray women as victims of risk-taking men, advocates for men often find it necessary to acknowledge the suffering of women before they make the case for supporting men. If men are to be helped, it seems there must first be an acknowledgement of guilt.

Basing policy responses for men on the notion that some or even all men are engaged in a particular behaviour is punitive and possibly counterproductive. In cases where policymakers want to support one group more than another—choosing, between investments in prevention and investment in the former, because they believe it to be more "deserving", for example—such value judgements should be subject to public debate. The simple ability to raise money more easily for one group than for another should not serve as the basis on which to engage or provide support.

Public debate and involving those affected in policy and programme development are necessary for effective policy design and implementation. Public debate must occur at the local and national levels, where policies are made; discussion in a distant country is likely to be of little benefit. Similarly, policy formation without public debate in affected countries may produce suboptimal results. Obviously, this point has broader implications, extending beyond men, families and HIV and AIDS; but the issue does highlight the importance of shifting the balance of power in policymaking towards those affected.

## Conclusions for social and family policy

Family policy has the potential to improve HIV prevention, treatment, and care and support outcomes. To do so in ways that are effective and sustainable requires that family policy support men's involvement in the family and family services more generally. If such policies target only affected families, opportunities will be missed.

Supporting greater male involvement in family services may have many benefits (for both male and female family members) that extend beyond mitigating the impact of HIV/AIDS. Policies aimed at strengthening families will help those that are unaffected by HIV to remain so and will enhance the capacity of affected families to deal with the attendant challenges. Policy effectiveness is likely to be limited if responses target families only when they are in crisis.

Identifying best practices and facilitating their implementation can be difficult. The types and levels of men's involvement in families varies widely, as do the individual, social, cultural and economic factors that influence men's involvement. This diversity needs to be considered in the design of policies that seek to promote men's involvement in families. When examining how family-based policies and programmes can be used to support men's engagement with families affected by HIV/AIDS, it is useful to review the policies and programmes that have promoted and supported paternal involvement in recent years in different regions and to assess experiences and consider the lessons learned. Fatherhood policy initiatives that have included programmes targeting marginalized fathers and fathers at risk of limited or negative involvement also offers insights into potentially effective interventions.

Programmatic initiatives directed at men and families affected by HIV/AIDS should not be limited to mitigating the impact of ill health and bereavement but should allow for different points of intervention. Some innovative programmes have sought to engage men as partners and fathers during antenatal and delivery periods, during which PMTCT and voluntary counselling and testing services are provided (Tijou Traoré and others, 2009). School-based programmes have also begun to direct more attention and resources towards engagement with male family members (Baptiste and others, 2006).

Although the design of family policy will need to be adapted to specific contexts, the goals will remain fairly consistent. Essentially, HIV and AIDS family policies relating to men should incorporate provisions for the following:

- Promoting and supporting men's positive engagement with and involvement in families.
- Improving and initiating efforts to increase men's engagement with health services targeted at addressing their own health concerns as well as those of their partners, children, and other family members.
- Fostering positive social and service sector attitudes towards the involvement of men in providing support and care (including intimate personal care) for children and other family members, as well as recognition of the full range of parenting and childcare roles and responsibilities that men assume.

Policymakers can work to achieve these goals in many different ways. For example, policies might focus on educating men in order to change their attitudes and attendant behaviour or on developing media campaigns to modify community attitudes. Other policies could be designed to increase men's involvement in social protection, though underlying assumptions would likely need to be examined first; in this instance, policymakers might question the commonly held belief that children will benefit from increased income only if the money is given to a female caregiver. Action could also be taken at the policy level to combat discriminatory attitudes that hinder or preclude male involvement in certain family contexts. For example, policymakers might work to reduce the prevalence of negative social attitudes towards the involvement of homosexual men in the lives of their children. Again, policy approaches will need to be tailored to specific needs—but in all policy contexts, the best practice is to keep an open mind.

# References

Alkenbrack, B.S.E., and others (2008). Confirming the impact of HIV/AIDS epidemics on household vulnerability in Asia: the case of Cambodia. *AIDS*, vol. 22, supplement 1, pp. S103-S111.

American Psychological Association (2004). Sexual orientation, parents, and children. Resolution adopted by the APA Council of Representatives on 28 and 30 July 2004. Available from http://www.apa.org/about/governance/council/policy/parenting.aspx.

Antle, B.J., and others (2001). Challenges of parenting for families living with HIV/AIDS. *Social Work*, vol. 46, No. 2, pp. 159-169.

Bachmann, M.O., and F.L.R. Booysen (2004). Relationships between HIV/AIDS, income and expenditure over time in deprived South African households. *AIDS Care*, vol. 16, No. 7, pp. 817-826.

Baptiste, D.R., and others (2006). Community collaborative youth-focused HIV/AIDS prevention in South Africa and Trinidad: preliminary findings. *Journal of Pediatric Psychology*, vol. 31, No. 9, pp. 905-916.

Barker, G., and F. Verani (2008). Men's participation as fathers in the Latin American and Caribbean region: a critical literature review with policy considerations. Rio de Janeiro: Instituto Promundo and Save the Children-Sweden. Available from http://www.promundo.org.br/wp-content/uploads/2010/03/Mens%20Participation%20as%20Fathers%20in%20the%20Latin%20American(2008)-ING.pdf.

Beegle, K., and J. De Weerdt (2008). Methodological issues in the study of the socioeconomic consequences of HIV/AIDS. *AIDS*, vol. 22, supplement 1, pp. S89-S94.

Belsey, M.A. (2005). *AIDS and the Family: Policy Options for a Crisis in Family Capital*. United Nations publication, Sales No. E.06.IV.1.

Bila, B., and M. Egrot (2009). Gender asymmetry in healthcare-facility attendance of people living with HIV/AIDS in Burkina Faso. *Social Science and Medicine*, vol. 69, No. 6, pp. 854-861.

Birdthistle, I.J., and others (2008). From affected to infected? orphanhood and HIV risk among female adolescents in urban Zimbabwe. *AIDS*, vol. 22, No. 6, pp. 759-766.

Blum, R.W., and others (2000). The effects of race/ethnicity, income, and family structure on adolescent risk behaviors. *American Journal of Public Health*, vol. 90, No. 12 (December), pp. 1879-1884.

Booth, A., and P. Amato (1991). Divorce and psychological stress. *Journal of Health and Social Behaviour*, vol. 32, pp. 396-407.

Bor, R., and J. Elford, eds. (1994). *The Family and HIV*. London: Cassell.

Braitstein, P., and others (2008). Gender and the use of antiretroviral treatment in resource-constrained settings: findings from a multicenter collaboration. *Journal of Women's Health*, vol. 17, No. 1, pp. 47-55.

Brook, D.W., and others (2008). Risk factors for distress in the adolescent children of HIV-positive and HIV-negative drug-abusing fathers. *AIDS Care*, vol. 20, No. 1 (January), pp. 93-100.

Case, A., C. Paxson and J. Ableidinger (2004). Orphans in Africa: parental death, poverty and school enrolment. *Demography*, vol. 41, No. 3, pp. 483-508.

Clarke, L., E.C. Cooksey and G. Verropoulou (1998). Fathers and absent fathers: sociodemographic similarities in Britain and the United States. *Demography*, vol. 35, No. 2, pp. 217-228.

Cluver, L., and D. Operario (2008). Inter-generational linkages of AIDS: vulnerability of orphaned children for HIV infection. *IDS Bulletin*, vol. 39, No. 5, pp. 27-35.

Cooper, D., and others (2007). «Life is still going on»: reproductive intentions among HIV-positive women and men in South Africa. *Social Science and Medicine*, vol. 65, No. 2, pp. 274-283.

Cornell, M., and others (2009). The impact of gender and income on survival and retention in a South African antiretroviral therapy programme. *Tropical Medicine and International Health*, vol. 14, No. 7 (July), pp. 722-731.

Day, R. D., and M. E. Lamb, eds. (2004). *Conceptualizing and Measuring Father Involvement*. Mahwah, New Jersey: Lawrence Erlbaum Associates, Inc.

Delvaux, T., and C. Nöstlinger (2007). Reproductive choice for women and men living with HIV: contraception, abortion and fertility. *Reproductive Health Matters*, vol. 15, No. 29 supplement, pp. 46-66.

Denis, P., and R. Ntsimane (2006). Absent fathers: Why do men not feature in stories of families affected by HIV/AIDS in KwaZulu Natal? In *Baba: Men and Fatherhood in South Africa*, R. Morrell and L. Richter, eds. Cape Town: HSRC Press.

Denton, R.E., and C.M. Kampfe (1994). The relationship between family variables and adolescent substance abuse: a literature review. *Adolescence*, vol. 29, No. 114 (summer), pp. 475-495.

Desmond, C. (2009). Consequences of HIV for children: avoidable or inevitable? *AIDS Care*, vol. 21, supplement, No. 1 (August), pp. 98-104.

Donahue, J. (2006) Strengthening households and communities: the key to reducing the economic impacts of HIV/AIDS on children and families. In *A Generation at Risk: The Global Impact of HIV/AIDS on Orphans and Vulnerable Children*, Geoff Foster, Carol Levine and John Williamson, eds. New York: Cambridge University Press.

Drimie, S., and M. Casale (2009). Multiple stressors in Southern Africa: the link between HIV/AIDS, food insecurity, poverty and children's vulnerability now and in the future. *AIDS Care*, vol. 21, No. S1 (August), pp. 28-33.

Dunkle, K.L., and others (2008). New heterosexually transmitted HIV infections in married or cohabiting couples in urban Zambia and Rwanda: an analysis of survey and clinical data. *The Lancet*, vol. 371, No. 9631 (28 June), pp. 2183-2191.

Fisher, L., and others (1993). Families of homosexual men: their knowledge and support regarding sexual orientation and HIV disease. *Journal of the American Board of Family Practice*, vol. 6, No. 1 (January-February), pp. 25-32.

Fitzgerald, M., M. Collumbien and V. Hosegood (2010). No one can ask me «Why do you take that stuff?»: men's experiences of antiretroviral treatment in South Africa. *AIDS Care*, vol. 22, No. 3 (March), pp. 355-360.

Garfield, C.F., E. Clark-Kauffman and M.M. Davis (2006). Fatherhood as a component of men's health. *Journal of the American Medical Association*, vol. 296, No. 19, pp. 2365-2368.

Glenn, B.L., A. Demi and L.P. Kimble (2008). Father and adolescent son variables related to son's HIV prevention. *Western Journal of Nursing Research*, vol. 30, No. 1 (February), pp. 73-89; discussion, pp. 90-75.

Gove, W.R. (1973). Sex, marital status and mortality. *American Journal of Sociology*, vol. 79, No. 1 (July), pp. 45-67.

Gupta, G.R. (2004). Globalization, women and the HIV/AIDS epidemic. *Peace Review: A Journal of Social Justice*, vol. 16, No. 1 (March), pp. 79-83.

Haour-Knipe, M. (2009). Families, children, migration and AIDS. *AIDS Care*, vol. 21, No. 1, pp. 43-48.

Hart, G., and others (1994). Gay men, social support and HIV disease: a study of social integration in the gay community. In *The Family and HIV*, Robert Bor and Jonathan Elford, eds. London: Cassells.

Henwood, K.L., and J. Procter (2003). The «good father»: reading men's accounts of paternal involvement during the transition to first-time fatherhood. *British Journal of Social Psychology*, vol. 42, pp. 337-355.

Heymann, J., and R. Kidman (2009). HIV/AIDS, declining family resources and the community safety net. *AIDS Care*, vol. 21, No. S1 (August), pp. 34-42.

Hill, C., V. Hosegood and M.L. Newell (2008). Children's care and living arrangements in a high HIV prevalence area in rural South Africa. *Vulnerable Children and Youth Studies*, vol. 3, No. 1 (April), pp. 65-77.

Hobson, B. (2002). Introduction: making men into fathers. In *Making Men into Fathers: Men, Masculinities and the Social Politics of Fatherhood*, B. Hobson, ed. Cambridge, United Kingdom: Cambridge University Press.

Hosegood, V. (2009). The demographic impact of HIV and AIDS across the family and household life-cycle: implications for efforts to strengthen families in sub-Saharan Africa. *AIDS Care*, vol. 21, No. S1 (August), pp. 13-21.

Hosegood, V., and S. Madhavan (2010). Data availability on men's involvement in families in sub-Saharan Africa to inform family-centred programmes for children affected by HIV and AIDS. *Journal of the International AIDS Society*, vol. 13, supplement, No. 2, pp. S5.

Hosegood, V., and others (2007). Revealing the full extent of households' experiences of HIV and AIDS in rural South Africa. *Social Science and Medicine*, vol. 65, No. 6, pp. 1249-1259.

Hosegood, V., and others (2008). Fathers' involvement during infancy: factors influencing social and residential dynamics in rural South Africa. *Available as a* working paper of the *Africa Centre* for Health and Population Studies.

Hutchinson, M.K., and A.J. Montgomery (2007). Parent communication and sexual risk among African Americans. *Western Journal of Nursing Research*, vol. 29, No. 6 (October), pp. 691-707.

Jewkes, R., and R. Morrell (2010). Gender and sexuality: emerging perspectives from the heterosexual epidemic in South Africa and implications for HIV risk and prevention. *Journal of the International AIDS Society*, vol. 13 (9 February), p. 6.

Jewkes, R., and others (2008). Impact of Stepping Stones on incidence of HIV and HSV-2 and sexual behaviour in rural South Africa: cluster randomised controlled trial. *British Medical Journal*, vol. 337 (7 August), p. a506.

Joseph, E.B., and R.S. Bhatti (2004). Psychosocial problems and coping patterns of HIV seropositive wives of men with HIV/AIDS. *Social Work in Health Care*, vol. 39, No. 1-2, pp. 29-47.

Joseph, S., and others (2010). Examining sex differentials in the uptake and process of HIV testing in three high prevalence districts of India. *AIDS Care*, vol. 22, No. 3 (March), pp. 286-295.

Kadushin, G. (1999). Barriers to social support and support received from their families of origin among gay men with HIV/AIDS. *Health & Social Work*, vol. 24, No. 3 (August), pp. 198-209.

Kimberly, J.A., and J.M. Serovich (1999). The role of family and friend social support in reducing risk behaviors among HIV-positive gay men. *AIDS Education and Prevention*, vol. 11, No. 6 (December), pp. 465-475.

Lamb, M.E. (2000). The history of research on father involvement: an overview. *Marriage & Family Review*, vol. 29, No. 2 & 3 (May), pp. 23-42.

_____ (2002). Nonresidential fathers and their children. In *Handbook of Father Involvement: Multidisciplinary Perspectives*, C.S. Tamis-LeMonda and N. Cabrera, eds. Mahwah, New Jersey: Lawrence Erlbaum Associates, Inc.

_____ and others (1987). A biosocial perspective on paternal behaviour and involvement. In *Parenting across the Lifespan: Biosocial Perspectives*, J. Beckman Lancaster and others, eds. New York: Academic Press.

Le Coeur, S., and others (2009). Gender and access to HIV testing and antiretroviral treatments in Thailand: why do women have more and earlier access? *Social Science and Medicine*, vol. 69, No. 6 (September), pp. 846-853.

Levine, C. (1990). AIDS and changing concepts of family. *The Milbank Quarterly*, vol. 68, pp. 33-58.

Levine, J.A., and E.W. Pitt (1995). New expectations: community strategies for responsible fatherhood. New York: Families and Work Institute.

Madhavan, S., and N. Townsend (2007). The social context of children's nutritional status in rural South Africa. *Scandinavian Journal of Public Health*, vol. 35, No. S69 (August), pp. 107-117.

Madhavan, S., N.W. Townsend and A.I. Garey (2008). «Absent breadwinners»: father-child connections and paternal support in rural South Africa. *Journal of Southern African Studies*, vol. 34, No. 3 (September), pp. 647-663.

Makusha, T., and L. Richter (2010). A review of family issues among marginalised groups in the context of the HIV epidemic: men who have sex with men (MSM), injection drug users (IDU) and sex workers (SW). Paper prepared for the XVIII International AIDS Conference, Vienna 18-23 July.

Mathambo, V., and Andy Gibbs (2009). Extended family childcare arrangements in a context of AIDS: collapse or adaptation? *AIDS Care*, vol. 21, supplement 1, pp. 22-27.

McCann, K., and E. Wadsworth (1992). The role of informal carers in supporting gay men who have HIV related illness: what do they do and what are their needs? *AIDS Care*, vol. 4, No. 1, pp. 25-34.

McGrath, N., and others (2008). Age at first sex in rural South Africa. *Sexually Transmitted Infections*, vol. 85, supplement 1, pp. i49-i55.

McLanahan, S., and J. Adams (1987). Parenthood and psychological well-being. *Annual Review of Sociology*, vol. 13 (August), pp. 237-257.

McLanahan, S., and J. Adams (1989). The effects of children on adults' psychological well-being: 1957-1976. *Social Forces*, vol. 68, No. 1 (September), pp. 124-146.

McMahon, T.J., J.D. Winkel and B.J. Rounsaville (2008). Drug abuse and responsible fathering: a comparative study of men enrolled in methadone maintenance treatment. *Addiction*, vol. 103, No. 2 (February), pp. 269-283.

McMahon, T.J., and others (2005). Looking for poppa: parenting status of men versus women seeking drug abuse treatment. *American Journal of Drug Alcohol Abuse*, vol. 31, No. 1, pp. 79-91.

McMahon, J., and others (2007). Drug-abusing fathers: patterns of pair bonding, reproduction, and paternal involvement. *Journal of Substance Abuse Treatment*, vol. 33, No. 3 (October), pp. 295-302.

Miller, C.L., and others (2002). Females experiencing sexual and drug vulnerabilities are at elevated risk for HIV infection among youth who use injection drugs. *Journal of Acquired Immune Deficiency Syndromes*, vol. 30, No. 3 (1 June), pp. 335-341.

Mkhize, N. (2006). African traditions and the social, economic and moral dimensions of fatherhood. In *Baba: Men and Fatherhood in South Africa*, Robert Morrell and Linda Richter, eds. Cape Town: HSRC Press.

Monasch, R., and J.T. Boerma (2004). Orphanhood and childcare patterns in sub-Saharan Africa: an analysis of national surveys from 40 countries. *AIDS*, vol. 18, supplement 2 (June), pp. S55-S65.

Montgomery, C.M., and others (2005). Men's involvement in the South African family: engendering change in the AIDS era. *Social Science and Medicine*, vol. 62, No. 10 (May), pp. 2411-2419.

Morrell, R. (2006). Fathers, fatherhood and masculinity in South Africa. In *Baba: Men and Fatherhood in South Africa*, R. Morrell and L. Richter, eds. Cape Town: HSRC Press.

Munro, I., and K.L. Edwards (2009). The burden of care of gay male carers caring for men living with HIV/AIDS. *American Journal of Men's Health*, vol. 10 (22 December). Doi:10.1177/1557988309331795.

Muula, A.S., and others (2007). Gender distribution of adult patients on highly active antiretroviral therapy (HAART) in Southern Africa: a systematic review. *BMC Public Health*, vol. 7, pp. 63-68.

Myer, L., C. Morroni and K. Rebe (2007). Prevalence and determinants of fertility intentions of HIV-infected women and men receiving antiretroviral therapy in South Africa. *AIDS Patient Care and STDs*, vol. 21, No. 4 (April), pp. 278-285.

Myer, L., and others (2005). Focus on women: linking HIV care and treatment with reproductive health services in the MTCT-Plus Initiative. *Reproductive Health Matters*, vol. 13, No. 25 (May), pp. 136-146.

Myer, L., and others (2010). Impact of antiretroviral therapy on incidence of pregnancy among HIV-infected women in sub-Saharan Africa: a cohort study. *PLoS Medicine*, vol. 7, No. 2 (9 February), e1000229.

Ochieng-Ooko, V., and others (2010). Influence of gender on loss to follow-up in a large HIV treatment programme in western Kenya. *Bulletin of the World Health Organization*, vol. 88, No. 9 (September), pp. 641-716.

Paiva, V., and others (2007). Desire to have children: gender and reproductive rights of men and women living with HIV: a challenge to health care in Brazil. *AIDS Patient Care and STDs*, vol. 21, No. 4 (April), pp. 268-277.

Peacock, D., and A. Levack (2004). The Men As Partners program in South Africa: reaching men to end gender-based violence and promote sexual and reproductive health. *International Journal of Men's Health*, vol. 3, No. 3 (fall), pp. 173-188.

Peacock, D., and others (2009). Men, HIV/AIDS, and human rights. *Journal of Acquired Immune Deficiency Syndromes*, vol. 51, supplement 3 (1 July), pp. S119-S125.

Posel, D., and R. Devey (2006). The demographics of fatherhood in South Africa: an analysis of survey data, 1993-2002. In *Baba: Men and Fatherhood in South Africa*, R. Morrell and L. Richter, eds. Cape Town: HSRC Press.

Pulerwitz, J., and G. Barker (2008). Measuring attitudes toward gender norms among young men in Brazil. *Men and Masculinities*, vol. 10, No. 3 (April), pp. 322-338.

Ramchandani, P., and others (2005). Paternal depression in the postnatal period and child development: a prospective population study. *The Lancet*, vol. 365, No. 9478 (25 June-1 July), pp. 2201-2205.

Reichman, N.E., H. Corman and K. Noonan (2004). Effects of child health on parents' relationship status. *Demography*, vol. 41, No. 3, pp. 569-584.

Remien, R.H., and others (2009). Gender and care: access to HIV testing, care, and treatment. *Journal of Acquired Immune Deficiency Syndromes*, vol. 51, supplement 3 (1 July), pp. S106-S110.

Rhodes, T. (2009). Risk environments and drug harms: a social science for harm reduction approach. *International Journal on Drug Policy*, vol. 20, No. 3 (May), pp. 193-201.

Richter, L. (2006). The importance of fathering for children. In *Baba: Men and Fatherhood in South Africa*, Robert Morrell and Linda Richter, eds. Cape Town: HSRC Press.

_____ and others (2009). Strengthening families to support children affected by HIV and AIDS. *AIDS Care*, vol. 21, supplement 1 (August), pp. 3-12.

Risser, J., and others (2010). Gender differences in social support and depression among injection drug users in Houston, Texas. *American Journal of Drug and Alcohol Abuse*, vol. 36, No. 1 (January), pp. 18-24.

Robinson, B.E., L.H. Walters and P. Skeen (1989). Response of parents to learning that their child is homosexual and concern over AIDS: a national study. *Journal of Homosexuality*, vol. 18, No. 1-2, pp. 59-80.

Rose, L.L. (2006). Children's property and inheritance rights and their livelihoods: the context of HIV and AIDS in Southern and East Africa. LSP Working Paper 39. Rome: Food and Agriculture Organization of the United Nations, Access to Natural Resources Sub-Programme.

Sherr, L. (2010). Fathers and HIV: considerations for families. *Journal of the International AIDS Society*, vol. 13, supplement 2 (23 June), p. S4.

Sherr, L., and N. Barry (2004). Fatherhood and HIV-positive heterosexual men. *HIV Medicine*, vol. 5, No. 4 (July), pp. 258-263.

Sherr, L., and B. Talia (2003). Fatherhood and HIV: overlooked and understudied. Paper presented at the 2nd IAS Conference on HIV Pathogenesis and Treatment, Paris 13-17 July 2003.

Sikkema, K.J., and others (2000). Coping strategies and emotional wellbeing among HIV-infected men and women experiencing AIDS-related bereavement. *AIDS Care*, vol. 12, No. 5 (October), pp. 613-624.

Sinha, G., D.H. Peters and R.C. Bollinger (2009). Strategies for gender-equitable HIV services in rural India. *Health Policy and Planning*, vol. 24, No. 3 (May), pp. 197-208.

Skogmar S., and others (2006). Effect of antiretroviral treatment and counselling on disclosure of HIV-serostatus in Johannesburg, South Africa. *AIDS Care*, vol. 18, No. 7 (October), pp. 725-730.

Skovdal, M., and others (2009). Young carers as social actors: coping strategies of children caring for ailing or ageing guardians in Western Kenya. *Social Science and Medicine*, vol. 69, No. 4 (August), pp. 587-595.

Solomon, S.S., and others (2010). The impact of HIV and high-risk behaviours on the wives of married men who have sex with men and injection drug users: implications for HIV prevention. *Journal of the International AIDS Society*, vol. 13, supplement 2 (23 June), p. S7.

Stowe, A., and others (1994). Significant relationships and social supports of injecting drug users and their implications for HIV/AIDS services. In *The Family and HIV*, R. Bor and J. Elford, eds. London: Cassell.

Tamis-LeMonda, C.S., and N.J. Cabrera, eds. (2002). *Handbook of Father Involvement: Multidisciplinary Perspectives*. Mahwah, New Jersey: Lawrence Erlbaum Associates, Inc.

Tangmunkongvorakul, A., and others (1999). Factors influencing marital stability among HIV discordant couples in northern Thailand. *AIDS Care*, vol. 11, No. 5, pp. 511-524.

Tasker, F. (2005). Lesbian mothers, gay fathers, and their children: a review. *Journal of Developmental and Behavioral Pediatrics*, vol. 26, No. 3, pp. 224-240.

Tekola, F., and others (2008). The economic impact of HIV/AIDS morbidity and mortality on households in Addis Ababa, Ethiopia. *AIDS Care*, vol. 20, No. 8 (September), pp. 995-1001.

Tijou Traoré, A., and others (2009). Couples, PMTCT programs and infant feeding decision-making in Ivory Coast. *Social Science and Medicine*, vol. 69, No. 6 (September), pp. 830-837.

Timaeus, I.M., and T. Boler, (2007). Father figures: the progress at school of orphans in South Africa. *AIDS*, vol. 21, supplement 7 (November), pp. S83-S93.

Townsend, N. (2002). Cultural contexts of father involvement. In *Handbook of Father Involvement: Multidisciplinary Perspectives*, C.S. Tamis-LeMonda and N.J. Cabrera, eds. Mahwah, New Jersey: Lawrence Erlbaum Associates, Inc.

Umberson, D. (1987). Family status and health behaviours: social control as a dimension of social integration. *Journal of Health and Social Behaviour*, vol. 28, No. 3 (September), pp. 306-319.

Umberson, D. (1989). Relationships with children: explaining parents' psychological well-being. *Journal of Marriage and the Family*, vol. 51, No. 4 (November), pp. 999-1012.

van Leeuwen, E., and others (2007). Reproduction and fertility in human immunodeficiency virus type-1 infection. *Human Reproduction Update*, vol. 13, No. 2, pp. 197-206.

VanDevanter, N., and others (1999). Heterosexual couples confronting the challenges of HIV infection. *AIDS Care*, vol. 11, No. 2 (April), pp. 181-193.

Verma, R.K., and others (2006). Challenging and changing gender attitudes among young men in Mumbai, India. *Reproductive Health Matters*, vol. 14, No. 28 (November), pp. 135-143.